W9-BGA-778

Mosi-oa-Tunya : A Handbook to the Victoria Falls Region

Editor: David W Phillipson

M.A., Ph.D., F.S.A., Curator, Cambridge University
Museum of Archaeology and Anthropology

Longman Zimbabwe

LONGMAN ZIMBABWE
Associated companies, branches and
representatives throughout the world

© Longman Group Ltd 1975, 1990

All rights reserved. No part of this
publication may be reproduced, stored
in a retrieval system, or transmitted
in any form or by any means, electronic,
mechanical, photocopying, recording, or
otherwise, without the prior permission
of the Copyright owner.

First published 1975
Second edition 1990

ISBN 0 582 64170 5

Printed by National Printing and Packaging
Simon Mazorodze Road, Harare

48.85

Contents

Frontispiece Vertical air view of the Victoria Falls and gorges.

Colour Plates

Maps

Acknowledgements

The editor and publishers wish to thank the Zambia National Monuments Commission for consenting to the preparation of this volume, which succeeds *The Victoria Falls Handbook* (1st ed. J. D. Clark 1952, 2nd ed. B. M. Fagan 1964) published by the National Monuments Commission of the then Northern Rhodesia.

The handbook was first published in this form in 1975. In 1988–9 it was extensively revised and up-dated. For information and help with the revision the editor is grateful to Mr N. Katanekwa of the Zambia National Monuments Commission, Mr G. Mahachi of the National Museums and Monuments of Zimbabwe, Mr R. Mpofu of Victoria Falls, Dr F. Musonda of the Livingstone Museum and Ms M. Poole of Longman Zimbabwe Ltd.

We are grateful to the following for permission to reproduce illustrations:
Barnaby's Picture Library, plate III; M. S. Bisson, Chap. II, figs. 1, 4; D. K. Blake, Chap. 13, figs. 1, 3; the late G. Bond, Chap. 2, fig. 1; D. Broadley, Chap. 13, figs. 2, 4–15, plates XVa,b; Camera Press Ltd., plate XIII (Jan Kopec); J. D. Clark, Chap. 4, fig. 3; Bruce Coleman Ltd., plate XIV (David Hughes); D. B. Fanshawe, Chap. 10, figs. 1, 3, 9; Dr L. Holỳ, Chap. 6, fig. 14; Dr Jane Lancaster, Chap. 11, fig. 6; Livingstone Museum, Chap. 1, figs. 9, 11 (J. D. Clark), Chap. 2, fig. 2, Chap. 5, figs. 2–4, 6–10, Chap. 6, figs. 3 and 5 (Royal Family of Mukuni), 7–10 (Barbara Tyrell), 11–13, Chap. 7, fig. 8 (F. Coillard), Chap. 8, figs. 2 and 4 (Orlando Baragwanath), 5–7 (P. M. Clark), 8, 9, 11–13, Chap. 9, fig. 1; the late Kafungulwa Mubitana, Chap. 6, fig. 2; C. Nugent, Chap. 3, fig. 1; David W. Phillipson, Chap. 1, figs. 1, 6, 7, 10, 12, Chap. 4, figs. 1, 2, 8, Chap. 5, fig. 5, Chap. 7, figs. 1, 2, Chap. 8, figs. 1, 3, 10, chap. 10, figs. 2, 4–8, plates IVa,b; Picturepoint Ltd., plates I, II, VI–IX and cover; R. Pletts, National Museums and Monuments of Zimbabwe, Chap. 11, figs. 2, 3; Per B. Rekdal, Chap. 9, figs. 2–18; Royal Geographical Society, plates XI, XII; Peter Steyn, Chap. 12, figs. 1–12, plate XVI; Tourist Photo Library, plate V (Peter Fraenkel); Joseph O. Vogel, Chap. 5, fig. 1; G. Webb, Chap. 1, fig. 8, Chap. 11, fig. 5; Dr H. Wilson, plate X; Zambia National Monuments Commission, Chap. 5, fig. 5 (D. W. Phillipson); Zambia Survey Department, frontispiece.

We are grateful to the following for permission to base illustrations on their material: Mrs Betty Clark, Chap. 4, figs. 4–7; Dr and Mrs Rex Jubb, Chap. 14, figs. 1–5; Zambia Survey Department, Chap. 1, fig. 5; Dr. E. Pinhey, National Museums of Zimbabwe, Chap. 15, figs. 1–10; South African Archaeological Society and J. D. Clark, Chap. 3, fig. 2; Survey Departments of Zimbabwe and Zambia, Chap. 1, figs. 2, 3, 4, Chap. 16, figs. 1, 2.

Figs. 1, 4 and 6 in Chap. 5 are reproduced from E. Holub, *Seven Years in South Africa*, London, 1881. In Chap. 6, fig. 3 is from W. D. Cooley, *Inner Africa Laid Open*, London, 1852; fig. 4 from H. Waller (ed) *The Last Journals of David Livingstone*, London, 1874; fig. 5 from W. Baldwin, *African Hunting from Natal to the Zambesi*, London, 1863; figs. 6, 9, 10 from C. W. Mackintosh, *Colliard of the Zambesi*, London, 1907; and fig. 7 from F. Colliard, *On the Threshold of Central Africa*, London, 1897.

Artwork is by Richard Bonson.

The Contributors

W. F. H. ANSELL, now retired, was formerly Deputy Director (National Parks and Wildlife) in the Zambia wildlife department.

GRAHAM BELL-CROSS, Lic. (Biol.), M.I.A.F.S., F.Z.S., was formerly Curator of the Queen Victoria Museum in Harare and is now Curator of the Bartolemeu Dias Museum, Mossel Bay, South Africa.

The late G. BOND, B.Sc., Ph.D., F.G.S., was Professor of Geology at the former University of Rhodesia.

DONALD G. BROADLEY, M.Sc., Ph.D., F.Z.S., is Curator of Herpetology at the Natural History Museum of Zimbabwe, Bulawayo.

J. DESMOND CLARK, C.B.E., M.A., Ph.D., F.B.A., F.S.A., is Emeritus Professor of Anthropology, University of California, Berkeley.

R. J. DOWSETT, formerly Keeper of Natural History at the Livingstone Museum, is now Director of Tauraco Press, Jupille-Liège, Belgium.

D. B. FANSHAWE, B.A., now retired, was Principal Scientific Officer, Division of Forest Research, Kitwe, Zambia.

JOHN L. MINSHULL, B.Sc., M.Sc., T.R.E., is Curator of Ichthyology, Natural History Museum of Zimbabwe, Bulawayo.

The late KAFUNGULWA MUBITANA, M.Sc., was Director of the Livingstone Museum, Zambia.

CHRIS NUGENT is a graduate student in the Geology Department, University of Zimbabwe.

DAVID W. PHILLIPSON, M.A., Ph.D., F.S.A., formerly Secretary/Inspector of the Zambia National Monuments Commission is now Curator of the Museum of Archaeology and Anthropology and Fellow of Gonville and Caius College in the University of Cambridge.

ELLIOT PINHEY, now retired, was formerly Keeper of Entomology at the National Museum, Bulawayo.

PER B. REKDAL, Ph.D., formerly Keeper of Ethnography at the Livingstone Museum, is now Head of Information, Museum of Contemporary Art, Oslo, Norway.

The late REAY H. N. SMITHERS, O.B.E., D.Sc., F.Z.S., was Director of Museums in Zimbabwe.

JOSEPH O. VOGEL, M.A., D.Phil., formerly Keeper of Prehistory at the Livingstone Museum, is now Associate Professor of Anthropology, University of Alabama.

Editor's Introduction

There can be few areas of Africa which have been subject to such intensive scientific investigation as that surrounding the Victoria Falls; and this book sets out to provide an outline multidisciplinary account of the present state of the results of this work. Displays illustrative of much of this research may be found in the Livingstone Museum in Livingstone and, further afield, in the Natural History Museum of Zimbabwe in Bulawayo. There is also a Railway Museum in Livingstone, and a small Field Museum, illustrating the archaeology and history of the Falls area, situated beside the Eastern Cataract.

This book attempts to provide a complete account of the entire area, both Zambian and Zimbabwean; and aims to help the visitor whose sightseeing is restricted to one country to obtain a more comprehensive understanding of the Falls. The book does not provide details about access, accommodation, and other tourist logistics, since these rapidly change; up-to-date information is obtainable from the Zambia National Tourist Board, P.O. Box 30017, Lusaka, or from the Zimbabwe National Tourist Board, P.O. Box 8052, Causeway, Harare.

David W. Phillipson

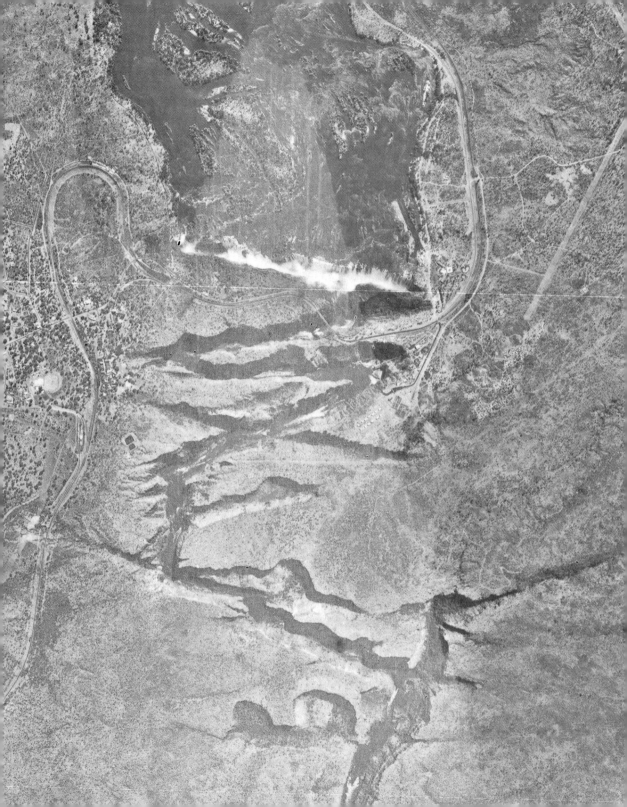

CHAPTER 1

The Victoria Falls Region

David W. Phillipson

In the far interior of south-central Africa the great Zambezi River emerges from the Caprivi Swamps and flows eastwards through a broad flat-bottomed valley. The river, except where interrupted by occasional rapids, is placid and smoothly flowing. Then, with very little advance warning, the river falls into a vast chasm stretching from side to side of its bed, forming the largest curtain of falling water known anywhere in the world. Thence the Zambezi, compressed in places almost to one thirtieth of its former width, flows on an angry tortuous course through a deep rocky gorge which traverses some of the wildest and most unfrequented country in this part of Africa, before emerging into a more open valley now flooded by the waters of Lake Kariba. It is with the detailed description and explanation of this great waterfall – known to local people as Mosi-oa-Tunya, loosely translated as 'smoke that thunders' – and its fascinating environs that this book is concerned.

Mosi-oa-Tunya is the name given to the waterfall by the Kololo people who invaded this area from the south in about 1838. The earlier Toka-Leya name Shongwe has now fallen into disuse. In 1855 their first European visitor, Dr David Livingstone, gave them the name of Victoria Falls by which they are today generally known.

The Zambezi River itself rises in the Mwinilunga District of north-western Zambia as a small and insignificant spring bubbling up between the roots of a tree, very close to where the modern countries of Angola, Zambia and Zaïre all meet. Rapidly growing through the addition of the water of many tributary streams, the Zambezi embarks on its 2700-kilometre journey to the Indian Ocean, flowing first westwards into Angola, then swinging to the south to re-enter

1

Fig. 1 The Victoria Falls at low water: the view along the chasm from the Eastern Cataract.

Zambia at Cholwezi Rapids. Next it passes in a general south-south-easterly direction through the flat country of Zambia's Western Province, which is covered by a thick mantle of sand, evidence of a past northern extension of the Kalahari Desert. Here it traverses the broad, annually inundated Barotse Plain, then returns to more rocky country where its course is broken by the Ngonye Falls and numerous rapids, finally emerging into the Caprivi Swamps where it is joined by the Chobe River. From the Chobe confluence eastwards past the Victoria Falls the Zambezi for some 500 kilometres forms the border between Zambia and Zimbabwe. For about one fifth of this distance below the Falls, the river flows through the narrow, steadily deepening Batoka Gorge, ending in the broad Gwembe Valley, at the eastern end

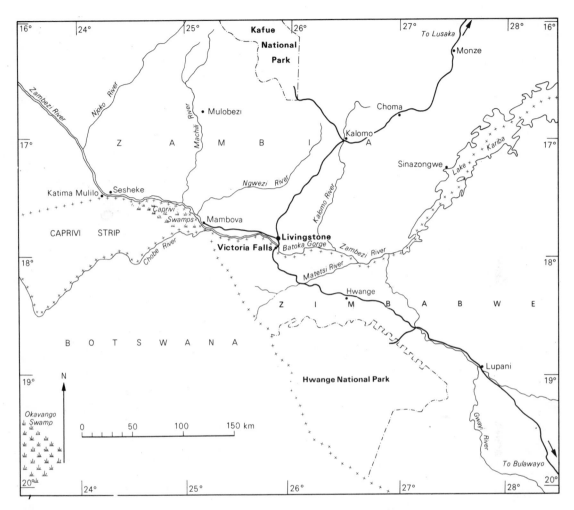

Fig. 2a Location of the Victoria Falls region (1).

of which the river has been dammed to form Lake Kariba. Below Kariba, the Zambezi is swollen successively by the affluence of the waters of the Kafue and the Luangwa; at its junction with the latter river the Zambezi enters Moçambique. It then passes the Cabora Bassa rapids, where another dam has been constructed, and eventually issues into the Indian Ocean almost 1500 kilometres from the Victoria Falls.

The Victoria Falls themselves are 1708 metres in width and have a maximum height of 103 metres. They are formed by the waters of the Zambezi falling over one side of a vertical-sided slot or chasm which has eroded in the basalt rock from side to side of the river-bed roughly at right angles to the river's direction of flow. The opposite side of the chasm is at the same height as the lip of the Falls and is broken only at the one

3

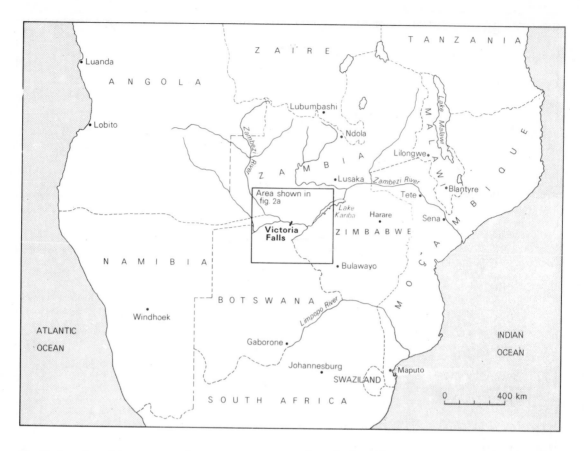

Fig. 2b Location of the Victoria Falls region (2).

point, some two-thirds of the way from the chasm's western end, where the river makes its exit through a gorge which, at its narrowest point, is only 60 metres in width. Within range of the spray of the Falls this gorge is spanned by the bridge, built in 1905, which carries road and railway between Zambia and Zimbabwe at a height of over 100 metres above the roaring water. Downstream of the bridge the gorge forms a series of close zigzags, each of which represents the line of a previous waterfall. Because of the great lateral compression of the almost two-kilometre-wide river into such a narrow gorge the depth of water in the latter must be very great, but no accurate figures are available. A rise of one metre in the level of the river above the Falls produces a five-metre rise in the water level in the gorge.

There is such great seasonal variation in the flow of water that the Falls can produce widely differing impressions on the visitor at various times of the year. Virtually all the rainfall in this region, which averages some 76 centimetres per year, falls in the five months between November and March. This summer rainy season is also the hottest time of the year, when temperatures can reach 52

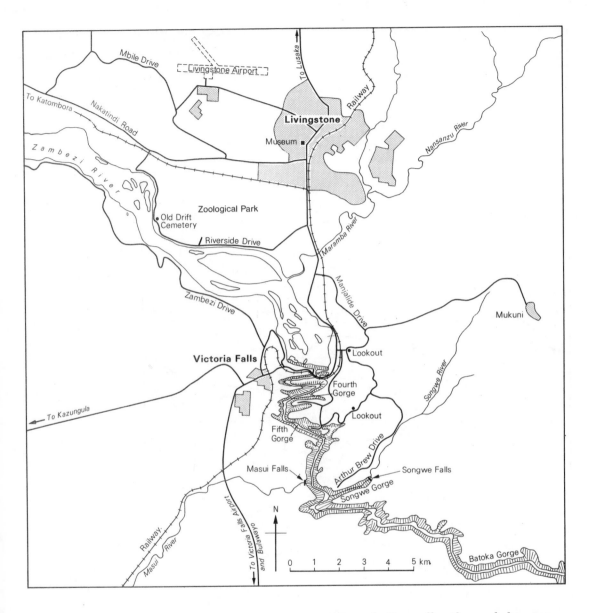

Fig. 3 Map of Livingstone and the Victoria Falls.

degrees Centigrade; it is, however, only when the rains are interrupted for several weeks that such extreme temperatures are experienced. Generally, the cool dry season of June and July has occasional night frosts and is followed by steadily increasing temperatures until October, which can be uncomfortably hot. The advent of the rains

5

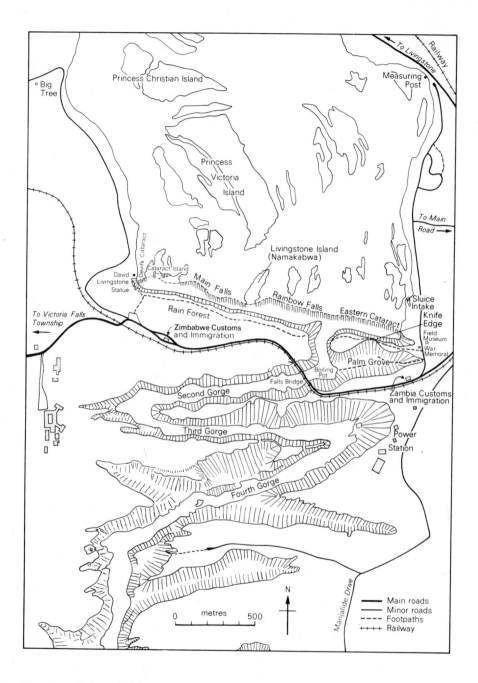

Fig. 4 Detailed map of the Victoria Falls.

brings immediate relief and when the rains peter out in March or April temperatures are again falling.

Since the bulk of the water which passes over the Victoria Falls is derived not from rainfall in their immediate vicinity but from that in regions far upstream, there is an appreciable time-lag between the season of peak rainfall and that of the highest flow of water over the Falls. The Victoria Falls have their lowest water level generally in late November or early December, well after the start of the rainy season. At this period the mean flow of water over the Falls is less than 20 000 cubic metres per minute; the clear steely-blue water breaks into thin white veils and, since comparatively little spray is produced, it is at this season that the geological formation of the Falls can most easily be appreciated. As the rainy season proceeds the water level rises rapidly and generally reaches its peak in March or April, although there is considerable variation in this from year to year. At peak flood, water passes over the Falls at about thirty times its dry-season volume, averaging 550 000 cubic metres per minute. Flows of 700 000 cubic metres per minute were recorded in the record flood of March 1958. At this season the water is stained a golden reddish-brown by the sediment which it carries and it rolls over the lip of the Falls in a continuous stream. Spray is so dense that the drenched spectator can neither see to the bottom of the chasm nor fully appreciate the width of the Falls; everything but the wall of water immediately before him is hidden in a swirling mist of rising spray. To be appreciated and understood in all their moods the Victoria Falls are to be visited not once but many times.

The physical formation of the Falls enables the visitor to obtain close views of almost all sections from paths which run along the lip of the narrow chasm opposite to that over which the water pours. Except when the water is low, the spray prevents him from seeing along the whole length of the chasm from either end; at such times the only complete view which can be obtained is from the air.

Starting at the Zimbabwean end of the Falls, the westernmost section is that known as the Devil's Cataract, separated from the rest of the Falls by Cataract Island, formerly Boaruka. The Devil's Cataract has cut its bed down almost ten metres below the level of the other sections; and it thus carries a large volume of water at all seasons. It is probably here that the next fall-line will start to form as more and more water is directed to this western section. The alternative position for the next fall-line is through the cleft which has formed obliquely to the present Falls through Cataract Island. The Devil's Cataract is 62 metres high and its water breaks over a pile of high rocks at its base, rising some distance above the general level of the base of the Falls.

To the east of Cataract Island are the 830-metres-wide Main Falls which carry a substantial volume of water even when the river is at its lowest level. They can best be viewed from the Rain Forest, a stretch of lush vegetation nourished by the spray which has fallen almost incessantly for many centuries upon the lip of the chasm opposite the Falls. The eastern boundary of the Main Falls is marked by Livingstone Island, also known as Kaseruka. This island projects slightly from the general line of the Falls and it was from here that David Livingstone, having descended the river by canoe, obtained his first view of the Victoria Falls in 1855. Today it is not easy for the visitor to reach Living-

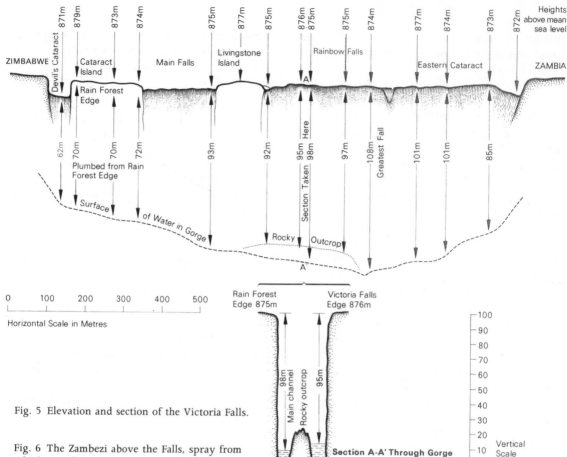

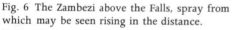

Fig. 5 Elevation and section of the Victoria Falls.

Fig. 6 The Zambezi above the Falls, spray from which may be seen rising in the distance.

stone Island, but an impression comparable with that obtained by Livingstone – of being perched on the brink of the precipice surrounded by roaring falling water – may be experienced at Danger Point. This rocky promontory is the furthest point east that can be reached through the Rain Forest, being situated at the angle of the main Falls chasm and the narrow gorge which directs the water into the First Gorge now spanned by the Victoria Falls Bridge.

To the east of Livingstone Island are the Rainbow Falls, now easily seen from the promontory on the Zambian side which corresponds to Danger Point described above. The narrow Knife Edge which joins this promontory to the mainland is now spanned by a footbridge. Because of the smaller volume of water carried by this section of the Falls, the spray is less dense than it is further to the west and rainbows, often double, may frequently be seen when the sun is shining on the spray. Between the Rainbow Falls and the eastern extremity of the Falls is the Eastern Cataract. When the river is low hardly any water passes over this section of the Falls and consequently the geological formation of the chasm is here most clearly seen.

The Victoria Falls look particularly beautiful by moonlight, especially when a lunar rainbow is formed in the spray. Floodlighting on the Zambian side unfortunately means that the lunar rainbow is now very rarely seen there, but the Zimbabwean side of the Falls has not been desecrated in this way.

At all times but those of the very lowest water level, the spray of the Falls rises to a considerable height and may easily be seen from a distance of 30 kilometres on the main road from Livingstone to Lusaka, and from a similar distance at a viewpoint close to the

Fig. 7 Danger Point, seen from across the Gorge. The Rainbow Falls are on the right.

main road to Bulawayo. Here, the spray is best seen in the cool hours of the early morning. In the flood season, when the spray-clouds rise to their greatest altitude, they are visible over twice this distance, but the vantage points are less easily accessible.

Downstream of the Victoria Falls the Zambezi gorge follows a tight zigzag course for some eight kilometres, the general direction being to the south. This configuration is due to the repeated cutting back of the line of the Falls and the successive formation and abandonment of each of seven broad waterfalls, all broadly comparable with the present

9

Fig. 8 Above the Eastern Cataract.

one. Beyond the confluence of the Zambezi and Songwe, at an impressive meeting of two nearly precipitous gorges which may be reached by road on the Zambian side, the main river turns again to a more easterly course. The gorge, here known as the Batoka Gorge, now becomes progressively deeper; its walls are more weathered and less steep, indicating its progressively greater antiquity. These features may be clearly seen on the aerial photograph which forms the frontispiece to this book. Since these lower stretches of the gorge are inaccessible by road, the best way for the visitor to see them for himself is from a low-flying aeroplane.

Much of the rugged country, bisected by numerous deep tributary gorges, through which the Batoka Gorge runs, is uninhabited and is accessible only on foot. Throughout the 90-100 kilometre length of the Batoka Gorge the Zambezi drops approximately 260 metres from its level at the base of the Victoria Falls. Over this distance the top of the basalt rock through which the gorge has been cut remains more or less horizontal; much of this drop is thus due to the progressive deepening of the gorge. This is some 110 metres deep at the Victoria Falls themselves; but at its downstream end the depth of the gorge approaches 350 metres. Although of such great depth, the gorge here is considerably weathered and lacks the precipitous walls of bare rock which are characteristic of its upper reaches. There are no major waterfalls in the gorge itself and consequently most of this drop is accounted for by several series of rapids. Only at Chimamba Rapids (called Moemba Falls by Livingstone) is there anything approaching a true waterfall in the gorge. Here, some 36 kilometres east of the Victoria Falls, the whole Zambezi passes through a defile less than 20 metres in width, best described in the words of W. G. Lamplugh:

> Insignificant in height it is true, but when one stands on the brink of the lower cataract and sees the whole volume of the great Zambesi converging into a single pass only fifty or sixty feet in width, shuddering, and then plunging for twenty feet in a massive curve that seems in its impact visibly to tear the grim basaltic rocks asunder, one learns better than from the feathery spray-fans of the Victoria Falls, what force there is in the river, and one wonders no longer at the profundity of the gorge. (Lamplugh, 1908: 150–1.)

There are, however, numerous waterfalls on the tributary rivers which join the Zambezi in the Batoka Gorge, but the majority of these carry an impressive flow of

Fig. 9 (top) The Victoria Falls bridge and Second Gorge, as seen from the Boiling Pot at the foot of Palm Grove.

Fig. 10 (bottom) The foot of the Eastern Cataract. This unusual photograph was taken in 1936 while the water was diverted during construction work on the hydro-electric scheme.

Fig. 11 The lower fall at Chimamba Rapids.

water only in the rainy season. Several of the more spectacular of these falls are on the Kalomo and Chibongo Rivers far downstream of the Victoria Falls and are extremely difficult of access. Closer at hand are the Songwe Falls on the river of that name, one kilometre from its confluence with the Zambezi. Nearby is the point where the Masui River flows over the near-vertical side of the Sixth Zambezi Gorge in a 110-metre

waterfall which is a most impressive sight when the water level is high. Although situated in Zimbabwe, the Masui Falls are best seen from the Zambian side of the Zambezi gorge.

The easiest descent into the gorge is at Palm Grove, immediately upstream of the railway bridge on the Zambian side. Here, stairs lead down at the end of the previous fall-line to the bank of the whirlpool where the Zambezi sweeps from the foot of the Falls themselves into the first stretch of the gorge.

Archaeological evidence demonstrates that the Victoria Falls region has been occupied by man since the Earlier Stone Age. It is also clear that the Falls themselves are, in geological or archaeological terms, a comparatively recent phenomenon. It has proved possible to correlate the process of formation of the Falls with the archaeological succession and to demonstrate the position of the Falls at various phases of the prehistoric past. In Middle Stone Age times, for example, the waterfall was about eight kilometres downstream of its present position. This was probably at least 100 000 years ago and since then there have been no fewer than seven separate and distinct lines of the Falls. As there is evidence that the Middle Stone Age extended over a very long period of time in this area, the cutting back of the Falls may have been even more rapid. It is clear that each stage in the Falls' retreat has been comparatively short-lived. In due course, perhaps in only a few thousand years' time, the Victoria Falls we see today will be no more and a new waterfall will have formed a short distance upstream. Eventually the Falls will retreat as far as the point, some three kilometres above their present line, where the Zambezi, previously flowing in a general eastward direction, takes a great bend to the south. Upstream of this bend it seems probable that wide falls such as the present one will not generally be formed, but that the river will cut back more gradually in a series of rapids. Since, as the Falls retreat, each successive waterfall is slightly lower than its predecessor, the time must eventually come when there will be no Victoria Falls at all, and the river will traverse the entire area in a gradually deepening gorge.

The sheer size and variety of the Victoria Falls present insurmountable difficulties to representation by painting, by photography, or by the written word. The illustrations of this book show some attempts by the first two methods; this chapter will conclude with a selection of prose descriptions taken from the writings of several early visitors.

Descriptions and Impressions of the Victoria Falls

. . . the Victoria Falls have been formed by a crack right across the river, in the hard, black, basaltic rock which there formed the bed of the Zambesi. The lips of the crack are still quite sharp, save about three feet of the edge over which the water rolls. . . . When the mighty rift occurred, no change of level took place in the two parts of the bed of the river thus rent asunder, consequently, in coming down the river, to Garden Island, the water suddenly disappears, and we see the opposite side of the cleft, with grass and trees growing where once the river ran, on the same level as that part of its bed on which we sail. . . . Into this chasm, of twice the depth of Niagara-fall, the river, a full mile wide, rolls with a deafening roar;

Fig. 12 The Masui Falls seen from the Zambian bank.

13

and this is Mosi-oa-Tunya or the Victoria Falls.

The whole body of water rolls clear over, quite unbroken; but, after a descent of ten or more feet, the entire mass suddenly becomes like a huge sheet of driven snow. Pieces of water leap off it in the form of comets with tails streaming behind, till the whole snowy sheet becomes myriads of rushing, leaping, aqueous comets.

Much of the spray, rising to the west of Garden Island, falls on the grove of evergreen trees opposite; and from the leaves, heavy drops are for ever falling, to form sundry little rills, which, in running down the steep face of rock, are blown off and turned back, or licked off their perpendicular bed, up into the column from which they have just descended.

The morning sun gilds these columns of watery smoke with all the glowing colours of double or treble rainbows. The evening sun, from a hot yellow sky, imparts a sulphureous hue, and gives one the impression that the yawning gulf might resemble the mouth of the bottomless pit. No bird sits and sings on the branches of the grove of perpetual showers, or ever builds its nest there. . . . The sunshine, elsewhere in this land so overpowering, never penetrates the deep gloom of that shade. In the presence of the strange Mosi-oa-Tunya, we can sympathise with those who, when the world was young, peopled earth, air, and river, with beings not of mortal form. Sacred to what deity would be this awful chasm and that dark grove, over which hovers an ever-abiding 'pillar of cloud'?

The ancient Batoka Chieftains used Kazeruka, now Garden Island, and Boaruka, the island further west, also on the lip of the Falls, as sacred spots for worshipping the Deity. It is no wonder that under the cloudy columns, and near the brilliant rainbows, with the ceaseless roar of the cataract, with the perpetual flow, as if pouring forth from the hand of the Almighty, their souls should be filled with reverential awe.

(D. and C. Livingstone, 1865: 152–8)

We approached the brink with trembling, and carefully parting the bushes with our hands, looked at once on the first grand view of the Falls at the west end. Picture to yourself a stupendous perpendicular rent in a mass of basaltic rock, extending more than a mile (scarcely the half of which, however, is visible) and only sixty to a hundred yards wide, right across the river, from one end to the other, into which pours this mighty river, roaring, foaming and boiling. Then immediately before you, a large body of water, between eighty and ninety yards wide, stealing at first with rapid and snake-like undulations over the hard and slippery rock, at length leaping at an angle of thirty degrees, then forty-five degrees, for more than one hundred yards, and then with the impetus its rapid descent has given it, bounding bodily fifteen or twenty feet clear of the rock, and falling with thundering report into the dark and boiling chasm beneath, seeming, by its velocity, so to entrance the nervous spectator that he fancies himself being involuntarily drawn into the stream and by some invisible spell tempted to fling himself headlong into it and join in its gambols; but anon he recovers himself with a nervous start, and draws back a pace or two, gazing in awe and wonder upon the stream as it goes leaping wildly and with 'delirious bound' over huge rocks. It is a scene of wild sublimity.

. . . Nothing can be more delicately beautiful and pleasing to the eye than the milky streams, broken at the top by dividing rocks and widening to the base, pouring down in one unbroken flow of snowy whiteness from a height of upwards of three hundred feet. Little juvenile cataracts steal quietly aside, as if fearful of the overpowering crush of the great ones, and these skip and sport down the greasy steps from rock to rock, while long, downy, snowy streamers, sometimes thick and voluminous, at other times light and airy, are swayed and wafted to and fro when the wind finds an entrance at the narrow outlet of the mighty river, which from the breadth of a mile or more, is here condensed into the narrow space of from thirty to fifty yards, or even less, then flowing out near its eastern extremity between high cliffs, running away to the west, and nearly doubling upon itself, then back again to the east in a very compact zigzag manner for about five miles, finally turning away to the east. The stream pours playfully into this narrow rent, sending up volumes of spray, and the waters from the base flow westward, and, meeting there the great body of water from the west, which here slackens its speed before the entrance, steals slowly round, at the solemn pace of a funeral procession, before it escapes from its confinement between the massive columns of rock. A large semi-circular gap having been broken away in the bank of the river forms a large, shady, almost cavernous enlargement, in which the deep, dark waters quietly eddy about, then dash up against the rocky shore, which drives them foaming and hurrying backwards.

(J. Chapman, 1868, II: 116, 130–1)

It seemed to me as if my own identity were swallowed up in the surrounding glory, the voice of which rolled on forever, like the waves of eternity. . . . No human being can describe the infinite; and what I saw was a part of infinity made visible and framed in beauty.

(E. Mohr, 1876: 327)

To my mind the Victoria Falls of the Zambesi are one of the most imposing phenomena of the world. . . . Let the reader then imagine himself to have taken a position upon a spot facing a rugged dark brown rocky wall about 200 yards away, rising 400 feet above its base, which is out of sight. Over the top of this are dashing the waters of the Zambesi. About 100 yards from the western bank he sees several islands adorned with tropical vegetation in rich abundance; further on towards the eastern shore and close to the edge of the abyss his eye will light upon nearly thirty bare brown crags that divide the rushing stream into as many different channels. To the left again, between the bright green islands and the western shore, he will observe that the great wall of rock is considerably lower, allowing a ponderous volume of water to rush impetuously as it were into a corner, whence it is precipitated in a broad sheet into the gulf below; beyond this and the next cascade he will see another portion of the surface of the rock, and as he carries his eye along he will be struck with admiration at the jutting peaks that stand out in vivid con-

15

trast to the angry foam that seethes between them. The countless jets and streams assume all colours and all forms; some are bright and gleaming, some dark and sombre; but as they plunge impetuously into the depth below they make up a spectacle that cannot fail to exite a sensation of mingled astonishment and delight. . . .

Nor does the magnificence of the view end with the prospect of the giant waterfall itself. Let us raise our eyes towards the blue horizon; another glorious spectacle awaits us. Stretching far away in the distance are the numerous islands with which the river-bed is studded, the gorgeous verdure of their fan-palms and saro-palms standing out in striking contrast to the subdued azure of the hills behind. All around them, furnishing a deep blue bordering, lies the expanse of the mighty stream that moves so placidly and silently that at first it might seem to be without movement at all; but gradually as it proceeds it acquires a sensible increase in velocity, till checked by the rocky ridge that impedes its flow, it gathers up its force to take its mighty plunge into the deep abyss. . . .

Nor less striking is the effect when we turn towards the chasm or rocky trough that receives the rolling flood. The rock on which we stand is rich with varied vegetation. . . . In a large measure this peculiar vegetation owes its existence to the perpetual fall of spray from the cataract; from every separate cascade clouds of vapour incessantly ascend to such a height that they may be seen for fifty miles away; at one moment they are so dense that they completely block out the view of anything beyond; another moment and a gust of wind will waft them all aside, and leave nothing more than a thin transparent veil; as the density of this increases or diminishes, the islands that lie upon the farther side will seem alternately to recede or advance like visions in a fairy scene. . . .

The incessant roar that rises from the mighty trough below fills the air for miles around with a rolling as of thunder; . . . the seething waters before us crash against the crags; we find the ground beneath our feet tremble as though there were some convulsion in a subterranean cave beneath . . . no infernal crater in which the elements were all at strife could produce a more thrilling throb of nature! Truly it is a scene in which a man may well become aware of his own insignificance!

(E. Holub, 1881, I: 191–6)

One stands . . . on the very verge of the chasm, on a level with the river above, and only separated from the cataract by the breadth of the opening . . . into which it dashes, so that when a sudden puff of wind blows away the spray immediately in front one sees the beautiful blue river, studded with thickly-wooded, palm-bearing islands, seemingly as still and quiet as a lake, flowing tranquilly on heedless of its coming danger, till with a crash it leaps in one splendid mass of fleecy, white foam into an abyss four hundred feet in depth. At whatever part one looks the rays of the sun, shining on the descending masses of foam, form a double zone of prismatic colours, of whose depth and brilliancy no one who has only seen the comparatively faint tints of an ordinary rainbow can form any conception. Such are the Victoria Falls – one of, if not *the*, most transcendentally beautiful natural phenomena on this side of Paradise.

(F. C. Selous, 1881, 109–10)

This (the Devil's Cataract) is the smallest of the falls, but it is the most beautiful, or, more correctly speaking, the only one that is really beautiful, for all else at Mozi-oa-tunia is sublimely horrible. That enormous gulf, black as is the basalt which forms it, dark and dense as the cloud which enwraps it, would have been chosen, if known in biblical times, as an image of the infernal regions, a hell of water and darkness, more terrible perhaps than the hell of fire and light. As if to increase the sensation of horror which is experienced in (the) presence of this prodigy of nature, one must risk one's life in order to survey it. . . . At times, when peering into the depths, through that eternal mist, one may perceive a mass of confused shapes, like unto vast and frightful ruins. These are peaks of rocks of enormous height, on to which the water dashes and becomes at once converted into a cloud of spray, which rolls and tumbles about the peaks where it was formed, and will continue to do so as long as the water falls and the rocks are there to receive it. . . . I could perceive from time to time, as the mist slightly shifted, confusedly appear a series of pinnacles, similar to the minarets and spires of some fantastic cathedral, which shot up, as it were, from out of the mass of seething waters. . . . The islands of the cataract and the rocks which lie about it are all covered with the densest vegetation, but the green is dark, sad-coloured and monotonous, although a clump or two of palms, as they shoot their elegant heads above the thickets of evergreens which surround them, do their best to break the melancholy aspect of the picture.

(A. A. de Serpa Pinto, 1881, II: 158–63)

I expected to find something superb, grand, marvellous. I had never been so disappointed. . . . It is hell itself, a corner of which seems to open at your feet: a dark and terrible hell, from the middle of which you expect every moment to see some repulsive monster rising in anger.

(L. Decle, 1898: 96–8)

As the vast masses of foaming water are precipitated, with the constant roll of thunder into the abyss, they are broken up into comet's tails, again into spray, and still again are comminuted into driving mist. The air forced down with them sets up a current along the canyon and, ascending in eddies in the chasm, carries with it the spindrift of the dashing spray, and rises in vapoury clouds and columns far above the Falls. . . . Amidst this sunlit vapour is born the crowning spectacle of the Falls . . . the glorious double rainbow follows one, whether in the rich prismatic colours of the daytime or the neutral tints of the moonlight.

(A. J. C. Molyneux, 1905: 53–4)

The name (Rain Forest) is appropriate as well as picturesque, for the spray from the Falls, rising in a stupendous column from the chasm below, falls in an incessant rain-shower on this tongue of land – three parts tree jungle and one part grass; a rain so overpowering that it drips in torrents from every branch and leaf, rustles in the coarse grass, lies in pools on the ground and in a very few minutes soaks the sightseer to the skin. . . . A man may walk to the very brink; immediately opposite him, and so close that he can almost pitch a stone into it, is the descending wall of foam, and from the pit below there leaps up in volleys like small shot, and with a fury that blinds and stuns, the eternal spray-storm. Sometimes it completely obscures the cataract . . . and renders it almost impossible for a man to stand upright. Then as it drifts with the wind, through the seams are visible the yellow and white crests as they flash along the opposite summit, and the descending squadrons as they pitch into the booming depths below.

(Lord Curzon of Kedleston, 1923: 133–4)

A truly magnificent sight, and one which brings home the tremendous glory of the whole mighty work of Nature, and the comparative insignificance of humanity.

(P. M. Clark, 1925: 3)

Select Bibliography

CHAPMAN, J. *Travels in the Interior of South Africa*, London, 1868.

CLARK, J. D., 'Introduction' in B. M. Fagan (ed.) *The Victoria Falls*, Livingstone, 1964, pp. 11–20.

CLARK, P. M., *Guide to Victoria Falls*, Victoria Falls, 1925.

CURZON OF KEDLESTON, *LORD*. *Tales of Travel*, London, 1923.

DECLE, L. *Three Years in Savage Africa*, London, 1898.

HOLUB, E., *Seven Years in South Africa*, London, 1881.

LAMPLUGH, G. W. 'The gorge and basin of the Zambesi below the Victoria Falls', *Geographical Journal*, xxxi, 1908.

LIVINGSTONE, D. and LIVINGSTONE, C. *Narrative of an Expedition to the Zambesi and its Tributaries*, London, 1865.

MOHR, E. *To the Victoria Falls of the Zambesi*, London, 1876.

MOLYNEUX, A. J. C. 'The physical history of the Victoria Falls', *Geographical Journal*, xxv, 1905.

SELOUS, F. C. *A Hunter's Wanderings in Africa*, London, 1881.

DE SERPA PINTO, A. A. *How I Crossed Africa*, London, 1881.

CHAPTER 2

The Geology
of the Victoria Falls

G. Bond

More than two kilometres wide, over one hundred metres high, the Victoria Falls form the largest known curtain of falling water in the world. Above the Falls the river is wide and placid, below them it is a narrow angry torrent, and it is natural to ask why it behaves in this way. David Livingstone concluded that the earth had been split by some shattering cataclysm, and that the water of the Zambezi had simply fallen into a ready-made cleft. More recent work by geologists has not confirmed this idea, but the story of the development of the Falls remains a remarkable one.

The southern part of the African continent is rather like an inverted dish. There is a low-lying narrow strip round most of the coast, which is very flat. This strip is of varying width and is backed by an escarpment which may be precipitous, or merely a long and appreciably steeper slope. This separates the coastal plain from the interior plateau which, at an average height of 1000 to 1400 metres above sea level, forms the greater part of the country. In comparatively late geological times this huge and more or less level plain was gently bent into undulating depressions and swells. The streams rise on the swells, and collect into major rivers in the depressions. These major rivers then have to find their way to the sea across the rim of the continent and down the escarpment. As a result, all the main rivers of southern Africa have falls, or at least rapids, somewhere on their journey to the sea from the interior. What form these take depends upon the types of rocks across which they run, and the descent is generally accomplished in several stages. In the case of the Zambezi, the Victoria Falls are the most spectacular stage in the descent. The existence of so large a fall at this point depends upon the coincidence of a number of favourable factors.

Waterfalls are formed by the erosive action of fast-moving water, but certain regional and local conditions are needed before a fall can develop. Niagara and many other waterfalls have a horizontal stratum of hard rock, such as limestone, forming the lip of the fall, but underlain by a thick stratum of much softer shale. Water, plunging over the edge, swirls round in a deep pool and undercuts the lip of the fall by removing the soft rock below. Fragments then fall off the unsupported edge and are reduced in size by churning and grinding in the plunge-pool until they are carried away by the stream. However, the sides of the gorges at the Victoria Falls are in basalt from top to bottom, and this is confirmed by deep boreholes at the Third Gorge Power Station and again at the Fifth Gorge. It is obvious, therefore, that the local mechanism of cutting and erosion at the Victoria Falls differs from that at Niagara.

A waterfall can also develop where the junction of hard and soft rocks crosses a river bed, with the soft one on the downstream side. The softer rock is then eroded faster than the hard one and a fall may result.

The gorges below the Falls provide many kilometres of natural section, nearly 120 metres deep, in which the rocks may be examined. There is only one rock type exposed, and that is basalt lava. The valley of the Zambezi runs in these rocks for some 200 kilometres from Kazungula, at the junction of the Chobe and Zambezi, to a point some 130 kilometres below the Falls, where a fault crosses the river and brings comparatively soft sandstones against the very hard basalts.

These basalts belong to great sheets of lava which were erupted long before the Zambezi River was in existence, in the period of geological time known in South Africa as the Upper Karroo System and elsewhere as the Jurassic. This means that the eruptions took place about a hundred and fifty million years ago. They covered an enormous area stretching right down to Lesotho, and from the east to the west coasts of the continent. They are now split up into isolated patches by erosion and earth movements, and are much obscured by later deposits. Although they are true lava flows, which were poured on to what was then the surface of the land, no craters have been found from which they could have come, and there are no signs that they were erupted with violence and explosion in the way that is typical of volcanic cones. They probably came from volcanoes which had no cones and no central craters, being merely long fissures in the earth's crust up which very liquid lava flowed quietly. Such eruptions have taken place in many other parts of the world at various times. They invariably produce basalt in enormous quantities, which is very mobile and flows for great distances before cooling and solidifying.

Basalt originates as a molten rock from one of the shells of the earth's crust and its mobility depends not only on its high temperature, but also on the amount of fluxes it contains, which reduce the temperature at which it solidifies. One of the commonest of these fluxes is water in the form of vapour. This has left plenty of evidence of its former presence in the lavas of the Falls area. Examination shows that there are two distinct types of basalt present. One is a fine-grained dark bluish rock, which forms bare cliffs with strong vertical jointing in the walls of the gorges. The second variety is purplish red in colour, full of almond-shaped inclusions of white minerals, often coated with a green skin. An example of this type can be seen on the paths from the Victoria Falls Hotel to the Falls. These two types alternate. The second variety forms bands up to six metres thick sandwiched between much greater thicknesses of the fine-grained massive variety. The vesicular bands are the slaggy tops and bottoms of individual lava flows. Each band consists of two parts, the top of the underlying flow and the bottom of the succeeding one. These bands are rather easily weathered and are picked out in the gorges (below the second) by lines of trees.

The slaggy parts of the flows were formed by the expansion of the water vapour and other gases in the molten lava, which were released when the liquid reached the surface. This produced innumerable more or less spherical holes. Sometimes these remained as open cavities, but more frequently they were filled with secondary minerals quite soon after their formation. These were deposited from solutions which found it easy to circulate in the basalts.

One kind belongs to the group of minerals called Zeolites. They occur as radiating needle-shaped crystal bunches in some of the larger cavities, and are white or pale pink in colour. Natrolite, Scolecite, and Laumontite are found, but they are all similar in appearance and chemical composition, being hydrated silicates of lime, soda and alumina. The name Zeolite means 'boiling stone'. When strongly heated these minerals froth up as the water in them is being driven off. Another kind of filling, not so common at the Victoria Falls themselves, is agate. This is a hydrated form of silica and fills cavities with a beautifully banded, semi-transparent material, which is generally pale grey or white, but may be stained orange or red. The banding follows the shape of the original hole, and occasionally the central part is still open. When this occurs beautifully clear crystals of rock crystal (quartz) project into the centre, and sometimes show the pale purple shade of amethyst. The outside skin of agate-filled cavities may be dark green from the presence of the mineral Chlorite.

Although the basalts were poured out on the surface, and each successive flow formed the land surface at the time of its formation, flow followed flow in quick succession. There are no intercalations of sediments, such as sandstone or shale, in the face of the gorges. There was not even time for the formation of the typical red soil which forms on their surface when they are weathered. If any was formed it was entirely removed before the next flow was laid down. Perhaps this is not surprising as the climate at the time was an extremely arid desert one. The total thickness of the lava at the Victoria Falls is not known exactly, since the gorge does not cut through to its base, but from evidence elsewhere it is probably more than 300 metres. This means that there may be at least as great a thickness of basalt below the river bed as there is in the walls of the gorge above.

After the formation of the basalts there was a long interval of time about which we know nothing. This vast period of time, which must have been more than a hundred million years, is a closed book, but at the end of it conditions changed and deposits again began to form on the eroded surface of the basalts. These record a very complex series of events and only a brief account can be given here.

The lowest – that is the oldest – rock, lying on the basalt, is chalcedony, which is rather like flint. This is only one or two metres thick, but is important as the source of raw material from which so many of the stone implements of prehistoric man were made. It is followed by a sandstone, of about the same thickness, with a very peculiar texture. It is fairly well consolidated but is pierced by a large number of pipes or holes, about the thickness of a large grass stem, which have given it the name Pipe Sandstone. Above it there is a thick mass of red unconsolidated sand. This is called the Kalahari Sand and it has a very wide distribution in southern Africa. This series is well seen in the railway cutting near the Falls Hotel or on the scarp below the Chalets Hotel near Livingstone Airport. The red sands were accumulated under desert conditions, and are typical wind-blown deposits. They form the low scarps which flank the Zambezi Valley on both sides, and lead up to the very level surface of the surrounding country. Livingstone town is built on the edge of the northern scarp. The sand scarps stretch far down the valley below the Victoria Falls themselves and they emphasise the peculiar double nature of the valley.

Standing on one of the sand scarps above the Falls and looking across and downstream, one can see that the river flows on the floor of a wide shallow valley. At the lip of the Falls the river channel changes its nature, but the gorge is cut in the continuation of the same broad shallow valley, which stretches for many kilometres downstream. This must have been the valley in which a placid Zambezi used to flow as it does now above the Falls. It was, in fact, above the Falls until the gorges were cut.

The most striking features of these gorges are their zig-zag shape and steepness. These features make the Victoria Falls unique among the great waterfalls of the world, because it is possible to walk almost the entire width along a platform at the height of the lip in front of the Main Falls. The diagrammatic plan shows that the gorge consists of at least eight more or less east-west sections connected by much shorter ones running from north to south. The most clearly defined of these short connections is at the Boiling Pot, between the first and second gorges.

If any of the bare horizontal surfaces of basalt are examined, the reason for this arrangement becomes clear. Any of these surfaces will show that the basalt is broken by systems of vertical cracks called joints. A very strong set has a more or less east-west direction, and there is another set running roughly from north to south. There are less prominent fractures at other angles but these are not so important.

These joints may have formed as shrinkage cracks when the lavas cooled, but the east-west sets have been emphasised by later crustal movements. In this way zones of very close jointing have been formed, some of them being filled with material almost as soft as clay. The present fall-line is along one of these zones and at once gives the explanation for all the other gorges below.

When the Zambezi, in cutting its gorge upstream, reached a zone of such soft material, the tremendous power of this large volume of water would very quickly scoop out the soft material from the fissures. As the fissures run from east to west, which is the general direction of the river valley, it is only where the river runs in a north to south direction that a broad fall can be formed in this way. It so happens that near Livingstone the general easterly course of the river suddenly swings southwards, and continues in this direction for a few kilometres. It is in this reach that broad falls are possible. Once the soft material has been removed and the fall established on an east-west line, a period of stability follows while the water searches out the weakest point in the lip. This is a relatively slow process because the north-south joint planes are not filled with soft material. Inevitably in time, a block is loosened, falls off, and the lip is lowered at this point.

Once the lip is lowered slightly at one place by this process, more water is concentrated at that spot, and the erosive power is increased. This leads to the removal of more blocks, and this point is lowered preferentially and cut further back until practically the full force of the river is concentrated into a narrow fissure and the broad fall-line is abandoned. Once this has happened it is only a question of time before the retreating narrow gorge cuts back into another transverse fracture zone of soft material. The whole force of the river is then employed in gouging out this soft zone, and another broad fall is established.

This process of retreat of the fall-line has happened several times. The northern lips of at least seven transverse gorges were once full-scale Victoria Falls, which flourished for a time, until one point of the lip gave way. This generally happened near one end; the old fall was abandoned, and in time a new one established. Those farthest downstream, which have been abandoned longest, are least easy to recognise, but the Second Gorge and the Boiling Pot show clearly how the process has operated. The northern lip of the Second Gorge is clearly moulded by water action, and the north-south Boiling Pot Gorge marks the point where this lip gave way. The present line is, therefore, only a temporary pause in the process of retreat, which is still continuing and will probably go on until the Falls reach the point, near the Maramba con-

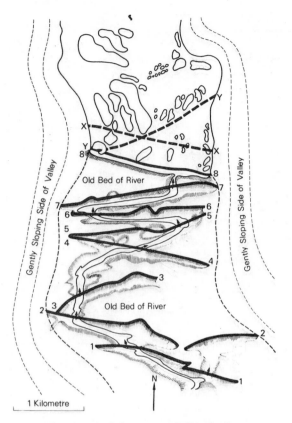

Fig. 1 The retreat of the Victoria Falls. The heavy numbered lines 1–7 are abandoned lines of the Falls; 8 is the present position; X and Y are probable future fall-lines. The arrows mark the point where the lip of the fall gave way at each stage of the retreat. Compare the vertical air photograph (frontispiece).

fluence, where the river swings back again to a west-east course.

The present fall-line is at a stage when it is possible to see where it may give way. The lip is level right across from the Eastern Cataract to Cataract Island. The extreme western Fall (Devil's Cataract) has given way and is several metres lower than any other point. There are the beginnings of a short connecting gorge already in evidence. The process is very slow judged by the span of human life and there is

23

Fig. 2 The Victoria Falls and Gorges from the air.

practically no change to be seen since the first accurate pictorial records were made. There is no fear that the Falls will change any more rapidly in the near future. Yet change they must; and the Devil's Cataract is the probable line along which they will develop. There is, however, a deep cleft in Cataract Island which has already cut back some distance, forming a deep narrow cleft parallel with the Second Gorge below. This cleft does not normally carry a great volume of water, but in time of flood – and it is at such times that the river has the greatest power of erosion – there is a strong flow. It looks as though the Devil's Cataract has established a lead which it will be difficult for the more modest cleft in

Cataract Island to overhaul.

Aerial photographs show that no matter which of these two eventually gains the mastery, there are two possible lines of weakness which they will meet as they cut upstream. One runs north-eastwards along the margins of a long line of islands, and the other more or less eastwards through Livingstone Island. Perhaps they will both form fall-lines, first along the easterly and then along the north-easterly lines. Time alone will show. Perhaps later generations will see and record them, for it is certain that Stone Age man saw the Falls retreat several kilometres up the present system of gorges.

It was shown above that the valley below the Falls consists of two parts, the deep gorge and a wide shallow valley which is the continuation of the one above the Falls. While the Zambezi still flowed on this higher surface it formed various alluvial deposits of gravel. Stone Age tools,* made by prehistoric peoples who lived in the valley, have been found in these deposits. These gravels with stone implements are found for at least eighteen kilometres down the valley from the Falls. This shows that, since the time their makers lived there, the river has cut at least that length of gorge in the floor of its old valley. It is not possible to say with any exactness how long this has taken, but it probably covers a space of time between a quarter and half a million years long.

From this it is tempting to work out an average rate at which the excavation has been carried out, but this would be misleading as a guide to the rate at which erosion is now going on. It has been pointed out that the process is not uniform, because the excavation of the soft east to west shatter-zones must be much more rapid than the cutting of the connecting gorges between them. That means that the retreat proceeds by a series of alternating fast and slow stages. But that is not the only changing factor in the story.

There is evidence that the climate has changed from time to time. The alluvial deposits laid down by the Zambezi suggest that there may have been variations in the amount of rainfall at various past periods. Not only did the various prehistoric people see the Victoria Falls at different stages in their retreat, they probably also lived under differing climatic conditions.

Since the erosive power of the river varies with the amount of water in it, this factor

*See Chapter 4.

must also have influenced the rate of retreat. The kind of material which the river is bringing down today, in the placid reaches above the Falls, is mainly coarse sand. Yet at two periods at least in its history since the first men made their tools there, it seems to have been capable of rolling along coarse gravels, indicating a very much more powerful stream. There were also periods of reduced activity; indeed, the river is probably much smaller now than it has sometimes been.

The study of the present behaviour of the Falls gives us the clues to its past history, and from this we can guess its future. We are lucky to live at a time when the lip of the Falls is more or less intact, and the full width is used by the river in its plunge to the gorge below.

Select Bibliography

BOND, G. 'Pleistocene Environments in Southern Africa' in F. C. Howell and F. Boulière (eds.), African Ecology and Human Evolution, Chicago, 1963, pp. 308–335.

LAMPLUGH, G. W. 'Geology of the Zambezi Basin around Batoka Gorge', Quarterly Journal of the Geological Society, lxiii, 1907, pp. 162–216.

MAUFE, H. B. 'New Sections in the Kalahari Beds at the Victoria Falls, Rhodesia', Transactions Geological Society of South Africa, xli, 1938, pp. 211–224.

MOLYNEUX, A. J. C. 'The Physical History of the Victoria Falls', Geographical Journal, xxv, 1905, pp. 40–55.

CHAPTER 3

The Formation of the Victoria Falls

Chris Nugent

The Victoria Falls form the point where the waters of the mighty Zambezi pour off the Southern African Plateau into the chasm of Batoka Gorge and thence to the wide rift valley of the Gwembe Trough. As Professor Bond has shown in Chapter 2, this has not always been so. The river and the Falls have experienced a dramatic evolution since Early Stone Age times, which Stone Age man would have witnessed as he used and discarded his tools.

The story of the developments that led to the formation of today's Victoria Falls can be pieced together from the record preserved in sediments both upstream and downstream. Having left the seasonal swamps of the Barotse Plain, the Zambezi passes over a series of rapids in the underlying basalt before entering the Chobe Swamps at Katima Mulilo (Fig. 1). From there to the Mambova Rapids, the river flows with a very gentle gradient across its own alluvium.

The alluvial sediments of the Chobe Swamps fill a rifted basin, one of several still forming in the southern African interior, at the southern extension of the East African Rift System. These basins are linked by stream lines and contain river and lake sediments, dating from the last few million years, which broadly delineate them in Fig. 1. Whereas today the Okavango and Chobe basins contain swamps, the surface of the Makgadikgadi now forms a series of salt pans that are dry for most of the year. Fossil beach lines around the pans record the former existence of large lakes (Cooke, 1980). Middle and Late Stone Age sites occur on or near these ancient beaches, and dates obtained from associated carbonate and shelly deposits show that lakes have existed at various levels over the Makgadikgadi during periods ex-

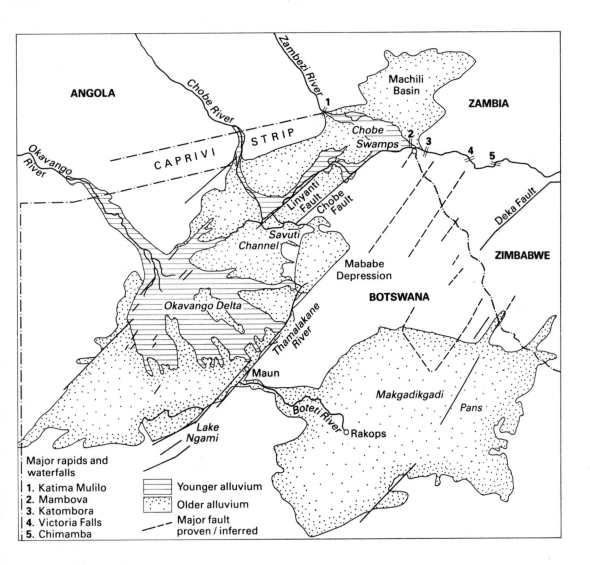

ANGOLA

Okavango River

Zambezi River

Chobe River

CAPRIVI STRIP

Machili Basin

ZAMBIA

Chobe Swamps

1

2 3

4 5

Linyanti Fault

Chobe Fault

Deka Fault

Savuti Channel

Mababe Depression

ZIMBABWE

BOTSWANA

Okavango Delta

Thamalakane River

Maun

Boteti River

Lake Ngami

Rakops

Makgadikgadi

Pans

Major rapids and waterfalls
1. Katima Mulilo
2. Mambova
3. Katombora
4. Victoria Falls
5. Chimamba

Younger alluvium	
Older alluvium	
Major fault proven / inferred	

Fig. 1 The distribution of alluvial and lacustrine sediments in Central Southern Africa, the basins of Greater palaeo-lake Makgadikgadi.

tending from at least 50 000 years ago into recent times.

The highest beach lines, at about 945 metres above sea level, lie some 65 metres higher than the lip of the Victoria Falls. They outline a lake which extended over the Makgadikgadi, the southern Okavango and most of the Chobe Swamps, known as Greater palaeo-lake Makgadikgadi. This lake had an area of about 60 000 square kilometres, roughly the size of present-day Lake Victoria. The combined modern inflows of the Okavango and Chobe rivers, together with

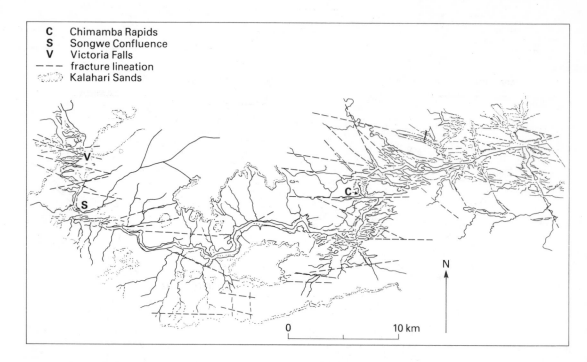

C   Chimamba Rapids
S   Songwe Confluence
V   Victoria Falls
– –   fracture lineation
    Kalahari Sands

Fig. 2 Sketch map of the upstream end of Batoka Gorge and the local fracture pattern (after Clark, 1950).

local rainfall, supply under modern climatic conditions less than half the water required to balance evaporation from the surface of such a large lake. This implies that the Upper Zambezi must have flowed into the lake, at least at its high stands. Under these circumstances the waters would have been lost in evaporation, without ever reaching the Victoria Falls.

So what caused the flow of the Upper Zambezi to be diverted along its present course and over the Victoria Falls, so that the huge old Makgadikgadi lake dried up? Technically, what happened is known as a river capture: the Middle Zambezi captured its upper catchment. This could have resulted from headwards erosion, caused by the Middle Zambezi cutting upstream into its water-shed until it cut back into the river supplying the former lake, or into the lake itself. Alternatively capture could have occurred through overtopping, by the lake rising and overflowing onto the basalt plateau upstream of the Victoria Falls.

Evidence for overtopping comes from downstream of Chirundu, in the Mana Pools National Park. Here a ridge of poorly sorted, unbedded, coarse-grained alluvium known as the Stony Ridge remains as evidence of a cataclysmic flood that swept along the former river channel. The Stony Ridge flood probably lasted only a few weeks, as several years' supply of water poured out of the lake, across the basalt plateau and into the pre-existing river system of the Middle Zambezi. As the waters drained rapidly away, they eroded downwards into the former lake margin at Katombora, some 15 kilometres downstream of Kazungula. This cut the proto-Katombora Gap, establishing the link between the Upper and Middle Zambezi that the river has used in modern times. This inferred cataclysmic flood thus marks the birth of the Victoria Falls and the Zambezi as we know them.

Was there a waterfall before capture? The answer is uncertain. The distribution of fish species within the river system (Chapter 14) suggests that certain species have never been able to move freely between the Upper and Middle Zambezi Rivers; and it may be that a waterfall or waterfalls had already formed on the river by the time the Upper Zambezi was captured. These falls would have formed a comparatively uninteresting spectacle, lying on a minor river supplied by a small catchment. Flow was almost certainly highly seasonal, similar to that of the present day Matetsi River which drains the basalt plateau to the south of the Zambezi and has cut several rapids and waterfalls along its descent into the gorge.

Whether or not the proto-Middle Zambezi once resembled the modern Matetsi, it was changed for ever when palaeo-lake Makgadikgadi overtopped. Such a flood would have eroded rapidly downwards into the stream's bed. Even after the flood had abated and much of the ancient lake had drained away, the Zambezi would have continued to erode downwards until it established a much gentler gradient, in equilibrium with the greater flow. This was the process that created Batoka Gorge, whose walls rise from the river at thirty degrees or more along its whole 110-kilometre length and are almost vertical near the Victoria Falls. The Zambezi loses some 270-metres of height within Batoka Gorge (not counting the drop at the Falls), an average gradient of about 1:400. Within the broad rift valleys downstream the gradient is reduced to 1:4 000 and the river is still cutting into its bed, albeit very slowly. We may conclude that the Zambezi is downcutting rather more rapidly within Batoka Gorge, which is thus being progressively deepened.

The tributary streams that flow into Batoka Gorge have cut gorges of their own (Fig. 2), dissecting the plateau on either side of the Zambezi into some of the roughest and least hospitable country in the world. Although no tributaries have developed waterfalls that equal the splendour of the Victoria Falls, many waterfalls and rapids have been created and these generally occur at changes in the hardness of the underlying rock. Where a stream flows onto a fault in the basalt, the soft rock in the fault zone has often been eroded away to form a gorge, and the harder rock upstream of the fault is thus the site of rapids or a waterfall.

As Professor Bond explained in Chapter 2, the Zambezi, downstream of Victoria Falls, crosses several east–west trending faults which mark a series of seven former Falls positions. At each in turn, the soft rock within the fault zone was eroded away to leave the harder bounding rock as the lip of a new waterfall. Flowing off the relatively gentle slope of the basalt plateau, the river eroded downwards into the Falls more slowly than it cut into the steeeper bed of the gorge downstream. This very slow downward erosion characterises most of the modern fall line at the present time. It is only after a part of the sharp lip had been cut back, the process that has started at Devil's Cataract, that erosion becomes more rapid, cutting downwards and backwards to the next fault zone upstream. Each time the process was repeated the Falls experienced a long period of relative stability during which the lip of the Falls was hardly eroded at all, although Batoka Gorge continued to deepen. The first Victoria Falls were created some time after river capture, which can tentatively be dated from the archaeological record preserved in the sediments downstream. The Zambezi's channel between Batoka and Devil's Gorges and beneath the waters of Lake Kariba is bounded by terraces, rising up to 55 metres above the river. The higher terraces contain Early Stone Age tools, which have been rolled and are therefore redeposited. The surfaces of all the higher terraces are littered with fresh, unrolled tools of Sangoan type (Bond and Clark, 1954; see also Chapter 4). The younger terraces, which may correspond in age with the Younger Gravels at the Victoria Falls (see Chapter 2), contain tools made by the first Middle Stone Age people. The youngest alluvium, bounding the channel, is associated with later Middle Stone Age and Late Stone Age remains.

It is believed that the Middle Zambezi River, prior to capturing its Upper Catchment, flowed at the level of the highest terraces, which were isolated, after capture, by the massively increased flow cutting into the river's bed. The archaeological record suggests that this degradation of the channel began around the time that Stone Age tools of Sangoan type were being made.

As Professor Clark indicates in Chapter 4, the date of the Sangoan is only imprecisely known. It probably falls within the general period 150 000–125 000 years ago. This was the time of the last interglacial period, when the world was on average some 2 degrees Centigrade warmer than it is today and rainfall over most of Africa was rather higher. Sangoan remains are overlain by a Middle Stone Age succession, of which the earliest Middle Stone Age stages may belong to a time of global cooling, marking the end of the last interglacial period and the start of the last 'Ice Age'

It seems that global climatic changes at the peak of the last interglacial were responsible for causing Greater palaeo-lake Makgadikgadi to rise to its maximum height and finally to spill onto the basalt plateau and into the Middle Zambezi River system (Nugent, 1990). It is intriguing to imagine the interior of southern Africa at that time, the huge lake (Fig. 1) fringed with dense Okavango-like vegetation: a time of plenty for the Sangoan people. Later, after the lake spilled into the Middle Zambezi and the river established its new course through the Katombora Gap and over the Victoria Falls, the climate began to cool and rainfall was probably reduced. Downstream, Middle Stone Age people lived on the terraces formed as the river cut down to bedrock.

We have seen how successive waterfalls developed relatively rapidly, then became stable for a long period of time. The retrogression of the Victoria Falls has been irregular for another reason. Flow along the Zambezi River and over the Victoria Falls has been much reduced and may have virtually dried up for periods of perhaps hundreds or thousands of years since the time of capture. Shoreline features around the Makgadikgadi Pans, up to and including 945-metre lake stands, have been dated to Middle and Late Stone Age times, long after Sangoan people witnessed capture and the great flood. Fossil beach lines around Lake Ngami and the Mababe Depression (Fig. 1) indicate a series of lakes at 936 metres in the recent geological past and as recently as 1 500 years ago (Shaw, 1985).

These diversions, which have occurred since capture and the cutting of the Katombora Gap, almost certainly resulted from tectonic rifting movements beneath the Chobe Swamps (Nugent, 1990). Rifting creates fault scarps, which divert the flow of water. The

Chobe River itself follows such scarps between the Savuti offtake and Kazungula (Fig. 1). In order to maintain a 945-metre lake over the Makgadikgadi and the Southern Okavango, an inflow more than twice that of the modern Okavango and Chobe Rivers is required. This implies that the lake was also supplied by the Upper Zambezi and that upper catchment waters were diverted away from the Victoria Falls. Shaw and Thomas (1988) show how such a lake (Lake Caprivi) was ponded behind the Mambova Rapids and may have drained, *via* the base of the Chobe Scarp, into a lake over the Okavango.

During the millennia that man has lived on the banks of the Zambezi, the River and the Falls have undergone immense change. From the flood that heralded the birth of the great river, through dry spells when its waters were diverted into lakes over the Kalahari, the Victoria Falls have been slowly and irregularly but inexorably cutting backward, exposing first one then another line of weakness to create the zig-zag gorges described in the previous chapter. It is intriguing to speculate on what exactly early man saw and understood by these early falls. There must have been times when the river was directed over a narrow fall line and perhaps other times when it was wider than it is today. We must remember that each generation lived, as we do, within a mere moment in the life of this great river. They too saw the Falls as being as permanent and immovable as Mosi-oa-Tunya appears today.

Select Bibliography

BOND, G. and CLARK, J. D. 'The Quaternary Sequence in the Middle Zambezi Valley', *South African Archaeological Bulletin*, ix, 1954, pp. 115–130.

CLARK, J. D. *The Stone Age Cultures of Northern Rhodesia*, Cape Town, 1950.

COOKE, H. J. 'Landform Evolution in the Context of Climatic Change and Neotectonism in the Middle Kalahari of North-Central Botswana', *Transactions Institute of British Geographers*, v, 1980, pp. 80–90.

DERRICOURT, R. M. 'Retrogression rate of the Victoria Falls and the Batoka Gorge', *Nature*, cclxiv, 1976, pp. 23–25.

NUGENT, C. 'The Zambezi River: Tectonism, Climatic Change and Drainage Evolution', *Palaeogeography, Palaeoclimatology, Palaeoecology, in press (1990)*.

SHAW, P. A. 'Late Quaternary Landforms and Environmental Changes in Northwest Botswana', *Transactions Institute of British Geographers*, x, 1985, pp. 333–346.

SHAW, P. A. and THOMAS, D. G. S. 'Lake Caprivi: a Late Quaternary Link between the Zambezi and Middle Kalahari Drainage Systems', *Zeitschrift für Geomorphologie*, xxxii, 1988, pp. 329–337.

CHAPTER 4

Stone Age Man
at the Victoria Falls

J. Desmond Clark

Visitors will often remark upon the finely
glazed and polished stones, chiefly chalcedony and agates, that make up most of the
gravel at the Victoria Falls, especially near
the Eastern Cataract and on the road to the
Fifth Gorge. The archaeologist studying
these gravels will find that a very large
percentage of the glazed and patinated
stones are flakes, cores and retouched tools
made by prehistoric man. This cultural
content of the gravels was first recognised in
the early years of the present century and
the first published account of them dates to
1905. An added interest attaches to these
gravels since they are found on the flat tops

of the spurs that demarcate the zigzag
course of the Zambezi downstream from the
Falls where they were deposited at a time
before the river had cut back to the present
line of the waterfall. On both the Zambian
and the Zimbabwean banks the gravels are
protected by the respective country's Monuments Commission from indiscriminate excavation, and good exposures of them are now
preserved. Those most easily seen are on the
northern side beside the Nakatindi Road
between five and seven kilometres west of
Livingstone, on either side of the main
Livingstone-Victoria Falls road about one and
a half kilometres south of the Maramba River

Fig. 1 (left) Eroded remnants of the 15-metre terrace
west of Livingstone.
Fig. 2 (right) Close-up of a section of the 15-metre
terrace, showing artefacts *in situ*.

bridge, on the road to the Fifth Gorge, and
on top of the basalt spurs which demarcate
the zigzags of the gorge.

Since these gravels are found resting on
terraces at different heights above the river,
and since their composition differs, they are
clearly not all of the same age; the stone
implements and rare fossil remains of
animals that they contain belong also to
widely different ages. The gravels themselves

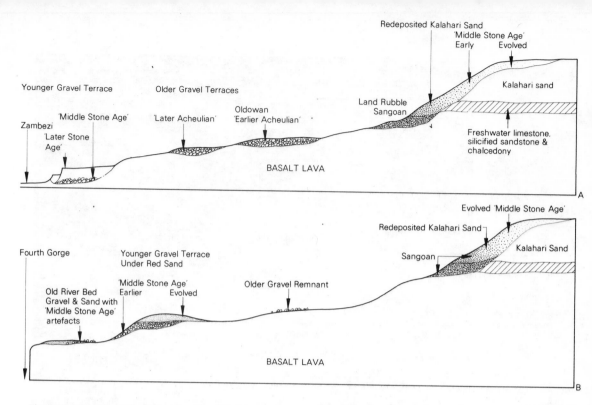

Fig. 3 Section through the north side of the Zambezi Valley: A – upstream of the Victoria Falls, B – at the Fourth Gorge.

are often all that remains of the sediments laid down by the Zambezi River at a time before its bed had been deepened to its present position and when the water was flowing over the basalt lava rock up to fifteen metres or more above the present level of the river. In the course of the millennia that have elapsed since the earliest of these waterlaid sediments were deposited and exposed to erosion by tropical rains, almost all the finer-grained material – sands, silts and clays – has been washed out and carried away to the main river by sheet erosion and by the numerous gullies and peripheral streams that have cut into them. The younger of these aggradation stages, however, have not been exposed to the same

amount of erosion as have the earlier ones, so that the later sediments are generally better preserved and have much of the fine-grained material still in place. Studies of sections exposed in gullies and stream banks will show a stratified sequence of these sediments, in which it is sometimes possible to recognise several periods of fluctuating river activity when more or less finer or coarser material was deposited. Such changes often reflect increased or decreased stream activity which can sometimes be shown to result from long-term variations in temperature and rainfall in the region of the catchment area.

Other deposits are to be found along the scarps of red sand that demarcate the edge of the valley. These consist of accumulations of land rubble, screes and sands which originated at different times in the past, more usually during periods of semi-aridity when torrential rains after a long dry season resulted in rapid run-off scouring the land and redepositing material at a lower level. Sometimes, also, increased wind activity under conditions of lowered temperature was a contributing factor to the redeposition of some of these sands, both on the scarps and in the valley proper. When all these different kinds of sediments are arranged in a sequence from oldest to youngest and the stone implements and fossils they contain are compared, a developing pattern of increasing technological and typological complexity is clearly seen. By comparing and matching up the artefacts from the river sediments with those from the scarp deposits it is possible to correlate the two sequences.

As a result of team studies by natural scientists, physicists, chemists and archaeologists, in particular in the East African Rift zone, not only has a chronological framework emerged from the use of various radiometric dating techniques, but we now have much more reliable evidence of the palaeo-ecological conditions that prevailed at different periods in the past and so of the habitats preferred by prehistoric man and the resources that he exploited for food and the other requirements of social and economic life. This knowledge derives from many different kinds of evidence. The geologist and palaeo-ecologist can show, from the nature of the sediments or chemically altered deposits that he studies, what were the temperature and humidity conditions that prevailed at any one time in the past. The surface texture of sand grains will show whether the agency that accumulated them was water or wind; a study of the heavy mineral content of sands will help to determine the source from which they were

derived; chemical deposition of calcium carbonates (surface limestone) is evidence of low humidity, while concentrations of iron oxides associated with a hard pan (ferricretes) are generally indicative of seasonally higher rainfall and fluctuating temperatures. Palaeontologists studying the fossil faunas have established a series of faunal zones, or spans, characterised by the presence or absence of certain extinct or living species and which show a steady evolutionary development from archaic to modern forms. When a sufficient number of species is represented in a fossil faunal assemblage, it is generally possible to show the relative time-range to which the assemblage belongs. As far as the Victoria Falls area is concerned, both past and present conditions have, unfortunately, been generally unfavourable for the preservation of bone. However, some fossil faunal remains have been found and we have evidence of an early form of elephant, a giraffid and several antelopes that provide valuable dating evidence as well as an indication of the prevailing environmental conditions in the past. They show, in fact, that the conditions under which these animals lived were not essentially different from those of the present day.

Evidence of past plant communities is best provided by studies of fossil pollen found in various kinds of fine-grained sediments, often from lakes or swamps. Studies in the northern part of Zambia cover, perhaps, the past 200 000 years and, with those from other parts of the continent, show that during much of the long period of time corresponding to the Last Glaciation in Eurasia – i.e. from about 70 000 to 10 000 years ago – temperature conditions in Africa were lower by some 6–8 degrees Centigrade and the climate was drier than it is today.

For example, the East African Rift Lakes and Lake Victoria were low until about 12 000 years ago when they began to rise and a more closed vegetation began to replace grassland and open bush. In northern Zambia at that time, some higher altitude plants and much grass pollen are associated with the *Brachystegia* woodlands.

This, then, is the background against which the remains of prehistoric man at the Victoria Falls have to be studied. The conditions of preservation have been such that all the perishable remains – wooden and bone implements, food-waste and any evidence of dwelling structures – have long since disappeared and only the imperishable remains – the stone implements – are preserved. These, especially when they are studied in relation to all the other artefacts in a concentrated assemblage from a single horizon, can, however, tell us not a little about their makers, their technological skill, economic requirements and hunting ability; they can also, perhaps, provide an estimate of the size of the group in which these people lived. Again, it is by comparison with similar artefact assemblages from East Africa and other areas as, for example, the Olduvai Gorge in Tanzania, where the camping places, butchery sites and workshops are preserved together with the scattered bone food-waste and a number of other most exciting features and finds, including the remains of the hominids themselves, that we now know a great deal more about man's biological and cultural evolution than we did when the first edition of this handbook was published in 1952.

We now know that the Pleistocene period, the time of generally lowered overall temperatures (often referred to in Europe as the Glacial Period), began about 1.8 million years ago. The earliest cultural stage, when man made simple chopping, pounding, cutting and scraping tools from local rock, began in the late Pliocene about 2.5 million years ago and lasted for more than a million years; the succeeding period when man made large, bifacial cutting and chopping tools – known as hand-axes and cleavers – lasted for almost as long. Modern man (*Homo sapiens*) with his much more sophisticated tool-kits did not make his appearance in the continent before about 100 000 years ago; in south-central Africa the hunting and gathering way of life was not generally replaced by food-producing economies until about the beginning of the present era. This new time-scale gives us a far more realistic indication of the time involved in bringing about each major biological and cultural advance, as well as of the increasing tempo of these changes which were at first incredibly slow and only perceptibly quickened throughout the world with the onset of village farming in the last six or seven thousand years B.C.

Archaeology, therefore, is the study of man's developing skills, his intellectual ability, manual dexterity and cultural attainments as these can be seen to emerge in his changing social and economic behaviour. When we hold in our hands one of the early stone tools from the Victoria Falls, it is of interest not for its intrinsic value, but for what it represents. A stone scraper, for example, supposes, first of all, a certain standard of skill and knowledge of stone technology on the part of the maker. Next it presupposes something to scrape – a skin, an arrow or spear-shaft – and this in turn indicates a certain level of hunting ability or behaviour such as the use of skins for thongs, clothing, hunting disguises and so on. The associated finds and circumstances indicate the cultural and intellectual level with which one· is dealing. When comparisons are made between assemblages, sites, localities and regions, various broad patterns of ecologically and geographically adapted behaviour emerge and can be seen to form distinctive artefact traditions of long duration. Each of these traditions will contain a number of local expressions or variants, relating to broadly contemporaneous time horizons and generally identified by the names of the sites where the characteristic assemblage was first recognised. In the Zambezi Valley we are concerned essentially with traditions that relate to the woodlands and grasslands of the central African savanna.

In the Zambezi Valley in the vicinity of the Victoria Falls, there exists a record of man's presence right back to the earliest cultural tradition of which we have evidence; this is known as the Oldowan Industry after the Olduvai Gorge where it was first recognised. Some time during the late Tertiary period the Zambezi carved out for itself the broad shallow valley, discussed in Chapter 2 by Professor Bond, and deposited a •series of sediments of which the gravels resting on the terrace at about fifteen metres above the river are the only remaining record. Within these highest and earliest gravels are found heavily abraded choppers made by flaking a nodule or cobble of chalcedony from one or two faces so as to form an irregular, heavy-duty edge for cutting and chopping (Fig. 4, nos. 2 and 3). Together with these there occur a number of intentionally struck flakes which show fairly steep and notched-edge retouch (Fig. 4 no. 1). These constitute a second kind of tool which, because of its small size, must generally have been used between finger and thumb in what has been called the 'precision grip', such as is required when using a pencil or screwdriver. A third type of artefact is a roughly polyhedral stone used for hammering and bashing.

These three classes of tool are also characteristic of the Oldowan Industry from Bed I and the lower part of Bed II at the Olduvai Gorge in Tanzania where they occur on old land-surfaces in discrete concentrations in such a way as to suggest that these were the home-bases or camping places of the hominids that made the tools. Sites of the Oldowan Industry have been dated to nearly two and a quarter million years ago in the Lake Turkana (Rudolf) basin and they continue until about one and three-quarter million years ago. At the Olduvai Gorge they are associated both with Australopithecines, whose remains have been found in East and South Africa, and with a more advanced form of hominid having a somewhat larger brain, known as *Homo habilis* – meaning man with the ability to make tools. Although the Australopithecines may have made some kinds of simple tools, it is more specifically with *Homo habilis* that tool-making is associated. The biological evolution that can be observed in the later *H. habilis* fossils, as also in later forms of man, is considered to be the result of a feedback relationship between increasing biological advancement – in brain size, intellectual ability and motor skills – and increased cultural activities.

These early hominids lived, it is believed, in small groups establishing a home-base where the young, who were dependent on their parents for about as long as children are today, were fed and cared for, learned skills and were taught their role as members of the group. Early hominid groups were organised for the hunting of small and per-

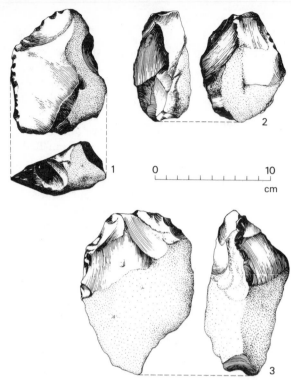
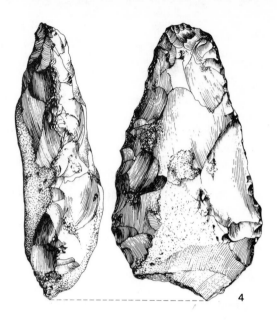

Fig. 4 Oldowan and Earlier Acheulian tools. 15-metre terrace, Nakatindi Road. (*1 End-struck flake, utilised; Oldowan. 2 Circular chopper; Oldowan. 3 End-chopper; Oldowan. 4 Handaxe; Earlier Acheulian.*)

haps some larger game and they also scavenged meat from carnivore kills and recently dead large animals; no doubt they also used a range of vegetable foods. Primate studies, especially of free-ranging chimpanzees, provide a basis for constructing a model for the behaviour patterns and capabilities of these early hominids which clearly lie somewhere between those of the chimpanzee and those of present-day hunting/gathering peoples.

Also in these same high-level gravels at the Victoria Falls are a small number of large, pear-shaped tools which are known as handaxes and are characteristic of the earlier stage of what is termed the Acheulian Industrial Complex (Fig. 4 no. 4). These earlier Acheulian artefacts, like those of the Oldowan, were shaped through the removal of a relatively small number of thick, broad flakes alternately from both faces, by means

of a hard hammer or stone anvil. They are all made to a generally similar pattern; and in this they show the beginnings of a standardisation in tool-form that is characteristic of the Acheulian Industrial Complex wherever it is found.

The Oldowan Industry, together with its makers, appears to be confined to the tropical parts of the African continent, thus confirming the suppositions of Darwin and Huxley that it was somewhere in the tropics, perhaps in Africa, that man the tool-maker had his origins. Towards the end of the Lower Pleistocene, between one and one and a half million years ago, the early hominids dispersed relatively rapidly into Europe and Asia. In south-east Asia and the Far East some of them continued to make tools like those of the Oldowan, while others carried the Acheulian (hand-axe) tradition to south-west

38

Asia and India and to southern and western Europe; the type-site from which the Acheulian takes its name is in northern France.

In Africa, both the Oldowan tradition (in a more developed form) and the Acheulian continue throughout the period of the Middle Pleistocene. It has been argued that this could imply that they were each made by a different kind of hominid. However, since the Acheulian has been found in Africa and Europe associated with a more advanced hominid, *Homo erectus*, and this form also occurs at sites in Java and north China, it is likely that any less efficient hominid stock competing for the same resources would have been eliminated by a process of natural selection. It is more probable, then, that these two tool-kits represent two basically different sets of activities and that the large cutting tools of the Acheulian are related to a new kind of behaviour.

The Acheulian tradition can be shown to have continued up to 100 000 years ago, or even later. By about 700 000 years ago, some significant changes are apparent in the assemblages. To begin with, there are many more of these later Acheulian occurrences; the living sites often cover larger areas; there are more tools associated with them and the tools show a greater degree of formalisation and a higher degree of skill in manufacture. In fact, the shapeliness displayed by many of these large cutting tools shows an amount of skill in stone-working often beyond what is necessary to make an efficient tool. This has been cited as one of the first indications of the emergence of man's sense of aesthetic appreciation.

Special techniques were developed for obtaining large flakes from boulder-cores. These flakes were made into hand-axes and axe-like 'cleavers' (Fig. 5 no. 2) by using what is known as a 'soft hammer' technique of retouch. A soft hammer of bone or hard wood (as opposed to stone) or a spherical anvil permits thinner and more accurately controlled flakes to be removed so that the finished tool is thinner and has straighter cutting edges.

Many fine examples of the later Acheulian stone-worker's craft have been found in a gravel terrace at somewhat lower elevations than that in which the earliest tools are found both in the Zambezi Valley and in that of its tributary the Maramba. Hand-axes were made mostly from chalcedony and basalt, but the cleavers are predominantly manufactured from large flakes of tough basalt lava. The broad working edge of the cleaver is formed by the intersection of two flake surfaces which thus provide a most useful chopping edge; in fact, the cleaver is the chopping tool or axe *sensu stricto*. In other parts of Zambia and Zimbabwe other materials were used and it becomes apparent that Acheulian man was in complete control of his raw materials. He could produce a hand-axe in quartz, quartzite or lava which was just as well made and efficient as that which he could make from more easily worked, fine-grained chert or chalcedony. His cleavers in the Zambezi Valley are just as well finished as his hand-axes. Two later Acheulian sites, which have, however, suffered some natural disturbance, were found and excavated about three kilometres upstream from the Maramba bridge; while another assemblage was found east of the Silent Pool where the canal for the Victoria Falls Hydro-electric Scheme was dug to lead water to the Power Station in the gorge below.

The purpose for which hand-axes and cleavers were made is not known. It is

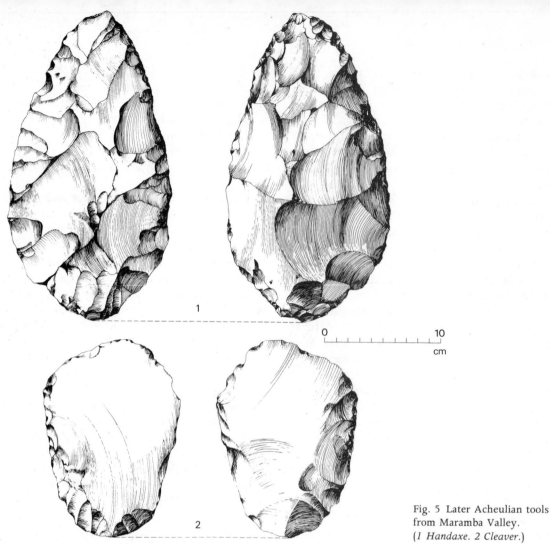

Fig. 5 Later Acheulian tools from Maramba Valley. (*1 Handaxe. 2 Cleaver.*)

usually supposed that they were some general-purpose kind of knife for cutting the meat from large animals but, at most of the butchery sites which have been found, the tools associated with the butchered bones are nearly always unmodified flakes and choppers. Hand-axes and cleavers are sometimes found concentrated in large numbers – some two or three hundred – over quite a small surface area, and they appear to relate more especially to the home-base activities.

Home-base sites are almost always situated in close proximity to water – a river, spring or lakeside – and in other parts of the continent where fauna is preserved they show that the inhabitants were possessed of no mean hunting skills. There is now evidence for the deliberate hunting and butchering of large game animals like elephant, giraffes, bovids and giant baboons. Unfortunately no undisturbed living site of this kind has yet been found in the Zambezi

Valley and the tools of this time have mostly been redeposited by stream action or dispersed by long exposure on the surface before being buried by sediments of a later age.

Besides these large cutting tools there are a number of light-duty tools – scrapers and knives – made from flakes, and also some heavy-duty forms including large scrapers and stone spheroids which were perhaps used for pounding. All these different tools indicate that the makers of the Acheulian industries were engaged in a number of different activities. While, however, there is a considerable variation between each assemblage in the kinds and proportions of the tools present, there is nevertheless an overall sameness about them from one end of the Acheulian world to the other. In Africa these populations occupied the more open, well-watered savanna where large numbers of grazing and browsing animals are to be found and where there is generally an abundance of vegetable foods throughout most of the year.

Remains of *Homo erectus*, a more advanced form of man than *Homo habilis,* have been found with Acheulian occupation sites in Algeria, Morocco, northern Tanzania and the Transvaal. While they were clearly much better organised than were the earlier hominids, they were not, apparently, capable of that degree of individuality exhibited by the tool-kits associated with man in the later part of the Pleistocene.

The Acheulian tradition appears to have continued, with increasing refinements in the tool-kit, until the onset of the Last Glaciation in higher latitudes – about 70 000 or so years ago. However, by the end of the Acheulian, there is evidence from the Cape that some of the population of southern Africa was closely similar to the form of man

represented by the remains found in the deep cave in No. 1 Kopje at the Broken Hill Mine near Kabwe, and named *Homo rhodesiensis.** At Kalambo Falls, on the northern border of Zambia, a number of undisturbed camping places of the terminal Acheulian have been excavated and we are most fortunate in that, owing to the perpetually waterlogged nature of the site, wood and other vegetable materials have been preserved. Among these are several wooden tools – a club, digging sticks and spatulate wooden artefacts. Several of these appear to have been shaped by the use of fire. Charcoals and charred logs present on some of these living floors also show that by this time man had already begun to make regular use of fire; and there can be no doubt that this was one of the important technological advances that led to the regional specialisation of the Upper Pleistocene. This was a time of advance of the Antarctic and Arctic ice-sheets, the influences of which were felt throughout the African continent and had an important effect on the eco-systems, so bringing about a redistribution of the animal and human populations. The lowered temperatures and increased effects of the trade-winds blowing from the south Atlantic over the cold Benguella current flowing up the west side of the continent resulted in generally drier, cooler conditions extending inland to the Victoria Falls. The climate became much more arid, though the lowered evaporation rate favoured a high water-table and the presence of numerous sources of permanent surface water.

In the Victoria Falls region at this time, quantities of the old Kalahari Sand that

* A small Acheulian occupation site was excavated at Broken Hill adjacent to the place where this skull and other remains had been found in 1921.

41

covered much of the west of south-central Africa were redeposited at lower altitudes along the upper slopes of the Zambezi Valley. The towns of Livingstone and Victoria Falls are built on these original and redeposited sands respectively. It is within the latter, as also in the ferricrete-cemented and partially reworked top of the Middle Pleistocene gravels, that assemblages of the next cultural stage are found. This was a time of population dispersal, when the Congo basin and the previously uninhabited West African forest regions began to be occupied on a permanent basis due, it would seem, to the retreat of the lowland rain-forest and its replacement by grass and woodland savanna with some higher altitude species.

Some of the most interesting sites of this time are situated on the sand-scarp along Mbwile Drive west of Livingstone and again exposed in railway cuttings just south of Victoria Falls on the Zimbabwean bank. The artefacts are in completely fresh condition and are associated with small workshop and living floors of what is known as the Sangoan Industrial Complex. These sites have not been disturbed in any way since they were abandoned by their occupants. From them excellent views over the valley may be obtained and they must have been favourable camping sites as they were quite close to the sources of raw material that outcropped at the base of the scarp. At these Sangoan sites there is an important emphasis on tools relating, it is generally believed, to woodworking activities. The hand-axe is still found but it no longer assumes the importance it did with the Acheulian. In shape, these new hand-axes are much more pointed and usually smaller, less well made, with the butts almost invariably left untrimmed, the emphasis being on the point and sides, thus further stressing the cutting nature of the tool (Fig. 6 no. 2). A new tool which makes its appearance is the pick or core-axe used, on analogy with that of the Australian aborigine, for removing boughs or sections of the trunk or bark from trees (Fig. 6, nos. 1 and 3). The chisel-like end shown by many of these tools tends to emphasise this method of use. By far the greatest number of tools are now made on flakes, however, and have been used for cutting and scraping. Examples are knifeblades made on flakes (Fig. 7 no. 2); scrapers (Fig. 6 no. 4) for scraping skins, wood or bone; 'points' (Fig. 7 no. 1) which may have been projectile heads but are more likely to have been used for working wood as in trimming spear-shafts; chisels and concave scrapers or spokeshaves.

At the Victoria Falls we have no direct means of dating these Sangoan occurrences, but evidence elsewhere suggests that they may have been made around 100 000 years ago; they are likely to be of similar age in the Zambezi Valley. The light-duty equipment of the Sangoan is very like that of the subsequent industrial tradition in Zambia and may, in part, also be contemporary with it. This technological tradition is referred to in general terms as the 'Middle Stone Age' and recent radiocarbon dates show that in South Africa its origins may go back to as much as 70 000 or 80 000 years ago. It is characterised by light-duty equipment made on flakes struck from specially prepared cores that are often discoid in shape, and sometimes also by long blades. Large numbers of these flake tools and disc cores are found in the gravels and fine-grained sediments of the next to the youngest terrace around the Victoria Falls. These are well represented upstream of the Falls in the area of the Mosi-oa-Tunya Zoological Park and also flanking the former river-

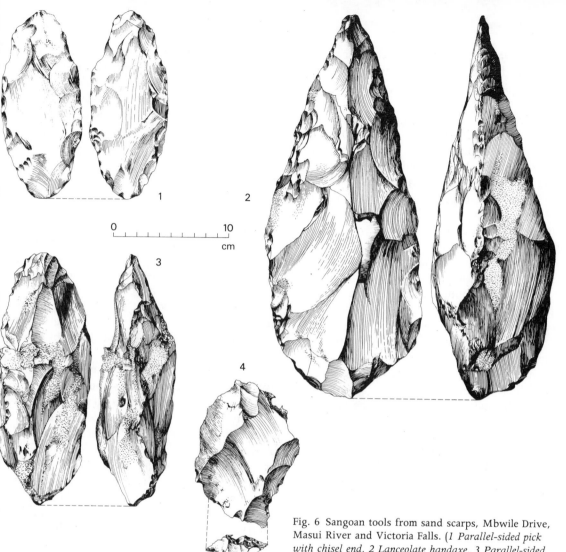

Fig. 6 Sangoan tools from sand scarps, Mbwile Drive, Masui River and Victoria Falls. (*1 Parallel-sided pick with chisel end. 2 Lanceolate handaxe. 3 Parallel-sided core-axe. 4 Denticulate side-scraper.*)

bed south of the Fifth Gorge.

Two industrial stages of the 'Middle Stone Age' have been recognised relating to two successive episodes of sedimentation; and, if the numbers of artefacts are anything to go by, the Zambezi Valley in the vicinity of the Falls was a particularly favoured locality for the hunting/gathering populations of this time. Characteristic artefacts of the 'Middle Stone Age' are illustrated in Fig. 7. The heavy-duty element present with the Sangoan is now much reduced and there is a concentration on smaller and more specialised forms of knives, scrapers and projectile points. Pre-determined forms of flakes were struck from the specially prepared faces of

43

discoid, oval or sub-triangular cores; and the flakes so derived were generally used with little further modification or retouch.

In the earlier stage of the 'Middle Stone Age' at the Falls two special kinds of tool are present. The first of these is a lanceolate or leaf-shaped 'point', bifacially retouched, which was probably used as a projectile head mounted with mastic on a shaft and serving double purpose as a knife. Some of the finest examples of this kind of tool are found in the Congo river basin where they may have been associated with the hunting of large game such as elephant or hippopotamus. The second implement is a carefully made stone spheroid about the size of a tennis ball. These may have been hafted by means of a rawhide sleeve for use as a throwing club, or perhaps two or three were enclosed in skin bags on the end of thongs and used, as is the South American *bolas*, to capture game by entangling the limbs as the animal runs away. Broken Hill man also used the stone ball and two of these were found in direct association with the famous skull and other remains. A few tools of bone, a conical-sectioned bone point and spatulate tools were also found in the Broken Hill cave, together with a number of light-duty tools – flakes and scrapers made in quartz.

It is not known when modern man (*Homo sapiens sapiens*) first made his appearance in the Zambezi Valley but it may have been during the closing stages of the Acheulian. He was present in the Omo valley in East Africa as early, perhaps, as 100 000 years ago. From South Africa, at Florisbad near Bloemfontein, another fossil skull dates to at least 50 000 years ago, while at Broken Hill a jaw fragment from a second skull associated with the first resembles Modern man more than it does *Homo rhodesiensis*,

thus confirming that a considerable amount of variability was present in the human populations of those times. Perhaps by the beginning of the 'Middle Stone Age', therefore, Modern man had everywhere started to replace all earlier or biologically less efficient forms of man. The earliest burials of Modern man in central Africa associated with 'Middle Stone Age' artefacts occur in the Mumbwa Caves in Zambia.

The artefact assemblages that belong to the later part of the 'Middle Stone Age' show a number of refinements and new techniques (Fig. 7, nos. 6–13). At the Victoria Falls finer-grained stones such as carnelian and agates were selected and, besides flakes struck from specially prepared cores, we now find numbers of thin, blade-like forms obtained by using a punch of horn, bone or hard wood. The lower end of the punch is rested on the edge of the core and, when the upper end is correctly struck with the hammer, a thin blade will be detached down the length of the flaking surface of the core. These blades and bladelets were retouched in various ways, often to form blunted-backed cutting tools similar to the blade of a penknife. Quite small, microlithic, backed pieces occur as well as trapeze-, triangular-, and lunate-shaped forms frequently made from snapped sections of blades. It is believed that these were hafted in series to form the cutting edges of composite tools such as knives, or the heads and barbs of projectile weapons. The shafts and handles would have been of wood and the stone cutting parts would have been held in position with a cement or mastic made of natural gums obtainable from certain trees and bushes. A common mastic used in the middle Zambezi Valley today to secure the tangs of iron spearheads into the socket is made from the

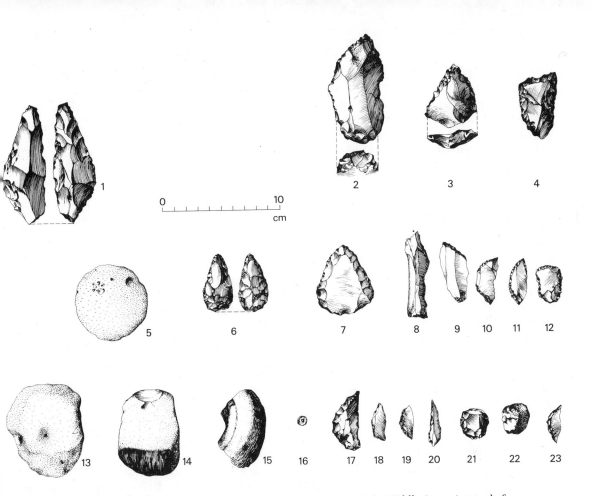

gum of the *Commifera* tree.

As well as these new small blade- and flake-tools, the various scrapers and points are more carefully finished and the triangular and leaf-shaped points in particular are thinner and much more shapely than those of the earlier stage. Sometimes this finishing process has been done by pressure as distinct from percussion flaking. If pressure is exerted in the right way, small flakes can be removed exactly where required, thus giving much greater control over the final shape and thickness of the tool. Some of these pressure-flaked points are among the finest examples of the prehistoric stone-worker's art. To this

Fig. 7 Nos. 1–5: Middle Stone Age tools from Younger Gravels and Sand Scarp, Victoria Falls. (*1 Lanceolate bifaced point. 2 Retouched flake from prepared core. 3 Unifaced point. 4 Angled scraper. 5 Spheroid.*)

Nos. 6–13: Evolved Middle Stone Age tools from Younger Gravels and Sand Scarp, Victoria Falls. (*6 Bifaced point. 7 Unifaced point. 8 Blade. 9 Truncated bladelet. 10 Trapeze. 11 Lunate. 12 End-scraper. 13 Dimple-scarred rubber.*)

Nos. 14–23: Later Stone Age tools from river bank and scarp sites between Victoria Falls and Old Livingstone. (*14 Edge-ground axe. 15 Fragment of bored stone. 16 Bead of ostrich eggshell. 17 Crescent-adze. 18, 19, 23 Lunates. 20 Straight-backed bladelet. 21, 22 Diminutive convex scrapers.*)

time also belong well-worn rubbing and grinding stones, suggesting the systematic use of wild plant seeds. No doubt, these had been collected since the earliest times, but it is not until the later 'Middle Stone Age' that such well-used stones become regular, though not common, pieces of home equipment.

These evolved 'Middle Stone Age' occurrences are found on camp-sites buried under two or three metres of red sand on the scarps overlooking the Zambezi Valley, as well sometimes as adjacent to the former river bank, usually on sands overlooking the younger series of gravels which was the source of the raw material. Some of these sites are probably between 20 000 and 15 000 years old, on dating evidence from other parts of Zambia and Zimbabwe, while certain dates from South Africa suggest that similar assemblages there could be appreciably older.

The recession of the ice-sheets in the northern and southern hemispheres about 12 000 to 10 000 years ago marks the end of the cooler and drier climate of the Upper Pleistocene and, in the Recent or Holocene period that followed, gradual increases in temperature and humidity took place. For example, the tropical, lowland forest in the Congo basin and in West Africa advanced to cover an even greater part of equatorial Africa than it does today. Comparable changes in the ecology of the savanna-woodlands and grasslands can also be shown to have taken place at this time and must have necessitated some readjustment and technological innovations on the part of the human populations that exploited them. There is now evidence from the coastal sites of the increasingly extensive use of sea-foods – mammals, molluscs, fowl and fish. In the same way, the resources of the inland lakes and rivers began to be systematically used. There is evidence from the coastal region and interior plateau of southern Africa for what appears to be a fundamental break with earlier technological tradition and certain industries making use of various forms of large scraper replace the evolved 'Middle Stone Age' tool-kits. These date between 15 000 and 8000 years ago and fall within what is known as the 'Later Stone Age'. They are often associated with large hearths consisting of compacted layers of white ash, charcoal and bone, presumably evidence for some important technological advance. Possibly these hearths are connected with the drying of meat, as if hunting skills had now produced a greater supply than the group could consume in the course of two or three days.

As yet this 'large scraper industry' (known in Zimbabwe as the Pomongwan, after the Matopos cave of Pomongwe) has not been recorded from the Victoria Falls, but one fairly large camp and workshop of this kind was found near Khotakhota Mountain in the middle Zambezi Valley before this was inundated by Lake Kariba. The tools consist of heavy core-scrapers and numerous end- and convex scrapers. There are even some of near microlithic proportions and at this site also there are a few microlithic lunates, though it is not certain that these might not be of later age.

Throughout Zambia and Zimbabwe the main part of the 'Later Stone Age' is characterised by fully microlithic flaked stone industries with which are associated certain larger tools and items of equipment. In parts of Zambia the earliest of these 'Later Stone Age' microlithic industries has been dated to about 16 000 years ago. In general, however, they fall in time between 8000 and 2000 years ago. The 'Later Stone Age' industry representative of the southern part of Zambia was first recognised in excavations at the Mumbwa Caves in 1939.

More recently, an important site – Gwisho Springs – in Lochinvar National Park near Monze has provided much valuable information about the equipment and way of life of the 'Later Stone Age' hunting groups. Here the camping places are close to hot springs which have preserved both bone and vegetable remains as well as burials, showing that the population of southern Zambia at that time was very similar to the present-day San or Bushman population of the central and northern Kalahari. These people hunted a number of large game animals with bows and arrows and there is indirect evidence, in the form of pods of the *Swartzia* tree, for the use of arrow poison by this time, as the northern Kalahari San use *Swartzia* seeds for this purpose today. Numerous bone and wooden points and the microlithic lunates with which they were tipped were found in the Gwisho deposits, together with digging sticks and even the remains of a collapsed, semi-circular windbreak. A number of different kinds of wild fruits and seeds were also being used; these were cracked and ground between stones to make flour.

'Later Stone Age' sites have been found on the top of the sand-scarps at the Victoria Falls but chiefly along the river-bank and in the *mopane* bush back from the river where the spread of occupation material shows that these sites were mostly small. They may be seen as the temporary camping places of no more than one or two families. The population would have made most use of the river at two main seasons of the year. During the later part of the dry season – late August, September and October – when permanent water-sources on the plateau would have been greatly reduced owing to the porous nature of the sands, and vegetable and animal resources would be concentrated on the river and tributary streams, the population can be expected to have split up into small family groups based on the more favourable localities, especially along the river bank. Again, when the flood-waters began to recede in late April and May, fishing would have been an important source of protein and groups of several nuclear families are likely to have joined in spearing and trapping fish behind weirs built across the mouths of the creeks.

The chief hunting weapon was now the bow and arrow and the occurrence of numbers of microlithic lunates and backed bladelets is believed to be related to the hunting of large game. Diminutive convex scrapers were probably the working parts of small hand-adzes for paring down bow-staves, arrow-shafts and other wooden tools. An interesting tool which appears to be confined to the Zambezi Valley is a large, clumsy lunate with a thick back and evidence of damage from use on the cutting edge. This implement has been called a 'crescent adze'. It may, perhaps, be more especially connected with the construction of equipment used in fishing – basket traps and fences made of reeds and bark-string, or the barbed wooden heads of fish-spears. This tool is very similar in appearance and has similar use-wear to the Australian *eloura* adze-blades. Fig. 7 (nos. 14–23) illustrates typical 'Later Stone Age' artefacts from the Victoria Falls region.

One of the Zambezi camping sites of this period is on a mound overlooking the river about two kilometres upstream from the

Falls on the Zambian bank. Here, the micro-lithic stone tools were made and there is much dispersed flaking waste. Besides upper and lower grindstones, the site produced a ground stone axe – a heavy-duty tool, presumably for working wood. Ostrich egg- and mussel-shell beads attest the use of simple items of personal adornment, and stone for making pigment in the form of red ochre and haematite shows that these people also painted. Occasionally round, flattish stones with an hour-glass perforation through the centre are found. These may have been weights for digging sticks like those of the Kalahari San, or a functional part of a hunting trap like some still in use today. Numerous fragments of semi-fossilised bone from large to medium-sized mammals occur and indicate that hunting was an important source of meat at these riverside sites. Fish bones have not been found but that is not surprising since only rarely are they likely to have been preserved under the climatic conditions that have pertained in the valley.

The principal vegetable staple would, without doubt, have been the *mungongo* nut from *Ricinodendron rautanenii,* one of the commonest trees growing on the sands that overlook the valley. This nut is the staple of the northern San and, because of its very hard shell, it is available all the year round. The kernel, rich in oil, is pounded and made into a porridge. Also available on the sand-scarp at different times of the year are the red outer skin of the *muzaule* (*Guibourtia coleosperma*) and the fruits of the *mabuyu* (*Parinari curatellifolia*), of the bao-bab (*Adansonia digitata*) and of the *marula* (*Sclerocarya caffra*) and *mulombelombe*, the African orange (*Strychnos struhlmannii*) both of which last are found also on the basalt soils in the valley itself. Among the riverine forest foods are the rind of the fan palm nut (*Hyphaenae ventricosa*), the fruit of the *mutoya*, the Barotse plum (*Syzygium guineense*), the mangosteen (*Garcinia living-stonei*), the *muchenje* (*Diospyros mespili-formis*) and also wild figs and dates. Water-lily bulbs and young stems of papyrus are also important food sources in several parts of the continent and orange-coloured spiny cucumbers are numerous in the riverside bush in the latter part of the dry season. The seasonally flooded *dambos* also support good stands of wild grasses such as *Echinochloa colona* and *Brachiaria brizantha* which, with others, are still regularly collected today by the Tonga people of the middle Zambezi Valley.

A wide range of game animals would have been available. Besides elephants and hippo-potamus, one of the most important is likely to have been the buffalo which is well represented in the 'Later Stone Age' fauna at Gwisho Springs. Eland, sable, roan antelope, kudu, waterbuck, bushbuck, dui-ker, and both warthog and bushpig would have been eaten and a number of smaller mammals also, of which the cane rat would have been a favourite. Some of these have limited territorial ranges; others, such as elephant and buffalo, migrate to the plateau during the rains and it may be expected that the hunting groups went with them, joining together for communal hunting.

The life of hunter/gatherers in the Zambezi Valley during the 'Later Stone Age' would indeed have been an optimum one, with the bands organised on a basis of regular seasonal transhumance between the river and the plateau. Competition for the resources would have been minimal until the coming of the first Early Iron Age cultivators and herders shortly after the beginning

I   The Main Falls.

II   The Victoria Falls from the air. The Rain Forest and Main Falls are in the foreground.

III   The Victoria Falls and Gorges from the air.

IVa   The Source of the Zambezi.

IVb   The Zambezi near the Old Drift, upstream of the Victoria Falls.

Table to Show the Associations of the Cultural Sequence at the Victoria Falls.

GEOLOGICAL PERIOD	YEARS BEFORE PRESENT	SIMPLIFIED SEDIMENTARY SEQUENCE	CULTURAL SUCCESSION		
					Iron Age Traditions
Holocene	2 000	Youngest Alluvial Terrace Formation	'Later Stone Age' Traditions	Developing Microlithic Industries	
	10 000	Redistributed Sands		('Large Scraper Industry')	
Upper Pleistocene		*Valley* *Scarp* Younger Terrace Gravels — Redeposited Kalahari Sand	'Middle Stone Age' Traditions	Evolved Industrial Variants Earlier Industrial Variants	
		Ferricretes — Ferruginous Land Rubble		Sangoan	
	100 000	Older Terrace			
Middle Pleistocene	700 000	Gravels 2	'Earlier Stone Age' Traditions	Late Acheulian	
	1·0 million	Older Terrace		Early Acheulian	Developed Oldowan
Lower Pleistocene		Gravels 1			
					Oldowan
	1·8 million 2·0 million				
Pliocene					

49

of the present era. Thereafter, economic pressures forced most of the 'Later Stone Age' groups to change their way of life from a hunting/gathering to a farming base, while others were absorbed into the communities of Iron Age peoples. In the Zambezi Valley this appears to have taken place well before 1500 A.D.

The prehistoric cultural succession as it is represented at the Victoria Falls, together with the sedimentary sequence of deposits to which it relates, is set out in the table on page 45, as is also the age of the industrial complexes according to the latest radiometric dating evidence. This sequence is further explained in the schematic sections of the Zambezi Valley given in Fig. 3.

A small site museum at the Eastern Cataract exhibits representative artefacts of the various industrial traditions referred to in this chapter. An excavation in the floor shows a section through the Younger Gravel terrace and the overlying sands, and includes a further selection of artefacts that relate to the different stratigraphical levels.

Fig. 8 The excavation through the Pleistocene gravels preserved in the Eastern Cataract Field Museum.

Select Bibliography

ARMSTRONG, A. L. and JONES, N. 'The antiquity of man in Rhodesia as demonstrated by stone implements of the ancient Zambezi gravels, south of the Victoria Falls, *Journal of the Royal Anthropological Institute*, lxvi, 1936.

CLARK, J. D. *Stone Age Cultures of Northern Rhodesia*, Cape Town, 1950.

CLARK, J. D. *The Prehistory of Africa*, London, 1970.

FAGAN, B. M. and VAN NOTEN, F. *The Hunter-Gatherers of Gwisho*, Tervuren, 1971.

KLEIN, R. G. (ed.) *Southern African Prehistory and Palaeoenvironments*, Rotterdam, 1984.

PHILLIPSON, D. W. *African Archaeology*, Cambridge, 1985.

CHAPTER 5

The Iron Age Archaeology

Joseph O. Vogel

The Iron Age in south central Africa represents a way of life which includes a metal-based technology, mixed agriculture, the production of pottery vessels, settled village communities and a tribal social structure. The development of this way of life is the subject of much intense study, but archaeologists still lack information on how the Iron Age came to sub-Saharan Africa. However, recent research indicates that for the Victoria Falls region it was introduced all at one time, early in the first millennium A.D. The developed nature of the Iron Age when we first perceive it suggests that the Iron Age way of life had undergone a long transitional history before its entry into this region. We know very little about the earliest agriculturalists of the sub-continent generally, but from the scattered data available archaeologists have pieced together the history of the Iron Age penetration of south central Africa and of its introduction into the Zambezi Valley.

The systematic archaeological investigation of the Iron Age in the Victoria Falls region began in 1962 with the Zambia National Monuments Commission's excavations at the Dambwa site near Livingstone. The results of this research were published in 1969 by S. G. H. Daniels and D. W. Phillipson. Between 1966 and 1972 the present writer carried out large-scale surveys and excavations in the region, under the aegis of the National Museums Board of Zambia. These investigations, at nearly thirty sites in and around the Victoria Falls region, allow us to describe the area's culture-history in some detail and to view these local developments within the broader context of the south central African Iron Age.

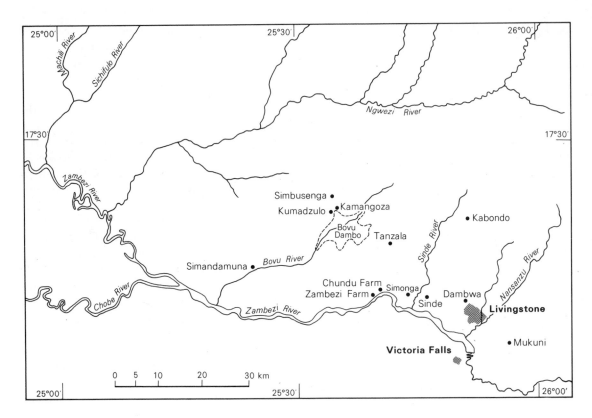

Fig. 1 Map showing Iron Age sites in the Victoria Falls region.

The Early Iron Age

Two thousand years ago the central African plateau south of the Congo-Zambezi watershed was occupied by small bands of stone-using hunter-gatherers. Although these Late Stone Age people practised neither metallurgy nor food production, they had achieved an efficient level of socio-economic integration. The hunter-gatherer band had been a viable cultural formation for thousands of years and, where not severely hampered by Iron Age settlement, it continued into fairly recent centuries.

In most of the Victoria Falls region, however, there is evidence for an early displacement of the Late Stone Age population. This was the direct result of competition within an environment of fairly low carrying capacity, which was unable effectively to maintain both hunters and mixed agriculturalists. Iron Age economy implies intensive land use, which effectively modifies the environment by forest clearance and soil depletion, as well as restricting the grazing available to game, as a result of keeping cattle. Domestic animals are usually grazed at a higher density than is normal to wild populations. They also utilise grazing more intensively than do game herds. The comparatively large settled village populations of a tribal society, the more complex relationship of the human society to land, and differing concepts of territoriality might further restrict the activities of the hunter-gatherers. Thus contact with an alien culture tended to undermine the established Late Stone Age people and, by the middle of the first millennium A.D., the region appears to have been occupied solely by a number of agricultural village communities.

We may suggest that the ancestors of these early farmers were Bantu-speaking negroids who had previously practised an essentially 'neolithic' way of life in the southern Congo basin. The Iron Age seems to have developed with the adoption of food plants, the introduction of iron-working and the development of a slash-and-burn agricultural system, using iron hoes and axes. This complex series of integrations was the result of a number of independent lines of movement and diffusion which are still incompletely understood by archaeologists. We may suggest that the economic efficiency so developed supplied the momentum for a rapid flow of peoples eastwards and southwards, producing a widely spread and culturally rather homogeneous population from the lacustrine regions of East Africa south to the south central African plateau. This expansion was neither an invasion nor a massive population expansion. Although we are unable to determine the numbers of individuals involved, the available evidence indicates that they need not have been very many.

Any impetus to this expansion beyond the search for better tillage, pasturage or other economic advantage is beyond our present resources to determine. It is usually assumed that the introduction of metallurgy acted as a catalyst to the rapid and widespread movements of people associated with the earliest manifestations of Iron Age culture in the sub-continent. It is apparent, however, that the spread of Iron Age culture is more complex than that. This question is beyond the scope of this chapter, and we shall concern ourselves here with the evidence of activities from early villages in the Victoria Falls region.

The most important evidence found in most Iron Age archaeological sites is the pottery. From a study of the form and design of early pottery we may make suggestions of cultural relationships and population distributions. We may identify several regional patterns of Early Iron Age ceramics in south central Africa. These patterns have sufficient similarity that we may consider them as part of one configuration with a common cultural origin, although we are unable to demonstrate the processes of a real differentiation as our data on the earliest period of the Iron Age are very incomplete. The Early Iron Age pioneers have left little trace in the archaeological record. However, by the middle of the first millennium A.D. we may detect regional centres of trait-dispersal. This suggests that, by at least the second quarter of the first millennium A.D., the sub-continent was entered by small numbers of immigrants who rapidly established centres of Iron Age life scattered throughout the area. The numbers of people grew and by the second half of the millennium they began to spread out from these population centres to many parts of the sub-continent. The first significant Iron Age occupation of the Victoria Falls region appears to have been instigated by one of these secondary expansions from a centre south of the Zambezi.

The available evidence allows us to draw up a comprehensive picture of the material life in an early community once a more

Fig. 2 Typical Early Iron Age pottery from the Victoria Falls region, dating from around the middle of the first millennium A.D.

sedentary settlement had become established. The inhabitants practised a wide variety of crafts, including pottery-making, the smelting of metal ores and the fabrication of artefacts from iron and copper. A small number of stone tools were also produced. Wood and bone were worked, but our evidence of wooden artefacts is indirect and very few bone tools have survived. Grass was used for thatching and presumably was woven into mats and baskets. Ivory was collected and may have been used in trade. Although the basic village economy was a simple subsistence one, the local lack of certain commodities, such as salt, iron ore or potting materials, as well as of gold, ivory and copper, led to extensive trading. Finds of cowrie shells and glass in the Victoria Falls region suggest that some form of trading network linking central Africa with the east coast was already in operation. The subsistence pattern depended upon the cultivation of cereals as well as vegetable crops. Small herds of cattle and flocks of sheep, goats and, presumably, fowls were kept. In addition to domestic food production, the diet was supplemented by hunting and the collecting of wild vegetable foods.

Village communities were probably organised along similar lines to some modern communities, with religious and political authority, although we lack archaeological evidence of this. Territorially adjacent communities were no doubt associated within some form of extended tribal society. From the very beginning, the cultural content of the village communities began to change in response to both cultural and environmental pressures as the generalised Iron Age way of life was adapted to the conditions of the Victoria Falls region. The history of Iron Age cultures here has been extensively investigated and we may describe a sequence of events which forms a continuous history leading to the more recent past.

While the earliest Iron Age farmers in the Victoria Falls region appear to have lived in small, semi-permanent, widely-scattered villages for short lengths of time, their descendants by the middle of the first millennium A.D. occupied a substantial number of much larger villages. These were permanently sited and appear to have housed as many as two hundred persons for periods of twenty years or more. These early villages are nearly always sited along the edge of a *dambo* (seasonally waterlogged, flat-bottomed valley). The *dambos* were important to the economy of Iron Age men in southern Zambia, for not only were cattle grazed

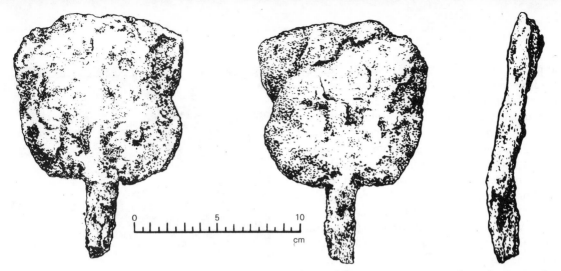

Fig. 3 An Early Iron Age hoe-blade.

upon their grassy surfaces and gardens planted along their edges, but throughout the year water may be drawn from wells dug into them.

Before the later decades of the seventh century A.D., we have no evidence of large permanent villages along the Zambezi Valley itself. Instead, the Iron Age farmers of the area congregated along a *dambo* system immediately south of the Ngwezi River in Zambia. We have no evidence of this period from Zimbabwe, but we may suspect that related peoples were living on the edges of highlands above the Zambezi Valley there as well. The point here is that these early communities consistently chose well-watered sites, adjacent to grassland and away from the valley. A wide range of artefacts and other evidence has been found at these early settlements and we may reconstruct the inhabitants' everyday activities with some accuracy.

The production of iron and iron artefacts was practised at each of the villages investigated and, although the product was utilitarian and technically simple, the technology practised was not vastly different from that current in most of southern Zambia into the last century. Techniques like welding or rivetting were not used, and all the known implements were forged. No specialised iron-working tools have been recovered and it is assumed that stone hammers and anvils were used. Large collections of iron artefacts from this period have been discovered, notably at Kumadzulo and Zambezi Farm, and in the basal horizon of the large stratified mound at Simbusenga. They include axes, knives, bodkins and spear and arrowheads. These objects imply the practice of woodworking, the use of skins and, possibly, barkcloth manufacture also. Unfortunately, none of these perishable materials remains in the archaeological record and the excavated evidence of Iron Age culture leaves us with a very limited view of the total cultural product of these communities in central Africa.

Copper, in the form of ornaments and currency bars, is known from several sites in the Victoria Falls region. Since copper ore deposits are unknown here, it is clear that the metal was brought into the area by means of trade. Both local and long-distance trade seems to have been well established. Although the Victoria Falls region never appears to have figured strongly in the trading activities of the sub-continent, we have sufficient evidence to describe some continued trade contact throughout the Iron Age sequence. Local trade seems to have brought pottery vessels from the Batoka highlands and the eastern parts of Zimbabwe into the region. It also introduced copper and presumably salt and other commodities which were not otherwise available, in the area. We also know that long distance trade brought objects from the coasts of East Africa into the region. At Kumadzulo, we found a fragment of green glass beneath the fallen debris of a burnt hut; and with the eighth-century burials discovered at Chundu Farm were located fragments of two cowrie shells. Other (generally more common) trade objects such as glass beads were still unknown in the region at this early date.

At Kumadzulo, archaeologists located the remains of a large village which was occupied during the early decades of the seventh century. Not only was a large collection of associated material culture recovered in the excavation but, since the village had been extensively burnt immediately prior to abandonment, sufficient of the wall posts and other architectural features were preserved to enable us to describe the houses of these people. These huts were sub-rectangular in shape with walls up to 2·3 metres in length. The floors were prepared with a surface of mud daub. The walls consisted of

Fig. 4 (top) Excavation of an Early Iron Age hut-floor at Kumadzulo.

Fig. 5 (centre) Collapsed remains of an Early Iron Age hut at the Dambwa site. Note the charred remains of posts and a pot partly covered by fallen wall fragments. (Scale in inches.)

Fig. 6 (bottom) Excavation of an Early Iron Age burial at Chundu Farm.

upright poles woven together with grass bundles and withies and covered with clay daub, as well. The roofs were probably thatched with grass in the traditional manner. These huts are quite small and probably just sufficient to house a nuclear family. Although one or two groups of aligned structures may be suggested, the various structural traces do not readily align themselves in patterns which may be interpreted as lanes or obvious family compounds. There is little evidence of internal posts or other furniture. A similar though slightly larger hut plan was discovered in the excavation at Zambezi Farm. Here, there was evidence of a definite entrance and additional corner support posts. At both sites a number of large pits were discovered as well as shallow depressions left in evidence of cooking-fires.

The pits discovered at Chundu Farm were of three kinds. Some were storage/refuse pits similar to those found at the other sites. Others contained human burials and funeral offerings. The burials were placed in shallow grave pits. The body was in a flexed position with the knees brought up to the chest and the arms folded across them. Although the grave of one of the Chundu burials was lined with pieces of pottery, the custom of the time appears not to have included the deposition of grave goods directly with the body. Instead, separate pits were prepared. In these we find pairs of pottery vessels, one enclosing the other, forming a container for iron and/or copper and other artefacts. Each of the caches contained at least a hoe and the largest one consisted of a hoe, an axe, and copper and iron bracelets, as well as cowrie shells and ostrich eggshell beads.

We may assume from the differences of the cache contents that certain differences in status and wealth existed within the early villages of the area. At the same time, the material evidence of the excavations suggests an economy and a way of life of an essentially subsistence kind. The life of the village revolved therefore around the maintenance of the domestic economy. The tools and other artefacts recovered are chiefly the most utilitarian kinds of object. The economy, generally, was a balance of food-production – by means of agriculture and stock-keeping – and the collection of wild food sources – by means of hunting and fishing as well as the gathering of wild fruit and vegetables.

During the period of the sixth and seventh centuries the area of the Bovu *dambo* south of the Ngwezi Valley was heavily occupied by farming settlements. By the eighth century, however, this was deserted in favour of the area immediately adjacent to the sandscarp overlooking the Zambezi Valley. In fact, this is the only time before the twelfth century that one finds evidence of a permanent settlement of the Kalahari Sand country this close to the river.

We may suggest from this fact that the Zambezi River itself played only a small part in the life of the early village peoples of the area, though it may have served as a source for fish. The valley floor is mostly composed of thin scoured soils or heavier clays which did not attract the Iron Age farmer. This eighth-century movement south from the more preferred areas along the Ngwezi and Kabondo rivers appears to be associated with a general decline in rainfall throughout south central Africa during the later centuries of the first millennium A.D. Further evidence of this is seen in the decrease in village population during the ninth and the next two centuries.

We may summarise the Early Iron Age as a

period during which the Iron Age way of life was brought into our area. By means of analyses of the pottery made at the various villages we can trace a continuity of this culture in time.

The Kalomo Tradition

The subsequent history of the region includes the development of the Kalomo Tradition and its expansion onto the Batoka highlands. Towards the end of the first millennium the evidence indicates a dwindling number of village occupants and a decrease in food production associated with a movement away from the Victoria Falls region into the grasslands associated with the headwaters of the Ngwezi and Kalomo rivers on the Batoka plateau.

This Kalomo Tradition was one of the first Iron Age manifestations to be studied on a large scale in Zambia. Originally, at the deep stratified mounds of Kalundu and Isamu Pati on the Batoka plateau, and later at the mounds of Kamangoza and Simbusenga near Livingstone, archaeologists described a uniform culture based upon small mixed agricultural settlements. While the earlier villages of the Victoria Falls region were relatively numerous and populous, the villages found associated with the period after the tenth century are quite small in area and held less than fifty inhabitants. In the Victoria Falls region, these villages are all situated upon the Bovu *dambo,* and we have no evidence of Iron Age settlement either in the valley or along the edges of the sandscarp during the period from the ninth to the eleventh century.

From an examination of the remains of foodstuffs from the various sites we are able to ascertain that the people associated with the Kalomo Tradition practised an economy very similar to that found in the earlier villages. Agriculture and husbandry accounted for no more than half, and possibly less, of the food available to the average diet. This means that these villagers still depended on the product of hunting and gathering activities as much as on the produce of their farms.

Finds from Kalomo Tradition sites illustrate a way of life not much different from that prevailing in parts of central Africa in quite recent times. Locally available iron ore was smelted and light wood-working tools and arrowheads were manufactured. Frequent finds of bodkins suggest the sewing of hides into clothing. Copper is found in the villages of the Kalomo Tradition; this attests to a continued trade contact with the copper-producing areas of the sub-continent. Despite such long-distance trade contact, village life seems to have been centred upon a daily routine typical of a subsistence-level agricultural village.

An important craft practised in these villages was the making of clay pottery vessels. From analysis of the types of vessels made and their decoration, archaeologists have been able to define the Kalomo population in time and to trace its penetration of the Batoka highlands from an origin among the Early Iron Age populations of the Zambezi Valley. By the beginning of the tenth century both the Victoria Falls region and the Batoka plateau were occupied by a culturally homogeneous population producing ceramics and other objects of essentially uniform type.

The Early Tonga Tradition

By the early twelfth century, however, villages in this area began to absorb elements of a new culture and population which were spreading southwards from what is

Fig. 7 A pair of pottery vessels from Zambezi Farm, dating to the eighth century A.D.; the small bowl forms a lid for the larger vessel.

now the northern part of Zambia's Southern Province. Investigations in various parts of the province have associated these new cultural traits with those known later in time as part of the culture of the Tonga-speaking peoples. For this reason, we may refer in a general way to Early Tonga culture to mean a tribally undifferentiated cultural stratum which existed throughout the province at this time. In time, the generalised similarities between the archaeological cul-tures located in different parts of the province changed into more regionally dis-crete entities. The traditional social and political structure of the area may not be discernible through archaeology alone; nevertheless, the results of archaeological investigations in the Victoria Falls region disclose that the area was occupied con-tinuously since the twelfth century by a cultural population at least partly ancestral to the present-day Leya inhabitants.

The Early Tonga apparently moved into the area and formed joint villages with the Kalomo people already living there. At least, from the twelfth century onwards there is no evidence of a Kalomo village which does not also include evidence of Early Tonga culture. At the same time, we discover villages not only on the edge of Bovu *dambo*, but also extending south to the edge of the sandscarp and north on to the alluvial clays of the Ngwezi Valley. In fact, this is the first time in the history of the area that we find villages occupying more than a single circumscribed eco-zone within the region. The settlement pattern now consisted of numbers of small village units scattered throughout the area and exploiting a greater number of soil types than had previously been the case.

These farming communities have been extensively investigated by archaeologists at sites like Sinde, Mukuni and Simbusenga. Although the general tenor of life in these villages was unchanged from earlier times, there is increasing evidence of the slight differences which were part of Early Tonga life and were introduced into the area by them. The huts associated with this period are small and round, usually about 2·5 metres in diameter, with a number of wall poles set in a shallow trench. The walls are plastered with mud daub. After the twelfth century we also find considerable evidence of the manufacture of figurines. These usually take the form of clay effigies of either human or animal figures. At Simbusenga we even found models of huts and a bird effigy. Many of these figurines were placed in pits near a baobab tree in the centre of the village. Iron hoe-blades are more frequently found in the post-twelfth-century villages of the area than in the earlier ones. This may indicate an increase

Fig. 8 A fourteenth-century Early Tonga hut-floor discovered at Simonga. The line of the wall is indicated by a ring of discoloured earth marking a trench dug to receive the wall-poles. Some of the burnt stubs of these poles, two interior poles and a grindstone may also be seen.
Fig. 9 Early Tonga clay figurine of an ox.

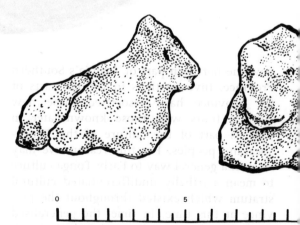

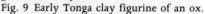

either in smithing activity or in farming; in any event, we know from increased finds of cattle bones at these villages that more domestic animals were kept.

The villages were much the same as earlier ones — a cluster of huts spread round a central clearing. An early hut of this period has been investigated at the Simonga site. Finds from the interior of this hut included a large flat grindstone and a grinder.

By the middle of the second millennium A.D. the local cultural tradition had established itself except for those slight modifications which allow us to distinguish between the modern tribes, and from this time onwards the area's culture-history becomes more accessible to the historian.

We may summarise the area's Iron Age prehistory briefly: sometime in the first half of the first millennium A.D. small groups of agriculturalists entered the area and introduced the Iron Age way of life. They do not appear to have been permanent residents, but their descendants established large settled villages and over a period of years occupied a large part of the Victoria Falls region, largely displacing the indigenous Late Stone Age inhabitants. Late in the ninth century this population began to dwindle. Their linear descendants are identified by the Kalomo Tradition which also spread on to the Batoka plateau. They were in turn superseded in the twelfth century by the Early Tonga who established the basis for the area's traditional culture, which has continued into recent times.

Select Bibliography

DANIELS, S. G. H. and PHILLIPSON, D. W. 'The Early Iron Age Site at Dambwa near Livingstone' in B. M. Fagan, D. W. Phillipson and S. G. H. Daniels, *Iron Age Cultures in Zambia*, ii, London, 1969, pp. 3–54.

PHILLIPSON, D. W. 'The Early Iron Age in Zambia: Regional Variants and some Tentative Conclusions', *Journal of African History*, ix, 1968, pp. 191–211.

PHILLIPSON, D. W. *African Archaeology*, Cambridge, 1985.

VOGEL, J. O. *Kamangoza*, Nairobi (Zambia Museum Papers, no. 2), 1971.

VOGEL, J. O. *Kumadzulo*, Lusaka (Zambia Museum Papers, no. 3), 1971.

VOGEL, J. O. *Simbusenga*, Lusaka (Zambia Museum Papers, no. 4), 1974.

VOGEL, J. O. 'Iron Age Farmers in Southwestern Zambia', *African Archaeological Review*, v, 1987, pp. 159–170.

Fig. 10 Early Tonga pottery, typical of the Victoria Falls region from the twelfth century onwards.

CHAPTER 6

The Traditional History and Ethnography

Kafungulwa Mubitana

The traditional history of the area surrounding the Victoria Falls has an important bearing on our understanding of central and southern Africa's major population movements and migrations; the growth and fall of empires and powerful chiefdoms; the intermixtures and interrelations of ethnic groups; the emergence of great leaders and social groupings and the customs and beliefs that have prevailed for many centuries. The ethnography of the area highlights the cultural differences and similarities, material and otherwise, between the various social groups.

Sources of Information

In November 1855, the missionary Dr David Livingstone, guided by Sekeletu's* men, visited the great falls on the Zambezi, then known to the Kololo as the *musi o'tunya* (the smoke that shoots and thunders). Livingstone renamed them the Victoria Falls after the then Queen of England. His eloquent reports about the great waterfall brought to the Zambezi many adventurers from Europe and the Cape, from whose writings much historical and ethnographical information may be gathered about the peoples of the Victoria Falls region as seen by outsiders. Although a few of these traders, hunters, travellers and missionaries made accurate observations about the people they found in the area, many regarded the human element a detraction from the 'natural' scenery, and only incidental derogatory remarks about the African population may be found in their

* Sekeletu was the Kololo leader, who succeeded his father Sebitwane. Sebitwane and his Kololo were a Sotho offshoot who left their original home in the south as a result of the wars of Chaka the Zulu. They fought their way north to the Zambezi where they defeated the various inhabitants of the Victoria Falls region, and also the Lozi and Tonga. They were finally crushed by the Lozi in 1864.

writings. Others were content to describe at face value what they saw and heard, but it is to the oral histories of the local inhabitants of the Victoria Falls region that we must sometimes turn for detailed or complementary information.

Histories of the Local Peoples

The San, or Bushmen, locally known as Kwengo, are the first traditionally recorded inhabitants of the region surrounding the Victoria Falls. There are today relatively few Kwengo, mainly of mixed stock, in this area which is now predominantly inhabited by the Leya, Toka, Subiya, Tonga, Nanzwa, Dombe, Mbukushu and Yeyi. The Leya and Toka live mainly on the north bank of the Zambezi, although the former once also occupied the south bank. The Subiya have always lived on both banks of the river, whereas the Nanzwa, Dombe, Mbukushu and Yeyi have, in the main, confined themselves to the south bank. Tonga live on both sides of the Zambezi in the Gwembe valley downstream of the Falls and also on the southern Zambian plateau.

The Leya

The Leya, who in 1962 numbered some 8000, are said by one authority to have been in existence as a component group of the Rozi* kingdom in about the seventeenth and eighteenth centuries, and to have lived on the southern side of the Zambezi 'somewhere in the vicinity of Zumbo, *i.e.* the country that is the cradle of the Rozi-Leya-Nyai' (von Sicard, 1948). On the other hand, A. D. Jalla's account (n.d.) of early Lozi invasions

* A distinction must be made between the Rozi (Rozwi) and Lozi kingdoms. The former was centred on the southern side of the Zambezi and the latter on the northern. There was no relationship between the two.

of Leyaland places the Leya of Sekute already in their present locality, on the islands and the north bank of the Zambezi. King Ngombala, 'the enslaver of nations', who led the Lozi in these campaigns against the Leya and Toka, must have reigned about the beginning of the eighteenth century as, according to Jalla (*op. cit.*), Mulambwa, who ruled the Lozi from about 1800 onwards, only came fifth from him in the line of succession.

At any rate, by 1853, the Leya were well established on the north side of the Zambezi River, as is shown by Livingstone's sketchmap of the middle Zambezi which was made at that time (Smith and Dale, 1920). There can be little doubt that some Leya also lived on the south bank since Leya chiefs often transferred their capitals from one bank to the other. Leya presence on both banks of the river up to the early 1930s is also confirmed by a report published in 1934 by J. Moffat Thomson, then Secretary for Native Affairs in Northern Rhodesia.

There are today two groups of Leya distinguished by political bounds. The larger group is under Chief Mukuni and the smaller under Chief Sekute. Mukuni and Sekute are hereditary titles of Leya chiefs; the incumbents of these offices may also be known by their own names. The Leya of Mukuni are commonly believed to have been in the Victoria Falls area longer than those of his counterpart. It is further believed that Mukuni's people came from the area of Kabwe in what is now the Central Province of Zambia and that they are of Lenje origin (Muntemba, 1970), those of Sekute being mainly of Subiya stock. This may be misleading as it is now almost certainly known that these traditions of origin apply mainly to the ruling clans and not to the subject peoples, who may be autochthonous. Thus

63

the Leya people, as opposed to the present Leya chiefs, may have first lived on the southern side of the Zambezi, possibly near Zumbo as von Sicard claims, but only started moving towards the Victoria Falls region at the beginning of the eighteenth century.

As has been pointed out above, Chiefs Mukuni and Sekute claim different origins. This has tended to divide the Leya into two groups with different orientations. According to von Sicard (1948), between 1693 and 1718 the founder of the Rozi kingdom sent a Leya chief named Ne-Mhanwe northwards on an expedition against the Shangwe living near the Zambezi in the Sebungwe district. Having conquered the Shangwe, Ne-Mhanwe settled there. If this account is accepted, it follows that Mukuni and, later, Sekute must both have gained ascendancy over their respective Leya groups after this period. On the other hand, according to Chief Mukuni

Fig. 1 View of 'Sesheke port' (Mwandi) by E. Holub (1881).

Fig. 2 Map of peoples and places mentioned in Chapter 6.

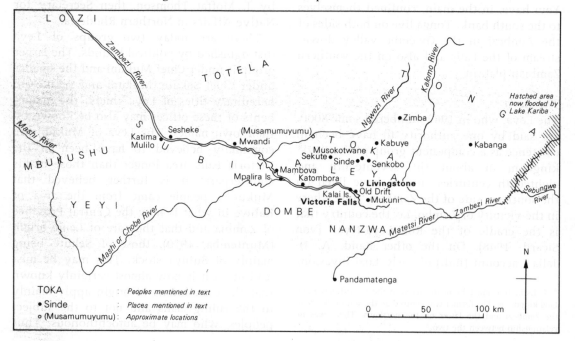

TOKA   : Peoples mentioned in text

• Sinde   : Places mentioned in text

o (Musamumuyumu): Approximate locations

Fig. 3 (left) Chief Mukuni Siloka II (reigned 1943–1971).
Fig. 4 (right) Mpalira Island, by E. Holub (1881).

Siloka II who reigned between 1943 and 1971, his Leya (then known as Lenje) left the Kabwe area between 1400 and 1500 and settled on the east bank of the Victoria Falls. However, if we accept Siloka II's claim that he was the seventeenth chief in the line of succession from the first Mukuni (Sichiyumuna), it is doubtful if the presence of his ancestors in the Falls area would date back as far as the fifteenth century, since this would require an average of thirty years' reign for each of the seventeen chiefs. It seems far more likely that the earliest Mukuni reigned about the beginning of the eighteenth century. This coincides with von Sicard's approximate dating of the invasion of the Shangwe by the Leya chief Ne-Mhanwe.

Some local oral traditions suggest that Sekute settled in the Victoria Falls region long after Mukuni had done so, but doubt is cast on this by other lines of enquiry. Although Mukuni Siloka II places Sekute's arrival at 1836 (Mukuni, 1957), many other sources indicate a much earlier date. David Livingstone reports having seen on Kalai Island, in 1855, the graves of the ancestors of the Sekute who had fled from Sebitwane

(Livingstone, 1857). According to Jalla, Sebitwane attacked and drove Sekute away from Kalai Island about 1836. This would indicate that Sekute's ancestors had been established in the area long before the date given by Mukuni. Indeed, nowhere does Livingstone indicate that Sekute, whom he called a Batonga chief, was a recent arrival in the area.

The claim by members of the Sekute royal family that the first Sekute settled in the Victoria Falls area by order of King Ngombala of the Lozi is not consistent with Jalla's version, which was taken from Lozi oral sources. Jalla states that, when Ngombala invaded the Victoria Falls area, probably early in the eighteenth century, he conquered the Leya under Sekute. It is thus probable that Sekute actually settled in this area long before the Lozi invasion. This view is shared by some traditional Leya historians who state that Sekute originally came to hunt hippopotami, a pursuit at which his people are said to have been particularly skilled.

The royal family of Sekute claims Nzanza origins. The Nzanza, who are closely related to the Subiya, are also said to have the same origin as the Mbowe. It may be concluded that Sekute acquired his Leyahood only after settling in the Victoria Falls region among the Leya proper. Like the people who came with the first Mukuni, the Nzanza or Subiya of Sekute soon incorporated Leya elements and eventually became identified as Leya, while retaining their traditional chieftainship. It may be pointed out that, to this day, the majority of the Leya of Sekute have Subiya connections.

The wars of the eighteenth and nineteenth centuries in southern Africa greatly reduced Sekute's power and influence. Soon after arriving in the Victoria Falls area, Sekute Koongo Ceete went to war with Mukuni because the latter had refused to allow him to settle on the mainland, confining him to the islands on the Zambezi. Sekute and his people were beaten. Soliciting the help of his uncle Liswaani, a Subiya-Mbukushu chief, and of the fierce Subiya leader Sundano, Sekute attacked again; but Mukuni still had the upper hand. He slew Sundano and took Sekute captive, also retaining the latter's royal drums. The situation was later resolved by Mukuni releasing Sekute and offering, in mitigation, his own sister as wife to him. It is said that Mujimaizi Mukuni was born from this marriage. Mujimaizi was to distinguish himself in battle against the Lozi at a place near Ngwezi known as Musamumuyumu (the dry tree) before the coming of the Kololo.

When the Kololo Sebitwane invaded Kalai Island about 1836, Siansingu was the incumbent Sekute. Although many of his people were massacred during the raid, Siansingu and a few others escaped and sought refuge at Malindi and Mpandeni near Nyamandhlovu, under the overlordship of the Ndebele leader Mzilikazi. Siansingu died of leprosy at Malindi, but some of his followers returned after the annihilation of the Kololo by the Lozi in 1864. Mungala, a nephew of

Siansingu, had assumed the Sekuteship. He and his people first settled at Lwanja in Mashi, but later moved back to the Victoria Falls area, where they settled at the 'Old Drift'.

During Mungala's reign, some of his Leya settled at Kabuye, south of Zimba, under the leadership of Katapazi, who was reputedly a brother of Mungala. A very close relationship existed between the Leya of Sekute and those of Katapazi until 1947, when the British Administration abolished Katapazi's chieftaincy and incorporated his area into that of Mukuni. Katapazi and his people naturally resented this move and argued their preference for Sekute, since they had more family and ethnic affinities with the latter's people. This was impracticable from the Administration's point of view, because Native Trust Land and the land alienated for European farming and settlement separated Sekute's chiefdom from that of Katapazi. On the other hand, Mukuni's chiefdom adjoined that of Katapazi and the two could thus conveniently be merged.

The Toka

The Toka are probably the largest of the societies inhabiting the north bank of the Zambezi in the immediate vicinity of the Victoria Falls. Culturally and linguistically they are similar to the Leya, the only difference between them being in the historical origins of their ruling chiefs. Tradition has it that the ruling clan of the Toka were originally Tonga who came from Kabanga, to the south-east of Kalomo, under a leader named Sianalumba. They settled in the Ngwezi, Sinde and Senkobo areas, which are separated from the Zambezi River by the territory occupied by the Leya and Subiya. Having arrived in the Victoria Falls region,

Sianalumba's followers intermingled with the Leya elements they found there; and today many Leya are to be found in the Toka area and *vice versa*.

Musokotwane is the hereditary title of the Toka chief.* It is generally believed that this was a nickname given to the Toka leader by the Kololo when they first came to the Victoria Falls area between 1830 and 1836. The name is said to have originated from the Toka or Tonga word *kusotoka* (to cross or jump). It is stated that, when Sebitwane asked the then Toka leader whence he and his people originally came, the latter replied '*twakasotoka mwami*' (we crossed over, chief) — referring to himself and his people having crossed the Kalomo river from Kabanga to settle in the Ngwezi, Senkobo and Sinde areas; whereupon the Kololo called him Musokotwane (probably meaning 'the jumper'). Musokotwane's people also claim that it was the Kololo who first called them Toka, which is really a corruption of the word 'Tonga'.

It appears that the first Musokotwane was a later arrival on the Victoria Falls scene than either Mukuni or Sekute. Even the present Musokotwane holds no ritual power over his soil, this being exclusively exercised by Mujala, who was found by Sianalumba in the area, and whom Livingstone, in 1860, found living independently but under fear of the Ndebele.

While Sekute fled his islands and Mukuni went into humble submission, Musokotwane first resisted the invading Kololo and then, having been defeated, went on to serve them loyally. It was the Toka who led the

Kololo up north to the Tonga and Ila countries; it was with the help of Toka auxiliaries that Sebitwane and, later, Sekeletu kept peace on the north bank of the Zambezi in the Victoria Falls region. The Toka, with the encouragement of the Kololo, also plundered the surrounding villages. As Musokotwane told Livingstone in 1860: 'The Makololo have given me a spear; why should I not use it?'. He had personally killed his rival, Chief Mukuni. According to the Livingstones, Musokotwane (Mushobotwane) was so well nourished that he was 'the stoutest man we have seen in Africa' (D. and C. Livingstone, 1865: 248).

While the Kololo had spared the Toka in return for the help they could get out of them, the defeat of the former by the Lozi in 1864 spelled disaster for all those who had been in league with Sebitwane. Furthermore, after that year, the Toka and Tonga developed the habit of harbouring recalcitrant Lozi. It was in pursuit of such rebels that a Lozi detachment attacked the Toka and took Lusungo, the then Musokotwane, captive. He was released only after the Toka had made several representations to the Lozi king.

The Subiya

The Subiya, another large and important group in the Victoria Falls region, are also closely connected with the Leya. They occupy both banks of the Zambezi between Katombora and Sesheke. In the Katombora area the Subiya and Leya have so intermingled as to be indistinguishable from one another. The Subiya language is now rarely spoken on the north bank, having been replaced by Leya in the Katombora-Mambova area and by Lozi between Mwandi and Sesheke. It is still spoken in the pre-

---

* The Toka have also been under other chiefs, most of them petty or subordinate to Musokotwane. The most important of these was Siakasipa who was, until 1951, recognised as a full chief by the British Administration.

dominantly Subiya settlements of the south bank.

In the past, the Subiya have in turn been under the domination of the Lozi, the Kololo and the Lozi again. Unlike the Leya and Toka whose domination by foreign invaders was never total, the Subiya people successively became an integral part of both the Lozi and Kololo empires. They were under the Lozi when their territory was partitioned between the then Northwestern Rhodesia and German South West Africa. Today, the Subiya living in Zambia are under Subiya, Lozi and Leya chiefs.

During the first Lozi conquest the Subiya were ruled by an induna (chief) resident at Sesheke. During the second period of Lozi domination, after 1864, the Lozi still placed some of their important chiefs at Sesheke to govern the Subiya, although Subiya chiefs were also appointed to help them keep the peace. One such important Subiya chief, Mukumba, was strategically placed by the Lozi king Sipopa near Mambova to guard against people crossing the Chobe and Zambezi from the south, whether these were enemies to the Lozi king and empire, or simply traders or missionaries. It was Mukumba's unfailing duty to warn Sipopa of strangers intending to enter the Barotse valley. Not until permission was received from the king would Mukumba allow the strangers to proceed. As the French missionary Coillard wrote in 1878:

Mpalira is a sandy isle at the confluence of the Chobe and Zambezi. The Barotse chiefs, whose powers are subordinated to one another, are established there, governing the tributary tribe of Masubia, and guarding the principal ford of the river, the entrance to the country. No one can cross it without special authorisation. . . . The chief, Mokumba, a man of unusual intelligence, received me with many attentions. Still, before consenting to let me pass on to Sesheke, the headman of which sent me a pressing invitation, he had to forward a special message, and obtain formal permission, as all entrance to their country, even to the left bank of the river, is absolutely forbidden to strangers. (Coillard, 1897: 57)

The Subiya of Sekute's chiefdom by no means acknowledge Sekute as their rightful leader. For example, the descendants of Segwanyana, a powerful chief before British rule came to the area, still look upon themselves as the masters of the western part of the chiefdom. It would appear that the Segwanyana dynasty is of long historical standing. For instance, the village of 'Sekonyana' appears on Livingstone's *Map of the Zambezi river Territory*, made between 1853 and 1854. Livingstone places the village on the north bank of the Zambezi, near Kazungula in the Subiya area (Smith and Dale, 1920), but does not, unfortunately, say anything more about the village or the chief Segwanyana.

Other groups

According to the oral traditions recorded by Worthington, the Subiya have absorbed a substantial number of Mbukushu who 'came originally from the neighbourhood of Katima Mulilo rapids on the Zambezi river' (Worthington, 1902). The famous chiefs Sundano and Liswaani, generally regarded as Subiya, were actually of Mbukushu origin. Mbukushu chiefs, like their Subiya counterparts, were sometimes employed by the Lozi and Kololo to guard the fords of the Zambezi and

Chobe. According to Livingstone, Liswaani was once evicted from Mpalira Island by Sebitwane's Kololo for having assisted the Ndebele to cross the river in order to attack them (Schapera, 1963).

The Yeyi are a group closely related to the Mbukushu. They live further up the Chobe river. Like the Mbukushu, the Yeyi suffered defeat and subjugation at the hands of the Lozi and Kololo.

The Nanzwa and kindred groups have lived mostly on the southern bank of the Zambezi and further south. Early white travellers mistook them for the Makalaka, a term derived from Makalanga, but the Kalanga are in fact a separate group inhabiting the southern part of Zimbabwe, although ethnically related to the Nanzwa. The term 'Makalaka' was a derogatory one, referring to both the Nanzwa and the Kalanga as a disorganised, broken people. As the traveller and adventurer Chapman remarked of both:

> Having long been a conquered race, they have been subdued in everything, and their morality, if they had any, has been chased away by the conqueror; so subdued are they now that they have no thought of their own rights or feelings, and believe everything they have, even their women, to be at the mercy of any kind of person who is a superior being. (Chapman, 1886, II: 161)

Once upon a time, the Kalanga and the Nanzwa had been great and proud peoples with great empires of their own. It was not until about 1838 that the Nanzwa empire was destroyed by the Ndebele leader Mzilikazi.

The Dombe are closely associated with the Nanzwa and live immediately to the west of them. They are also related to both the Subiya and Leya. It may be noted that in the Sekute chiefdom many inhabitants claim Dombe ancestry.

Living further downstream of the Victoria Falls on both banks of the Zambezi, and somewhat related to the Toka, Leya and Nanzwa, are the Valley Tonga. They too have been harassed by foreign invaders, particularly the Ndebele who carried off many of their young men and women and their cattle. In 1860, the Valley Tonga were cleared away from the right bank of the Zambezi as the Ndebele did not want them to alert their enemies during invasions.

The Totela, who now live to the far west of our area, appear at one time to have occupied a large area to the north-west of the Victoria Falls from which they have been largely driven by Leya and Toka. They are said to have worked most of the iron-smelting sites to be found in the Leya chiefdom of Sekute. Many Totela now identify themselves with either the Lozi or the Toka as the term 'Totela' is applied to them derogatorily by their neighbours.

Languages, Customs and Beliefs

As might be expected of societies living in close contact with each other, the languages, customs and beliefs of the peoples of the Victoria Falls region tend to be similar. The Leya, Toka, Valley Tonga, Subiya and even the Nanzwa speak languages which are mutually intelligible. In particular, there is practically no difference between spoken Toka and Leya, both of which are dialects of Tonga. All these languages, except Nanzwa, belong to the *Bantu Botatwe* group. Whatever the similarities in their language structure, however, the origins of these people are now thought to be diverse.

Both the Leya of Mukuni and those of Sekute have a high priestess who formerly exercised a high ritual influence over the land. Known as Bedyango among the Leya of Mukuni and Ina-Sing'andu among those of Sekute, the priestess was selected from among the chief's sisters and aunts. She was competent in performing rituals to avert disaster during wars, droughts or epidemic onslaughts; she officiated during births, marriages and deaths and had the final say in the choice of a new chief (Muntemba, 1970). Today, there is not as much pomp and significance attached to the offices of Bedyango and Ina-Sing'andu as there was in the past. Occasionally, during a drought or during a chief's succession ceremony at Mukuni's headquarters, Lukambo, the priestess Bedyango goes into action and the Leya of Mukuni revive an institution that was once great. Sekute's Leya, however, appear to be satisfied with preserving only the title of Ina-Sing'andu. Missionary influences, reinforced by changed political conditions, have done much to weaken these ritual offices.

Minor rites and ceremonies among the Leya are carried out at the village level. The village headman offers prayers and libations at his own ancestral shrine for the benefit of the whole village. Such localised ritual is also common among the Toka and Tonga.

The Subiya are said to have been great conjurors and magicians, and were usually commissioned to perform before Lozi kings. Perhaps due to his Subiya origin, Siansingu, the Sekute who led the Leya into exile about 1836, was feared for his magical powers. Livingstone reports that it was believed that while on Kalai Island, Siansingu Sekute had kept a pot of medicine which, when opened, released an epidemic in the land (Living-

Fig. 5 Chief Mukuni Siloka II (right) with the Priestess Bedyango (centre) at a rain-making ceremony.

stone, 1857). Like the Lozi, the Leya of Sekute believed that they could cause a thick mist to blind their enemies in battle, and they now claim that they thus won a battle against Mukuni's people. It was, however, Sekute's Leya who were beaten in the two wars against Mukuni that are traditionally remembered.

The Leya of Mukuni do credit Sekute's magical powers generally, and in particular those of his four royal drums. One of these drums, *makuwakuwa*, is said to have performed miracles at the time when Koongo Ceete Sekute was leading his people from Lutaka in Mashi. It 'sailed' ahead of Sekute's fleet of canoes along the Chobe and Zambezi, sounding loudly at the approach of danger. As Chief Mukuni Siloka II has related: 'It is said that they could not leave camp if *makuwakuwa* did not give any signal, and that sometimes they had to spend a month or so if *makuwakuwa* remained silent.' (Mukuni, 1957.) Chief Mukuni goes on to say that when Sekute finally attacked and was defeated by Mukuni, the latter ordered his people to seize the royal drums, including *makuwakuwa,* so that they could be employed in local ceremonies. The drum *makuwakuwa* is then said to have escaped capture by leaping into the Zambezi and settling at the bottom of the river, where it kept sounding for many years afterwards.

Livingstone records that three different spots at the Victoria Falls were used by Sekute, Mukuni and Liswaani as places of worship for their Gods and ancestors, on account of the fear and awe which they evoked. Coillard, who visited the Falls some twenty years after Livingstone, says of the Falls that the local inhabitants

> believe it is haunted by a malevolent and cruel divinity, and they make it offerings to conciliate its favour, a bead necklace, a bracelet, or some other object, which they fling into the abyss, bursting into lugubrious incantations, quite in harmony with their dread and horror. (Coillard, 1897: 55)

Many more customs and beliefs of the area have been recorded by various missionaries or travellers. Livingstone, for instance, describes the custom of hanging human skulls on poles or stakes near the home. At Kalai Island, where Sekute had his capital, and at Mujala's* village he counted a number of human skulls placed in this way. These trophies were taken from the bodies of slain enemies. Also at Kalai and at Mujala's village, Livingstone found elephant tusks set

Fig. 6 Subiya grave, drawn by E. Holub (1881).

in the earth around graveyards. The Czech adventurer, Dr Emil Holub, records the same custom among the Subiya. The Leya of Mukuni also appear to have practised it, and one of their songs in praise of a great chief refers to 'the grave of the great one, who lives under the earth, his grave surrounded by elephant tusks'.* The Leya, Toka and Subiya no longer show reverence to their beloved dead in this manner, partly because elephants are now difficult to procure, and partly because the wildlife preservation laws forbid the wanton slaughter of elephants.

Holub has given a vivid picture of Nanzwa customs. He states that when a young man fancies a girl for a wife he sends an intermediary, usually an old woman, to carry the proposal:

> to portray the young man in glowing colours; to extol the excellence of his temper, to praise his skill in procuring *nyama* (game), to describe the productiveness of his garden, and to enumerate the skins with which he has made his bed soft and comfortable. (Holub, 1881, II: 206)

---

* The man Mujala was probably Toka.

* It is interesting to note that a similar song, with similar words, is sung among Sekute's Leya also.

The burial custom of the Nanzwa is described thus:

> When anyone dies, his burial takes place in the evening near his own enclosure, the grave, if the soil permits it, being dug to the depth of five feet. An adult is wrapped in his mantle of skins and his assegai is buried with him. The interment is conducted in silence that is broken only by the sobs of the women. (Holub, 1881, II: 208)

Food and Dress

The area including the chiefdoms of Mukuni, Sekute and Musokotwane is dominated by the Kalahari type of soil and is thus mainly suitable for growing sorghum, millet and groundnuts. Between 1883 and 1887, when Holub made his second journey to this area, he found the Toka, Leya and Subiya growing pumpkins, millet, maize, beans and groundnuts, which they often traded to Europeans at Pandamatenga for lengths of calico. Wild fruits also abound in the area and in times of famine the people substituted these for their staple foods.

Much fishing has gone on in the Zambezi River for centuries; but today fishing on a large scale is restricted to certain parts of the river, such as Kazungula and Mambova. Fish is still an important food of the inhabitants of the Victoria Falls region. Livingstone residents consume much fish caught at Kazungula and Mambova.

Hippopotamus flesh was formerly regarded as a delicacy among the Leya, Subiya and Totela, but it is now rarely obtainable as there is government restriction on the indiscriminate slaughter of these animals.

The Toka, Leya and Tonga have always kept large herds of cattle, goats and sheep and have rarely been short of meat, milk and hides. It was mainly because of their large herds of cattle that they were repeatedly raided by the Lozi, Kololo and Ndebele. It is said that Sebitwane's first raid left the Toka, Leya and Tonga areas devoid of cattle, although goats and sheep were spared, as these were considered by the raiders to have little value for meat and milk. The vanquished peoples quickly recovered the size of their herds, only to attract more raids in the 1880s.

There was little variation in dress between the peoples of the Victoria Falls region. Holub observed that Subiya, Toka and Leya women wore leather skirts reaching to the knees. He also made a similar observation among the Nanzwa. Valley Tonga women are also known to have had a somewhat similar form of dress. The men of the area generally wore garments consisting of a length of calico or the skins of small animals fastened round the waist. The exception were Valley Tonga men whose only form of dress was red ochre smeared over their bodies. Consequently, they became known as *baenda pezi* (those who go about naked).

With regard to other forms of adornment, the Nanzwa, Subiya and some Leya file to points their upper central incisor teeth, while the Toka and Valley Tonga used to remove these teeth in order to resemble their cattle. Livingstone describes the Toka as having had a scanty dress, and their custom of knocking out the upper front teeth as having made them appear 'hideously ugly, especially when laughing or when they become old.' Yet the Toka themselves saw this custom both as a mark of ethnic identity and as fashionable.

Elderly Toka and Leya women still wear the *musisi,* a Lozi form of dress modelled on the style introduced by Victorian mission-

72

Fig. 7 (left) Woman wearing old-style Leya dress.
Fig. 8 (right) Man wearing old-style Leya dress.

Fig. 9 (left) Woman wearing more recent Barotse-style dress (*musisi*).
Fig. 10 (right) Man wearing Barotse kilt (*siziba*).

aries. It consists of a blouse left loose at the waist and several skirts joined and worn one over the other. Old Toka and Leya men still sometimes wear the Lozi kilt, the *siziba*. This 'consists of two many-pleated pieces of coloured cotton cloth joined at the top with a string for tying round the waist and open down the two sides.' (Clark, 1952: 76)

The modern people of the Victoria Falls region have largely adopted contemporary western dress, as have most other peoples in central and southern Africa.

Arts and Crafts

The people of the Victoria Falls region, like many others elsewhere, have highly developed oral literatures. Leya songs, connected with great events, chiefs, rituals and wars, are of the highest literary form, as Muntemba's (1970) renditions have shown.

The Leya, Toka, Valley Tonga, Subiya, Nanzwa and Totela have never been great sculptors like the Lunda, Chokwe, Luvale

and Mbunda. While the latter peoples have a sculptural tradition both of a representational and non-representational type, the people of the Victoria Falls area lack, in the main, the former element in their carvings. They are, however, highly skilled in carving and modelling utilitarian objects such as food bowls, water pots, mortars, stools and canoes. In the sphere of decorative art, both Toka and Valley Tonga women are renowned for their intricate beadwork. Subiya water pots are everywhere popular, not only for their original forms but also for their highly complex patterns and ornamentation.

The Totela are renowned for their metalwork. They formerly smelted iron and forged spears, axes and hoes which they traded to neighbouring societies. The smelting sites in Sekute's area are, according to local tradition, believed to have been worked by them.

The traditional architecture of the Victoria Falls area is similar to that found in many parts of central and southern Africa. The

Fig. 11 (top) Old-style architecture, Mukuni village.
Fig. 12 (bottom, left) Modern village architecture, Mukuni village.
Fig. 13 (bottom, right) Subiya pot.

houses are usually round and consist of mud smeared over a framework of poles stuck in the earth and bound fast with wattles; a grass thatched roof covers the structure. Villages are usually built in circular or semi-circular plan, leaving a large open space in the middle where a cattle kraal is constructed, to protect the animals at night.

Today, economic development and its accompanying urbanisation is having a steadily increasing effect on the traditional way of life and on the technology and customs described in this chapter. Away from the urban centres, many aspects of traditional African life remain comparatively unchanged. It remains to be seen in what form they will survive the rapid changes and disruptive influences with which they are now coming into contact.

Select Bibliography

CHAPMAN, J. *Travels in the Interior of South Africa,* 2 vols, London, 1886.

CLARK, J. D. 'The native tribes' *in* J. D. Clark (ed.), *The Victoria Falls,* Livingstone, 1952.

COILLARD, F. *On the Threshold of Central Africa,* London, 1897.

HOLUB, E. *Seven Years in South Africa,* 2 vols, London, 1881.

HOLUB, E. *Von der Capstadt ins Land der Maschukulumbwe,* 2 vols, Vienna, 1890.

JALLA, A. D. *The History of the Barotse Nation,* manuscript in Livingstone Museum, n.d.

LIVINGSTONE, D. *Missionary Travels and Researches in South Africa,* London, 1857.

LIVINGSTONE, D. and LIVINGSTONE, C. *Narrative of an Expedition to the Zambesi and its Tributaries,* London, 1865.

MUKUNI, Chief. *Handbook of the Leya History,* manuscript in Livingstone Museum, 1957.

MUNTEMBA, M. 'Political and ritual sovereignty among the Mukuni Leya of Zambia', *Zambia Museum Journal,* i, 1970.

SCHAPERA, I. (ed.) *Livingstone's African Journal 1853–1856,* 2 vols, London, 1963.

SEKWASWA (Ex-Head Messenger) and MAHIRITONA, K. *History of the Livingstone District,* manuscript in Livingstone Museum, n.d.

SICARD, H. VON. 'The Humbe under Chief Bangwe'. *N.A.D.A.* no. 25, 1948.

SMITH, E. W. and DALE, A. M. *The Ila-speaking Peoples of Northern Rhodesia,* 2 vols, London, 1920.

THOMSON, J. M. *Memorandum on the Native Tribes and Tribal Areas of Northern Rhodesia,* Livingstone, 1934.

WORTHINGTON, F. *Note on the Mampuku-shu,* manuscript in Livingstone Museum, 1902.

Fig. 14 Toka stool.

CHAPTER 7

The Victoria Falls and the European Penetration of Central Africa

David W. Phillipson

During the final decades of the nineteenth century, the whole of the central African region surrounding the Victoria Falls came under the political control of the British South Africa Company and soon began to attract increasing numbers of European settlers. One of the most important themes in the subsequent history of the region was the struggle for supremacy, which still continues south of the Limpopo, between the settlers and the indigenous African population. It is therefore not only of historical interest, but also of relevance to southern Africa's major source of modern socio-political unrest, to examine the process by which foreign domination was established in the Victoria Falls region.

The physical presence of Europeans in this part of central Africa extends back for less than one and a half centuries, but the indirect effects of foreign activities and settlement had been felt there for many hundreds of years previously. One of the contributing factors to the northwards migration of the Kololo, which resulted in their conquest of the Lozi state and subjugation of several neighbouring peoples, as described by Kafungulwa Mubitana in Chapter 6, was pressure from rapidly expanding European settlement in South Africa early in the nineteenth century. At this time, if not before, the Lozi had come into contact with the west coast trade, and the availability of imported cloth and firearms, together with New World foodstuffs such as maize and cassava (manioc), must have had a pronounced effect on large sections of the population. Archaeological evidence has been presented in Chapter 5 which indicates that the Iron Age people of the Victoria Falls region were receiving trade goods, principally glass beads, imported into Africa *via* the east coast as early as the seventh century A.D.

It is, however, highly probable that the traders who brought these items to Africa from across the Indian Ocean never themselves penetrated so far into the continent's interior. The goods were presumably spread by means of successive middlemen, or were passed from hand to hand through barter, until they reached the Victoria Falls region, over a thousand kilometres from the sea.

The exploration of this part of Africa by people from the outside world is a very recent development; and it is interesting briefly to survey the process by which outsiders gradually built up their geographical knowledge of the area, culminating in the numerous planned journeys of exploration during the third quarter of the nineteenth century which finally laid the region open to European settlement and colonisation.

Roman trade with south India was well established by the beginning of the Christian era, but a contemporary Greek navigation handbook to the Indian Ocean suggests that the east coast of Africa was but sketchily known to the ancient Mediterranean world, and that only as far south as the modern Tanzania. Later trade between this area, India and the Red Sea region appears to have been primarily in Arab hands, with occasional Chinese exploratory voyages: and there is no further evidence for a significant European presence on the Indian Ocean for more than a thousand years. During this period contact with the Gulf and India was established, bringing to the Swahili people of the east coast trade goods some of which eventually found their way inland in exchange for interior products, notably Zimbabwean gold. By the time Portuguese navigators rounded the Cape of Good Hope at the end of the fifteenth century and began their exploration of the coast from the south, Muslims were probably well established on the coast of northern Moçambique and had – during the thirteenth and fourteenth centuries at any rate – been in control of parts of the more southerly Sofala coast also, probably as far as the Sabi mouth. It thus seems certain that Muslims were acquainted with the mouths of the Zambezi before the Portuguese arrived in the area.

Early in the sixteenth century the Portuguese established forts at Kilwa and Sofala in 1505, and at Moçambique Island in 1558. Penetrating up the Zambezi, they founded Sena in 1531 and Tete a few years later. Upstream of Tete the Cabora Bassa rapids form an effective barrier to navigation and to general penetration of the Zambezi valley from the coast. There are, however, indications that there may have been a Portuguese settlement at the confluence of the Luangwa and the Zambezi during the second half of the sixteenth century. The main interest of the early Portuguese, however, lay not in the Zambezi valley but in the gold-rich regions of Monomotapa to the south. Certainly, there were Portuguese trading posts or fairs established in northern Mashonaland by the seventeenth century, but these would have been most easily reached by way of Tete and the Mazoe valley. Be that as it may, it seems clear that the course of the Zambezi River for some five hundred kilometres downstream of the Victoria Falls remained largely unknown to the outside world until the middle of the nineteenth century. During the eighteenth century Portuguese settlements at Feira and Zumbo traded extensively with the people of the area that is now central and southern Zambia, but this appears to have been through African traders and travellers; there is no evidence that Portuguese themselves penetrated into the middle Zambezi region until the 1860s.

European knowledge or ignorance of the African interior can be illustrated to a certain extent through the study of early maps, but such sources present many pitfalls for the unwary. Only rarely do these maps accurately reflect the contemporary state of knowledge. For example, classical views concerning the sources and upper course of the Nile, some of which can be traced back to the fifth century B.C. writings of Herodotus, were formalised during the second century A.D. by Claudius Ptolemy of Alexandria, whose work formed the basis of much early Arab geography. In the fifteenth century, Ptolemy's work was rediscovered by European geographers and his picture of the centre of Africa, with the Nile flowing from two lakes fed by streams rising in the snow-capped Mountains of the Moon, formed a prominent part of all maps of Africa produced in Europe before the end of the seventeenth century, being retained well into the eighteenth century by some cartographers.

Nevertheless, the results of Portuguese exploration of the coasts of Africa were gradually incorporated into the maps of the period, although largely mythical interior details were retained. For example, a French world map produced by Pierre Descelliers of Dieppe in 1546 shows the mouths of both the Limpopo and the Zambezi, features which were unknown to Ptolemy, within half a century of the first reconnaissance of the East African coast by the Portuguese. Both rivers are, however, shown as branches of the same stream, rising in one of Ptolemy's two lakes which also forms one of the sources of the Nile. The same blend of fact and myth occurs on Abraham Ortelius' well-known map of Africa published in Antwerp in 1570, part of which is here reproduced.

Fig. 1 Part of *Africae Nova Tabula* by Abraham Ortelius (1570).

Some discoveries were much slower to make their mark on contemporary cartography; Lake Malawi, for example, was known to the Portuguese by 1616 but did not appear on a printed map until the 1722 edition by Guillaume de l'Isle, Chief Geographer to the King of France. Tete and Sena seem not to have appeared on any printed map until two centuries after their foundation.

By the nineteenth century most mapmakers had discarded the last remnants of the mythical or imaginary features with

Fig. 2 Part of a map of southern Africa by H. Chatelain (1719).

which their predecessors' work had been embellished, and no longer feared to present large blank areas reflecting their ignorance of much of the African interior. Gradually, these gaps were filled, at first tentatively and – as we shall see – not always accurately, with the reports and inferences of the steadily increasing numbers of European travellers penetrating into what was, to them, one of the last remaining really extensive unknown areas of the globe.

Accounts of the journeys of the nineteenth century European explorers of central Africa are readily available and many of their own journals and other publications have recently been reprinted. Here, we can only touch on those which relate directly to the Victoria Falls themselves. Books of prime importance include David Livingstone's *Missionary Travels and Researches in South Africa* and *Narrative of an Expedition to the Zambesi and its Tributaries* by David and Charles Livingstone, published in 1857 and 1865 respectively. Other contemporary sources are given in the bibliography at the end of this chapter.

It was on 16 November 1855 that David Livingstone became the first European to see the great waterfall which he named in honour of his Queen; but its presence had been known to his compatriots and, indeed, to Livingstone himself, for some years previously. At the beginning of the present century George Lacy, who had himself visited the Falls in 1868, enquired into the question of European knowledge of the Falls before Livingstone's visit:

Englishmen in the South had, as early as about 1840, heard reports of the existence, far away in the North, of a phenomenon called Mosivatuna, 'the smoke that sounds', but little attention had been paid to them. They were brought by Bechuana hunters, who had them from wandering Makalakas and so-called Bushmen, or who had ventured as far as the Chobe branch of the Zambesi where, at Linyanti, dwelt the Makololo . . . under the leadership of Sebituani. No European, however, was within a hundred miles of them until 1851. (Lacy, 1904)

79

Fig. 3 Part of the map of Africa published by W. D. Cooley in 1852, showing the Victoria Falls.

It was not until that year (1851) that the course of the upper Zambezi itself became known to outsiders. On 3 August 1851 David Livingstone and William Cotton Oswell, travelling from the south, reached the river at Old Sesheke, now Mwandi. There, they were told of the great waterfall which lay some distance downstream. However, they made no attempt to visit it on this occasion but, after a brief stay, retraced their steps southwards to the Cape of Good Hope. Oswell marked the position of the Victoria Falls – 'Waterfall, spray seen 10 miles off' – on a manuscript map which he produced on this occasion but which was not published for almost fifty years (Oswell, 1900). It appears almost certain that Oswell did not himself approach within sight of the Falls but that he obtained his information from Africans in what is now the Caprivi Strip. An interesting result of this report is that the Falls are marked, in very nearly their correct position relative to the upper Zambezi, on the map contained in William Desborough Cooley's book *Inner Africa Laid Open*, published in London in 1852, three years before

Livingstone actually saw the Falls. A portion of Cooley's map is here reproduced.

It is not commonly realised that there are two other candidates for the honour of being the first European actually to set eyes upon the upper Zambezi. A Portuguese trader in slaves and ivory, Silva Antonio Francisco Porto, travelled east from Bihe in Angola and entered Barotse country in 1848. It seems probable that he reached the Zambezi on this occasion, but when he met Livingstone in the Barotse valley in July/August 1853, the latter was able to satisfy himself that Porto's knowledge of the river did not predate his own. The second candidate is a Hungarian, Ladislaus Magyar, who travelled through what are now the Zambezi (formerly Balovale) and Mwinilunga Districts of Zambia, also in 1851. It seems probable that Magyar's route took him across the Zambezi headwaters, but this cannot be established with any degree of certainty.

Thus, whether or not Livingstone and Oswell were the first Europeans to see the upper Zambezi, they were the first to make its presence known to the outside world.

Although Livingstone quickly realised the identity of his newly discovered river with the lower reaches of the Zambezi, this was hotly disputed by some of the armchair geographers of the time. W. D. Cooley's map of 1852, to which we have already referred, showed both the lower Zambezi and also the river which Livingstone and Oswell had found at Old Sesheke, the two rivers being separated by a continuous mountain chain. Cooley thus satisfied himself that the two rivers were quite separate. It was also asserted in 1856 – after Livingstone had followed the Zambezi from the Falls to the ocean, thus demonstrating the identity of the rivers, but before he had published an account of his journey – that the river at Old Sesheke had 'no connection with the Zambezi but flowed under the Kalahari Desert and became lost'. Such speculations did not, of course, survive the publication of Livingstone's account of his travels in 1857.

To return, however, to Livingstone's exploration of the Zambezi: after his return to Cape Town in 1851–2, he sent his wife and children back to Europe, and then retraced his steps to the Zambezi. Arriving at Linyanti in what is now the Caprivi Strip in May 1853, he spent a month there with Sekeletu, the chief of the Kololo, who since the 1830s had ruled the autochthonous people of much of the area between the Falls and the Barotse valley. Livingstone felt the need for a mission to be established among the Kololo by the London Missionary Society, under whose auspices he was then travelling.

Realising, as others have done more recently, that the route to the Zambezi from the south was potentially difficult and unreliable, he determined to investigate the practicability of opening up a route from either the east or the west coast. In June 1853

he, Sekeletu and a large entourage of Kololo set out for Old Sesheke on the Zambezi and followed the river upstream to the Barotse Plain before returning to Linyanti. Livingstone then took leave of Sekeletu in November 1853 and retraced his journey up the Zambezi, before branching off to the west at about twelve degrees of south latitude, finally reaching the Atlantic coast at Loanda in May 1854.

Realising the impracticability of this western route into Barotse country, he set out again four months later in a courageous attempt to cross the African continent to the Indian Ocean; almost exactly a year later he once again arrived at Linyanti. Here, as previously, he heard tales of the great waterfall of Mosi-oa-Tunya and, on 3 November 1855, he set out to visit it. Accompanied by Sekeletu and, initially, by some two hundred other Africans, he left Linyanti for Old Sesheke. After acquiring provisions for the journey the party left Sesheke along the river on 13 November.

The rains had already broken and the party had an uncomfortable passage downstream to the Katombora Rapids. Storms raised waves which threatened to overturn the canoes and they were drenched by heavy rain. At the rapids the party was forced to leave their canoes and to proceed along the river bank on foot. Two days after leaving Old Sesheke, Livingstone reached Kalai Island on which he saw where Sekute was buried in a grave surrounded with a fence of seventy large elephant tusks.

After a night on the island, Livingstone set out to visit the Falls, of which he had heard such frequent reports from Africans. Sekeletu had intended to accompany him but, as only one canoe could be found, he had to stay behind. Livingstone reports that it

Fig. 4 David Livingstone.

was only twenty minutes after leaving Kalai that he first caught sight of the rising columns of spray, which he compared with the smoke from a large-scale bush fire. He was struck by the beauty of the river and its banks, which he described in the following terms:

The whole scene was extremely beautiful; the banks and islands dotted over the river are adorned with sylvan vegetation of great variety of colour and form. At the period of our visit several trees were spangled over with blossoms.... There, towering over all, stands the great burly baobab, each of whose arms would form the trunk of a large tree, beside groups of graceful palms, which with their feathery-shaped leaves depicted on the sky, lend their beauty to the scene.... The silvery *mohonono*, which in the tropics is in form like the cedar of Lebanon, stands in pleasing contrast with the dark colour of the *motsouri*, whose cypress-like form is dotted over at present with its scarlet fruit. Some trees resemble the great spreading oak, others assume the character of

our own elms and chestnuts; but no one can imagine the beauty of the view from anything witnessed in England. It had never been seen before by European eyes; but scenes so lovely must have been gazed upon by angels in their flight. (Livingstone, 1857: 519)

About one kilometre upstream of the Falls he transferred to a smaller, lighter canoe and proceeded in this to the island between the Main and Rainbow Falls which is today called Livingstone Island. Landing on the island, he obtained his first view of the Falls from what is surely the most impressive of all viewpoints. The moment is best described in Livingstone's own words:

No-one could perceive where the vast body of water went, it seemed to lose itself in the earth, the opposite lip of the fissure into which it disappeared being only eighty feet distant.... Creeping with awe to the verge, I peered down into a large rent which had been made from bank to bank of the broad Zambesi, and saw that a stream of a thousand yards broad leaped down a hundred feet, and then became suddenly compressed into a space of fifteen or twenty yards*... the most wonderful sight I had witnessed in Africa. In looking down into the fissure on the right of the island, one sees nothing but a dense white cloud which, at the time we visited the spot, had two bright rainbows on it.... The snow-white sheet seemed like myriads of small comets rushing in one direction, each of which left behind its nucleus rays of foam. (Livingstone, 1857: 520–1)

* These figures are, of course, a gross underestimate. 'Whoever may come after me will not, I trust, find reason to say I have indulged in exaggeration'. (Livingstone, 1857: 522.)

Livingstone went back to the island the following day, 17 November, in the company of Sekeletu, who had not seen the Falls before. On the island the missionary planted a number of peach and apricot stones and some coffee seeds. He arranged for one of the Kololo to return and make a hedge around the garden to protect it from the hippopotami. When the garden was prepared, Livingstone cut his initials and the date 1855 on a tree on the island.

'This was' he wrote, 'the only instance in which I indulged in this piece of vanity. I have no doubt that this will be the first of all the gardens which may yet be in this young country.' (Livingstone, 1857: 525)

Today there is no sign of a garden on Livingstone Island and the tree bearing indecipherable marks commonly thought to be the initials carved by the missionary cannot be the original. Elephant are the only regular visitors to the island and they have spread devastation over it from end to end. The few recent visitors to Livingstone Island have been rewarded with magnificent views, virtually unchanged since they formed Livingstone's first sight of the Victoria Falls.

Leaving the Falls, Livingstone headed north-eastwards to the Kafue which he followed to its confluence with the Zambezi. He followed the latter river, with only a minor detour near the Cabora Bassa rapids, to reach the Indian Ocean at Quelimane in May 1856. Thence he returned to England, but returned two years later, having severed his connections with the London Missionary Society and having been appointed 'H.M. Consul for the East Coast of Africa to the south of Zanzibar and for the unexplored Interior'. Livingstone's second African ex-pedition was thus, it is important to realise, under British Government auspices; he was Commander of an expedition 'to survey and report on the country watered by the lower Zambezi'. Several Kololo from Linyanti who had accompanied Livingstone on his trans-Africa journey of 1853–6 had remained at Quelimane awaiting his return. Consequently, after investigating the Shire River and the southern part of Lake Malawi, the expedition proceeded up the Zambezi to escort these Kololo home. It was on this occasion that Livingstone paid his second and last visit to the Victoria Falls.

Following Livingstone's first visit, the next European to visit the Falls was William Baldwin, who arrived on 2 August 1860. Baldwin was an English hunter who spent much of the decade from 1851 wandering widely between Natal and the Zambezi. He found his way to the Falls, *via* the Chobe River, by pocket compass. On his arrival there, Baldwin was involved in an argument with Chief Musokotwane; impasse was only resolved by the intervention of Livingstone who arrived, with his brother Charles and Dr John Kirk, on 9 August. Baldwin made the first reasonably accurate estimate of the size of the Falls; he considered them to be two thousand yards wide and three hundred feet high. For eye-estimates these are remarkably close to the true figures and a great improvement on the gross underestimates made by Livingstone in 1855.

On this occasion, however, David and Charles Livingstone stayed on at the Falls after Baldwin's departure and were able to make a much more detailed examination of the area than had been possible five years earlier. It is reasonably clear that they crossed to the south bank and explored the Rain Forest there; this was probably the only

Fig. 5
William Baldwin.

occasion on which David Livingstone set foot in what is now Zimbabwe. Detailed measurements were made, and the total width of the Falls was found

> to be a little over 1860 yards, but this number we resolved to retain as indicating the year in which the Fall was for the first time carefully examined. . . . The depth of the rift was measured by lowering a line, to the end of which a few bullets and a foot of white cotton cloth were tied. One of us lay with his head over a projecting crag and watched the descending calico, till, after his companions had paid out 310 feet, the weight rested on a sloping projection, probably 50 feet from the water below, the actual bottom being still further down. The white cloth now appeared the size of a crown piece.* On measuring the width of this deep cleft by sextant, it was found at Garden Island, its narrowest part, to be 80 yards. (Livingstone and Livingstone, 1865: 253)

Livingstone's subsequent explorations took him far away from the Victoria Falls region, and we must now turn to the steadily increasing numbers of Europeans who found their way to the Falls. A few Boer hunters are known to have visited them during 1861 but it appears that only one, Martinus Swartz, survived the return journey. The visitors of 1862 are again well documented, being

---

* Major A. de Serpa Pinto cast doubt on the practicability of taking measurements in the manner described by the Livingstones, but the present writer considers these doubts unfounded, having observed several spots where measurements could be taken in this way. Serpa Pinto himself, in 1878, measured the Falls by sextant, leaning over the edge and supported by a cloth around his waist held by two Africans. The results he obtained in this precarious fashion are no more accurate, in comparison with the most recent figures, than those given by the Livingstones. (Serpa Pinto, 1881, II: 161 and fig. 116E)

James Chapman and Thomas Baines, both of whom published accounts of their travels, accompanied by Edward Barry. Chapman, a hunter and trader, had been near the Chobe in August 1853 and, had he then been told of the proximity of the Falls, as Oswell was in 1851, would have been in a position to anticipate Livingstone's visit by over two years. In 1862 he and Baines reached the Victoria Falls on their great journey which had begun at Walvis Bay on the Atlantic coast. Baines records that he visited Livingstone Island and found that the garden which David Livingstone had planted there had been trampled by hippopotami and was completely overgrown. It was on this occasion that Baines executed the fine paintings of the Falls which he published in 1863; two of these are reproduced as colour plates XI and XII.

During the following decade several further Europeans, mainly hunters, reached the Victoria Falls. By 1870 the names of twenty-five such visitors are recorded, but there were undoubtedly several others whose names have not been preserved. During the two years 1874–75, however, these numbers were doubled, indicating the rate at which the area was being drawn into the sphere of European activity centred on South Africa.

One of the prime instigators of this was George Westbeech, an English trader who established himself at Pandamatenga, on the 'hunters' road' from Soshong to Kazungula, in about 1871. He travelled, more extensively than had earlier European visitors, throughout much of Barotseland, where he hunted and traded for ivory on a substantial scale. He employed and equipped African hunters and was thus able rapidly to accumulate large quantities of ivory, largely displacing in this trade the Ovimbundu from further west, as well as the Portuguese such as Silva

Fig. 6 George Westbeech's headquarters at Pandamatenga.

Porto. Westbeech brought waggons in which to transport his ivory; he thus had no need to acquire slaves for this purpose, unlike the Ovimbundu and Portuguese who relied almost exclusively on slaves. Westbeech also acted as local agent for the pioneers of the 'safari trade' in this part of Africa, such as Harry Ware who, as early as 1876, organised hunting expeditions and sightseeing visits to the Victoria Falls which were advertised in the London sporting journal, *The Field*.

The high esteem in which Westbeech was held by the Litungas (Barotse Kings) Sipopa (1864–76) and Lubosi (Lewanika, 1878–84 and 1885–1916) gave him considerable influence which was utilised by other Europeans, including missionaries, hunters and political agents, who sought to enter Barotseland. For a time it seems that Westbeech enjoyed a position of unofficial

Fig. 7 François Coillard.

adviser on many matters which concerned the Lozi rulers' relations with their steadily increasing number of European visitors. It was with Westbeech that Dr Emil Holub first visited the Victoria Falls in 1875; he was later to make valuable records and collections illustrating the ethnography of the upper Zambezi peoples.

Shortly afterwards, the first of the missionaries arrived, over twenty-five years after Livingstone had first planned the establishment of a mission on the upper Zambezi.* This was François Coillard of the Paris Evangelical Mission which had for some time been operating in Basutoland (Lesotho). This background proved of considerable

---

* The London Missionary Society, following the suggestions of Livingstone, had sent Messrs H. Helmore and R. Price, together with their wives and young children, to Linyanti in 1860, with a view to establishing a mission at the Kololo capital. Disease soon claimed the lives of many of the party and the survivors hastily retreated.

assistance to Coillard since a Sotho dialect had previously been introduced into Barotseland by the Kololo. Coillard and his wife reached Leshoma, one of Westbeech's trading stations some 20 kilometres south of the Zambezi at Kazungula, in 1878. They soon obtained the permission of the recently established Lewanika to open a mission in Barotse country, but were forced to leave again in the following year due to the civil unrest which then prevailed. While at Leshoma, the Coillards were visited by Major A. de Serpa Pinto, who was then heading for the Victoria Falls on his trans-African expedition.

In 1880, the Jesuits established a mission at Mwemba's on the north bank of the middle Zambezi, but this was a short-lived accomplishment and their subsequent attempts to obtain the authority of Lewanika to establish themselves in Barotse country were no more successful. In 1882, again with Westbeech's help, the Plymouth Brethren missionary Frederick Arnot obtained the cooperation of Lewanika and was briefly resident at the latter's capital of Lealui.

Coillard returned to Leshoma in 1884 and, in the next year, following the reinstatement of Lewanika after a brief period of deposition, he succeeded in founding a mission at Old Sesheke. Leaving Sesheke in the care of his colleague Jalla, he moved to Sefula near the Lozi capital, where he rapidly replaced Westbeech as the major European adviser of the Lozi rulers.

At this time the 'scramble for Africa' by the European powers was gathering momentum. Portugal, established for several centuries on the east and west coasts in Moçambique and Angola respectively, was pressing her claims to the vast belt of territory which lay between these two colonies. In 1886,

Britain came very close to accepting Portuguese claims to the territory north of the Zambezi stretching without interruption from coast to coast. The British Government was at that time reluctant to embark on further imperial expansion on its own account; 'there was no point in "painting the map red" as long as other countries did not discriminate against British merchants and investors' (Gann, 1964: 50). That this policy did not always appeal to the British merchants and investors whose interests it was intended to protect, soon became clear. Cecil Rhodes, who had acquired substantial control both of the Kimberley diamond fields and of the recently discovered gold of the Witwatersrand, was attracted by the reports of further mineral wealth between the Limpopo and the Zambezi, as well as further north. In 1888, treaties were obtained from Lobengula, King of the Ndebele in that region, and on the basis of these in 1889 Rhodes' British South Africa Company was granted a Royal Charter confirming its rights over an ill-defined area north and west of the Transvaal.

Concession-hunting at this time was by no means restricted to the country to the south of the Zambezi; Harry Ware, acting on behalf of a South African mining syndicate, was the first European to obtain such a document from Lewanika. George Westbeech had died in 1888, but it was largely due to Ware's previous association with Westbeech that he was able to travel to Lealui in June 1889 and to obtain from Lewanika a mineral concession covering the Batoka country between the Machili and Kafue rivers, over which area the Lozi at that time claimed suzerainty.

The relative importance of European persuasion, of Lewanika's self-interest and

Fig. 8 (above) Lewanika, photographed in 1886 at Lealui by François Coillard. The club, bangles and kaross were then symbols of royalty.
Fig. 9 (opposite) The meeting of Lewanika and Frank Lochner at Lealui in 1890.

of the latter's genuine care for the future security of his country in persuading the Lozi actively to seek European protection, are not clear. Lewanika felt himself threatened by the Portuguese on the west, by Lobengula and his Ndebele on the south, and by political rivals at home. Shortly before, in 1885, Khama, King of the Bamangwato, had agreed to place his country under British protection as security against pressure from the Transvaal Boers and from Loben-

gula. A similar solution to his own problems clearly recommended itself to Lewanika for, at the beginning of 1889, he wrote to Khama to enquire whether the latter was 'happy and quite satisfied' with being 'under the protection of the great English Queen'. Shortly afterwards, Coillard, apparently on Lewanika's request, wrote to the Administrator of British Bechuanaland stating that the Lozi desired to be placed under British protection. Whether or not Coillard shared in the instigation of this plan, there can be no doubt that he supported it, feeling that the security of his mission would be enhanced if a protectorate could be established. Before further action was taken, and before any reply was received to Lewanika's

formal request for British protection, Harry Ware arrived at Lealui and, with Coillard's connivance and support, succeeding in acquiring a concession. The Ware Concession was subsequently bought by Cecil Rhodes on behalf of the British South Africa Company, to whom knowledge was also passed of Lewanika's earlier request.

A Company agent, Frank Lochner, travelled to Lealui in the following year (1890) and eventually after prolonged negotiations, in which he and Coillard gave the Lozi cause to believe that the treaty into which they were entering was to all intents and purposes with the British Government rather than with a private commercial company, a document was signed which granted the Company mineral rights over the whole of Lewanika's domains (except the Lozi heartland itself) in exchange for an annuity of £2000. The Company also undertook to send a British Resident to Lealui and to establish schools and trading posts in the country. Around this time the Company's agents also secured concessions from African rulers further to the east.

This development, by means of which Lewanika hoped to maintain the integrity of his kingdom, did not prevent the arbitrary division of the region between the European powers. In 1890 a draft treaty between Britain and Portugal placed the boundary between their respective spheres along the upper Zambezi itself, thus threatening effectively to bisect the country of Lewanika, who was not consulted at all about the proposal. When, however, news reached Europe of the Lochner Concession, a revised agreement was drawn up reserving Lewanika's kingdom to the British sphere.* Also in 1890 an agreement with Germany established the Caprivi Strip giving German South-West Africa (now Namibia) access to the Zambezi. Thus were established the political boundaries of the Victoria Falls region, which survive to this day.

Effective British South Africa Company administration of the whole of Southern Rhodesia (now Zimbabwe) was established by Order in Council in 1894, but there was considerable delay in implementing any of

* The actual territory involved was not defined and remained uncertain until 1905 when arbitration by the King of Italy established the boundary, still retained today as the border between Zambia and Angola, in a position most unfavourable to Lewanika.

Fig. 10 Lewanika photographed in 1902 in Bulawayo, on his way to attend the coronation of King Edward VII.

the conditions of the Lochner Concession in Barotseland. Robert Coryndon was finally dispatched to Lealui as the long-awaited British Resident in 1897; in the same year the territory of the modern Zambia, north of the Zambezi, became known officially for the first time as Northern Rhodesia. Following a further Order in Council in 1899, Coryndon became Administrator of the western part of this territory, Northwestern Rhodesia.

Legal difficulties were now encountered since the Lochner Concession was of doubtful validity in terms of the British South Africa Company's Royal Charter; and in addition it did not specifically provide Lewanika's consent to the establishment of Company administration. A further concession was sought to dispose of these irregularities; by this time circumstances gave Lewanika little option but to agree and the new concession was finally signed by Coryndon and Lewanika at the Victoria Falls on 17 October 1900. The new concession was much less advantageous to Lewanika than the old one had been, but at least it enabled him to retain a greater degree of independence of the Company's Administration than most African rulers were allowed in other areas. The way was, however, open for European settlement on a previously unknown scale: by 1905 – only half a century after the arrival of the first European visitor – a busy colonial town was flourishing within sight of the Victoria Falls.

Select Bibliography

BAINES, T. *Victoria Falls, Zambesi River*, London, 1863.
BAINES, T. *Explorations in South-west Africa*, London, 1864.
BALDWIN, W. C. *African Hunting and Adventure from Natal to the Zambesi*, London, 1863.
CHAPMAN, J. *Travels in the Interior of South Africa*, London, 1868.
COILLARD, F. *On the Threshold of Central Africa*, London, 1897.
COOLEY, W. D. *Inner Africa Laid Open*, London, 1852.
GREGSON, R. E. 'Trade and Politics in South-East Africa', *African Social Research*, xvi, 1973, pp. 413–446.
HOLUB, E. *Seven Years in South Africa*, London, 1881.
LACY, G. 'The Victoria Falls' in *South Africa Handbook*, c. 1904.
LANE-POOLE, E. H. *African Discovery and Exploration*, Livingstone (Rhodes-Livingstone Museum Occasional Paper), 1961.
LIVINGSTONE, D. *Missionary Travels and Researches in South Africa*, London, 1857.
LIVINGSTONE, D. and LIVINGSTONE, C. *Narrative of an Expedition to the Zambesi and its Tributaries*, London, 1865.
MACINTOSH, C. W. *Coillard of the Zambesi*, London, 1907.
MAINGA, M. *Bulozi under the Luyana Kings*, London, 1973.
OSWELL, W. E. *William Cotton Oswell, Hunter and Explorer*, London, 1900.
PRINS, G. *The Hidden Hippopotamus: the early colonial experience in western Zambia*, Cambridge, 1980.
RANDLES, W. G. L. *The Empire of Monomotapa*, Gweru, 1981.
DE SERPA PINTO, A. *How I Crossed Africa*, London, 1881.
TABLER, E. C. *Trade and Travel in Early Barotseland* (*the Diaries of George Westbeech, 1885–88*), London, 1963.

CHAPTER 8

The Early History of the Town of Livingstone

David W. Phillipson

The town of Livingstone owes its origin and growth to two major factors: its place as the main port of entry to Northwestern Rhodesia and its proximity to the Victoria Falls. Through the combination of these advantages the town rapidly became the largest European settlement in Northwestern Rhodesia. It was consequently chosen as the capital of Northwestern Rhodesia from 1907 to 1911 when the territory was amalgamated with Northeastern Rhodesia. Livingstone remained the capital of Northern Rhodesia until 1935.

Whereas Northeastern Rhodesia, with its capital at Fort Jameson (now Chipata), was settled and originally administered from the east, Northwestern Rhodesia became a continuation of the British South Africa Company's northward thrust into Southern Rhodesia and for a long time its external links and communications were exclusively with the south. Barotseland received a British Resident in 1897, and a Protectorate of Barotseland-Northwestern Rhodesia was confirmed two years later. In the closing years of the nineteenth century European prospectors, notably George Grey, Frank Lewis and Orlando Baragwanath, working on behalf of Cecil Rhodes' British South Africa Company and related groups, reported the presence of rich copper deposits in the Kafue Hook region and on the Zambezi/Congo watershed. Although Lozi rule over these regions was, to say the least, nebulous, the Chartered Company claimed the land and minerals by virtue of the concessions and agreements which had been signed with Lewanika.

These developments north of the Zambezi, together with the discovery of coal deposits at Wankie (Hwange) in 1897, caused the axis of European expansion to shift significantly to the west. The route of the Cape to Cairo railway, originally planned to proceed north-eastwards from Bulawayo through Gwelo (Gweru) and Fort Salisbury (Harare), was changed, and plans were made to route the line to the northern copper areas, *via* the new coalfield. In this region the only practicable crossing-places over the Zambezi were between Kazungula and the Victoria Falls. Upstream of Kazungula lay the extensive Chobe swamps of the Caprivi Strip (ceded to Germany in 1890), while downstream of the Falls the Batoka Gorge formed a major barrier for over a hundred kilometres, below which lay the inhospitable Gwembe Valley with its formidable escarpments. Before the occupation of Matabeleland the route from the south into Barotseland was along the 'hunters' road' (followed by the present Botswana/Zimbabwe border) *via* Pandamatenga to Kazungula. This route, which had been in regular use, notably by George Westbeech, since about 1870, specifically bypassed Matabeleland, to pass through which Europeans had first to obtain Lobengula's consent.

With the final crushing of Lobengula's authority in 1897 the need to use the waterless and hazardous Pandamatenga route fell away. The establishment of a substantial European settlement at Bulawayo, reached by the railway in October 1897, made the shorter and easier route from Bulawayo to the Victoria Falls the obvious choice for travellers to Northwestern Rhodesia. A wagon-road, cut on this route, was completed in 1898 and a regular coach service established by Doel Zeederberg, the journey taking up to twelve days. By early in the same year (but possibly before) the first permanent European settler, F. J. 'Mopane' Clarke, had taken up residence at the Victoria Falls.

The developments outlined above ensured that all goods and personnel for the mining and prospecting companies (notably Tanganyika Concessions and the Northern Copper Company), the Administration and the steadily increasing numbers of hunters and traders, entered Northwestern Rhodesia by way of the Victoria Falls. 'Mopane' Clarke, quick to realise the commercial advantages which would accrue to the oldest resident, established himself as a trader, hotel-keeper and forwarding agent on the north bank of the Zambezi at the point above the rapids where goods were ferried across. At this point, some nine kilometres upstream of the Falls, the Zambezi is at its narrowest for some distance, being less than one kilometre in width. The northern end of this crossing, known as the Old Drift or Sekuti's Drift, after the Toka chief whose village was then nearby, soon became the first European settlers' town (as opposed to mission station, mine or administrative post) in Northwestern Rhodesia. The site is flat, marshy and malarial, being only a metre or so above high water level.*

Later, in 1898 and during the following year, further settlers and traders arrived. The British South Africa Company established a new administrative post, known as the Victoria Falls Station, five kilometres above the Falls. The Paris Missionary Society sent an Italian-born cleric, the Rev. Giovanni Daniele Augusto Coisson, and his wife to open a mission at the Old Drift. They brought with them a Lesotho-trained Lozi evangelist, Petrose Kasaa, who in 1899 established a small school at the mission.

In 1900 Coisson replaced the temporary mission buildings with more permanent structures. A contemporary account des-

* It was completely inundated by the 1969 Zambezi flood.

cribes 'the mission station, which Mr Coisson has entirely built and planned himself. It stands on the peninsula formed by a bend of the Zambezi which flows behind it, though the front of the house is quite a little walk from the landing stage. Within a stake fence stand a spacious church, a cottage with a verandah and a high-pitched thatched roof, . . . another much smaller cottage, . . . and three or four round huts'. For almost two years Mrs Coisson was the only European woman in the settlement.

Throughout this time the settler population continued to increase. Notable arrivals were, in 1902, Fred Mills who set up an eating house and hotel in competition with that of 'Mopane' Clarke, and Mr and Mrs Tulloch who attempted to grow fruit on a smallholding beside the Maramba River. In 1903 Percy M. Clark came to the Falls and lived for a while at the Old Drift, but soon moved to the south bank near the present Falls Hotel where he established the photographic and curio business which was continued into the 1980s by his son, Mr V. Clark. By 1903 the population had grown substantially and included sixty-eight Europeans, including seventeen women and six children. There seems to be no record of the number of Africans attached to the settlement, but it appears that no housing was provided for African workmen, who presumably continued to live in the nearby villages.

A visitor in the following year described 'the scattered camps known as Livingstone. Some of these camps were miles apart, with the main body still at old Sekuti's crossing'. At the Old Drift itself, goods were ferried

Fig. 1 (top) The site of the Old Drift settlement.
Fig. 2 (centre) Landing at the Old Drift, c. 1900.
Fig. 3 (bottom) The Old Drift landing today, seen from the Zambezi.

across the river on a pont towed by a small steam launch. Passengers were carried in an iron boat propelled by eight Barotse paddlers and the fare was one shilling each way. All this equipment was apparently owned or supplied by the Administration, but it was managed by 'Mopane' Clarke who was, to all intents and purposes, in control of the crossing. A number of smaller craft also plied between the Falls and the Old Drift settlement.

Clarke himself was a man of considerable importance in the settlement. One visitor described him as 'a kind of honorary Lord Mayor, exercising hospitality to strangers and organising festivals and everything else that is nobody's business in particular but everyone's in general'. In addition to controlling the river crossing he ran a forwarding agency, one of three stores, a bar and a hotel at which dinner cost four shillings, a bed fifteen shillings and a whisky and soda (the staple diet of the Old Drifters) one shilling.

Life in this predominantly male settlement centred on the bars. On any given evening it often happened that virtually the whole population congregated in one bar, so the others closed. Gambling was the central attraction at Clarke's bar, notably a roulette wheel with two zeros run by a loud-voiced American. The bar-owners had their staff sieve the sandy floors each morning for coins dropped by the previous night's revellers. In September 1904 the Rev T. Stones, a Methodist missionary, arrived to work among the settlers, but he left through ill-health eight months later.

The major problem facing the Old Drifters was malaria, which frequently developed into fatal blackwater fever. One settler stoically recalled that 'the Old Drift was not what one would call unhealthy, although there were plenty of mosquitoes and that sort of thing. Everyone went down with fever, though we took quinine'. However, the fact remains that in most years some twenty per cent of the settlers died. Percy Clark claimed that in one year the deaths totalled seventy per cent, but this appears to be an exaggeration. To avoid the fever-ridden Old Drift, the Administration in 1901 moved its offices and the Post Office to the sandbelt, the present site of Livingstone, which then became known as 'Constitution Hill'. A private clinic was set up at the Old Drift in 1902 by Dr J. N. Wilson and Nurse Chapman, but in December of that year the Rev Coisson wrote that 'almost everyone is sick'. The following month the doctor himself died of blackwater fever. Two chemists' businesses, that of Findlay and Guthrie and that of Southurst, failed successively through the ill-health or death of their proprietors.

By 1903 the Administration had decided in principle that the settlement should be moved to a more healthy location, but the new site had not yet been chosen. The railway was by then being built north-westwards from Bulawayo towards Hwange and the Victoria Falls and it was the railway which was to join the mosquito in finally sealing the fate of the Old Drift settlement.

The journey south remained long and uncomfortable, as is illustrated by the experience of the Coissons when they went on leave in April 1903. For two days they travelled by ox-cart from the Falls to the railhead. Henry Rangeley describes this part of the route: 'the cart simply bumped from boulder to boulder and there were bits of broken wheels and wagon parts all over the track'. The Coissons then embarked on the railway in a cattle-truck which they had to

95

clean out themselves and share with another family. However, their truck was parked at Gwaai for two days while the engine went off to help in the construction work and the Coissons finally reached Bulawayo five days after leaving the Old Drift.

The year 1904 saw the arrival of Leopold F. Moore, who was to be a leading figure on the Livingstone scene for the next four decades. Moore came to Bulawayo in 1898 from Mafeking and established a chemist's business, with a branch in Gweru. Later he became embroiled in a bitter controversy with the British South Africa Company's Administration of Southern Rhodesia over the proposal to import Chinese indentured labour to that territory. It was probably largely as a result of this heated argument that Moore and his wife left Bulawayo and established their chemist's shop at the Old Drift.

In such an isolated settlement, news from the outside world was obviously at a premium. Mail from the south was meant to arrive at weekly intervals, but was often delayed. Its arrival would be heralded by a bugle call from the south bank, whereupon everybody at the Drift promptly downed tools or whisky glasses and a canoe was sent across to collect the mail bags. These were emptied out on the floor of a hut and everyone took his own letters. After this impromptu sorting the postmaster would arrive from the Post Office on 'Constitution Hill', some seven kilometres distant from the Old Drift, and take possession of those letters intended for onward transmission. A perma-nent staff of mail runners, whose uniform consisted of a long belted tunic emblazoned 'B.S.A. Co. Mail' and a fez, were kept at wages of between ten and fifteen shillings per month. Mail runners to Kalomo took four days, to Lealui fourteen days.

Henry Rangeley had been appointed Magistrate and Adviser on Legal Matters to the Northwestern Rhodesia Administration in June 1902. He arrived at the Falls with a large consignment of Boer War surplus rum which he had bought in Bulawayo for one shilling and tenpence per gallon. Rangeley was based at the capital, Kalomo, but he came once a month to the Old Drift to hear cases. There, his office and Court House was a wood and iron building some five metres square. It had been erected under a 'German sausage tree' (*Kigelia africana*) with large heavy fruits. Rangeley records: 'it was shattering to the nerves when one of these fruits fell on to the iron roof, perhaps when I was in the middle of a case'. Elsewhere he notes:

The gaol [for Europeans] was an even smaller building of similar construction. Prisoners invariably sat outside. It was no use trying to prevent them doing this, for it was really too hot inside and a prisoner could always get out by unscrewing the hinges of the door – as one prisoner showed us when we told him to stay inside . . . only one white prisoner escaped, however.

The single constable-cum-gaoler, an Irish-man named W. T. B. G. Foley 'kept order by exercise of tact and humour'.*

* Foley's tombstone at Sijoba in the Gwembe Valley, now flooded by the waters of Lake Kariba, gives his Christian names as William Thompson Barron Galway. It was presumably the third of these names that gave rise to the mistaken but frequently repeated claim by 'Old Drifters' that their constable was really a baronet working *incognito*.

Fig. 4 (opposite, top) 'Mopane' Clarke's hotel at the Old Drift.
Fig. 5 (opposite, bottom) An auction conducted by Leopold Moore in front of his chemist's shop at the Old Drift.

The railway line from Bulawayo, for which the construction contractor was George Pauling, finally reached the south bank of the Zambezi at the Victoria Falls in April 1904. Tourists and engineers brought increased prosperity to the Old Drift settlement. A visiting hunter, J. W. B. White, described the railway construction workers as 'the most extraordinary collection of cosmopolitan toughs I have encountered anywhere'. The original Victoria Falls Hotel was a temporary wood and corrugated iron structure built primarily to house the workers on the bridge. The intention, unhappily never carried out, was that the hotel should be demolished once the bridge had been completed, so that no buildings should remain within sight of the Falls.

Work on bridge construction began almost immediately, although there had previously been considerable controversy over the siting of the bridge. Cecil Rhodes never saw the Falls, but in 1900 he had already expressed the wish that the railway should 'cross the Zambezi just below the Victoria Falls. I should like to have the spray of the water over the carriages'. Colonel Frank Rhodes was one of those strongly opposed to such a site. The suggestion was made for a much

Fig. 6 (above) 'The Victoria Falls Station', the British South Africa Company's administrative post.
Fig. 7 (opposite, top) Building the Victoria Falls bridge, 1904/5.
Fig. 8 (opposite, bottom) The Victoria Falls bridge nearing completion, 1905.

longer bridge over the river near the Old Drift, but this was rejected as being too expensive and equally damaging aesthetically. The possibility of siting the bridge over the gorges downstream of its present position, out of sight of the Falls, does not appear to have been considered. Not surprisingly, the will of Cecil Rhodes, who had died two years previously, prevailed.

First of all, the gorge was crossed by firing a rocket attached to a string, by which was hauled over a rope and then a steel cable. A bo'sun's chair was put into operation, by which the gorge crossing could be made in approximately ten minutes. The bridge was designed by Sir Douglas Fox and built by the Cleveland Bridge Company of Darlington, England, Imbault being the engineer in charge of the fourteen-month project. The bridge was built out from each side and the two halves were successfully joined and bolted together early in the morning of 1 April 1905, before the heat of the sun could

97

cause the metal to expand. Two men were killed during the construction, despite the use of a safety net. Before the bridge was completed an engine was dismantled, hauled across in pieces and reassembled on the north bank where it was used in construction of the line northwards to Kalomo. The bridge bore only a single railway track, although it was wide enough for two, and no roadway. The official opening ceremony was conducted on 12 September 1905 by Professor George Darwin, President of the British Association.

As soon as work began on the bridge it was apparent that, with the completion of the railway, the Old Drift would fall into disuse and the only argument for retaining the settlement in that unhealthy spot would therefore fall away. The Administration consequently decided to site a new township on the sandbelt at Constitution Hill. By the end of November 1904 the new township was being surveyed and the roads marked with small white flags. The railway through the town was levelled and awaiting tracks which were laid on completion of the Maramba bridge in January 1905. The township itself was laid out as a rectangular grid of streets and sanitary lanes forming fifteen blocks, in all covering an area of rather less than one square kilometre. The central street, Mainway (now Mosi-oa-Tunya Road) was to be forty-three metres wide. The central block was to be an open park, known as the Barotse Centre, which still survives. The remaining fourteen blocks comprised two hundred and four stands. Some of these were reserved for the Administration's offices and others for Old Drift residents who were to be forced to abandon their old settlement. The remaining stands were sold at an auction held on 23 January 1905 and attended by some seventy people, almost half of whom came

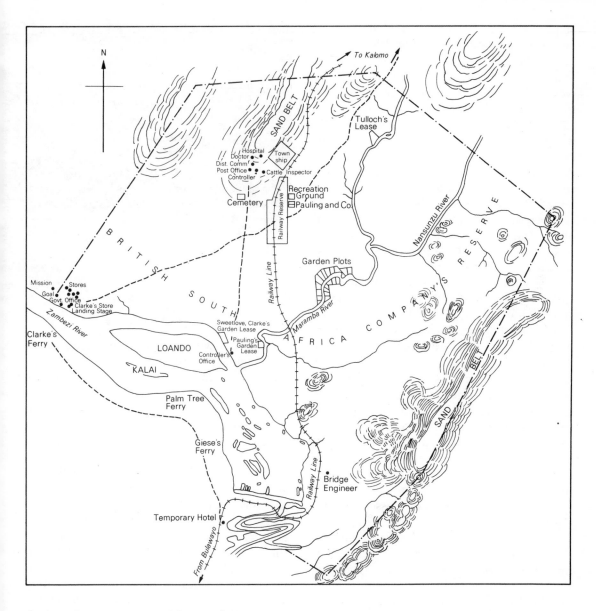

Fig. 9 Map of the Livingstone/Victoria Falls area copied from a survey prepared for the British South Africa Company in 1905.

from Bulawayo. To avoid speculation, purchasers had to agree to erect on their stands within twelve months a building to the minimum value of three hundred pounds. The siting and lay-out of the new township emphasised the importance which the Administration now attached to health.

The Old Drifters, however, were opposed to a site so far from the Falls, which they felt would deprive them of the profits of the tourist trade. They proposed instead that the town be situated at the camp of Imbault, the Bridge Engineer, which was on a well-drained site overlooking the river. The Administration did not agree to this proposal, since a town so close to the Falls would be bound to mar the natural beauty of the area. As a result of this disagreement several of the Old Drifters refused to move and at the end of June 1905 the District Commissioner was forced to issue the recalcitrant settlers with eviction notices, requiring them to cease trading at the Old Drift by 24 August and to leave that place altogether by 23 September. The mission alone would remain. A map of the Falls area, prepared for the British South Africa Company in 1905, shows the various settlements of the time and is reproduced on page 99. By January 1906 the few settlers still at the Old Drift were threatened with fines of one pound per day: this final resort at last had the desired effect. All that is now visible of the Old Drift settlement is the cemetery and some non-indigenous trees.

At this time, the Rev Coisson wrote: 'Personally, I do not think that Livingstone will ever be a big town unless some mineral deposits are discovered in the neighbourhood'. However, once it became clear that the move to Constitution Hill would be made despite the objections of the settlers, the new township developed rapidly. New settlers arrived and new businesses were established at a steady rate. By March 1907, only two years after the initial sale of uncleared stands, Livingstone could boast of two hotels, a

Fig. 10 The Old Drift Cemetery today.

restaurant, two mineral water factories, at least eight clothing and general stores, two butcheries, four building contractors, a chemist and a barber.

One of the first indications that Livingstone was becoming aware of its new status was the establishment of its own newspapers. The first of these, founded by William Trayner, had actually circulated, in an informal way, at the Old Drift during 1905. Trayner was an employee of 'Mopane' Clarke and worked the river crossing, a job which took him to Southern Rhodesia several times a day and thus gave him first access to news which was brought up by travellers from the south. By popular request he prepared hand-written news-sheets which were passed from hand to hand or pasted up in one of the bars. These impromptu 'newspapers' had varying headings, examples being *Trayner's Rag* or *The Livingstone Liar*. No copies are known to survive.

After the move to the new township the Administration asked Trayner to register his paper and to issue it at regular intervals with a fixed title, so that it could be used for the publication of official Administration notices. The name *Livingstone Pioneer and Advertiser* was suggested and agreed upon and the paper appeared at regular weekly intervals, with interruptions due to the indisposition of the editor/proprietor, from 13 January to 29 September 1906. The *Pioneer* was typewritten and duplicated by a gelatine process. Percy Clark described it as 'a very popular weekly with an enormous circulation – sometimes as many as fifty copies a week net sales'. Trayner was also pleased with it, and modestly wrote in an early issue:

The day we announced the publication of *The Livingstone Pioneer and Advertiser,* Chartered rose from thirty-five shillings to two pounds. No thinking man will credit the cynical suggestion of a jealous detractor that this was a mere coincidence, but we are as much amazed as gratified at the rapidity with which the market realized the significance of our advent.

Leopold Moore did not take kindly to the *Pioneer* and on 31 March 1906 he started a rival weekly newspaper, the *Livingstone Mail*. It was typewritten on wax stencils and produced on foolscap duplicating paper in purple ink. While concentrating on local settler news and views it contained a modicum of international matter: the first issue included the winner of the 1906 Grand National, run seven days previously. In Gann's words, 'the *Livingstone Mail* entertained its readers with Moore's musings on the evolution of humanity, the future of the soul, as well as other topics such as the current price of mealies'. The *Livingstone Mail* survived for sixty years and is a valuable source of information on the history of the town and country, particularly from the settler point of view. By May 1908 its circulation had risen to one hundred and seventy-five copies. In October of the previous year Moore had run into trouble: it was so hot that the wax on the duplicating stencils melted on the typewriter. Nothing daunted, he ordered a printing press which was installed in August 1908. The Livingstone Mail Printing Works still operates in Livingstone, as does the chemist's shop Moore founded.

In 1907 the first Northwestern Hotel was opened. According to the valuation roll for that year the building was worth sixteen thousand pounds. Later that same year the town became the capital of Northwestern Rhodesia, a territory almost half a million square kilometres in extent, and the Administration took over the hotel as Government House*. A new Northwestern Hotel, the present one, was built by 'Mopane' Clarke and opened in March 1909. A contemporary advertisement in the *Livingstone Mail* announced that the new hotel was 'now open for the reception of visitors. Accommodation is second to none in southern Africa. Carriages meet all trains'. An older hotel, known as the Livingstone Hotel, was owned by Fred Mills: he later bought the Northwestern as well.

The Standard Bank of South Africa opened a branch in Livingstone during September 1907. The following year two Lithuanian brothers, Harry and Elie Susman, who had been cattle trading in Barotseland since the beginning of the century, took over the

---

* It remained the residence of the Administrators and Governors until the capital was finally moved to Lusaka in 1935.

Pioneer Butchery. 'Mopane' Clarke's store and bar business, situated on the corner of Mainway and Empire Street, changed its name to Zambezi Trading Company in 1910.*

The European community was self-centred and the majority of the newly developing businesses and amenities were reserved for their exclusive use. Moore was a leading proponent of this philosophy. In 1907 the *Livingstone Mail* described the opening of a new shop in the following terms:

> . . . an up-to-date store. . . . a full and complete range of everything required in a White community will be carried and since this is to be imported direct from the coast, the reduction in prices will be considerable. None but White trade; ladies will not be required to rub shoulders with a crowd of clamorous and odorous natives.

At stores where Africans were served, they were generally forbidden to enter the building itself but had to remain outside and be served through a small hatchway. This practice continued into the 1950s. It was not until October 1907 that thought was given to the provision of housing for Africans working in Livingstone. The first 'native location' was for men only, four being accommodated in each wood and iron shelter, at a rent of one shilling per man per month.

Facilities for education were slow to develop. In the early years most European children went to boarding schools in Southern Rhodesia, the fees being subsidised by the Administration and by the Beit Trust.

Children too young for boarding school presented a particular problem. A Dutch Reformed Church minister from Kalomo offered to help but as he insisted on teaching Afrikaans his offer was refused. In May 1906 Miss Gladys Powell opened a private kindergarten and in the following year the Acting Administrator offered to rent and equip a schoolroom if the parents would meet Miss Powell's salary; there were at that time ten children enrolled in what later became the first Government primary school in the territory. African education remained in the hands of the Paris Missionary Society.

In 1906–7 the settlers established a council to raise funds for the establishment of an Anglican Church in Livingstone. Over one thousand pounds had been collected by 1910 when the foundation stone was laid. St. Andrew's Church, which still stands, was dedicated in 1911, the total cost of the building being one thousand three hundred and fifty pounds. A disagreement quickly arose

---

*The relationship between modern Livingstone trading companies and these early businesses is confusing. Clarke's Zambezi Trading Company has disappeared but its name is perpetuated in that of Zambezi Street, and the original store building survives, now occupied by Nanoo's Cash and Carry.

Fig. 11 (left) One of the early official's houses erected by the Company at the new township.
Fig. 12 (right) Leopold Moore with his first printing press.

with the Bishop because the settlers objected to services for Africans being held in the church. They eventually agreed to raise funds for the building of a separate church for Africans in the Maramba valley.

Life at the new township was somewhat more decorous than it had been at the Old Drift. Bars remained the centre of the male settlers' lives, but the gossip column of the *Livingstone Mail* suggests that bridge and chess parties were becoming frequent. On Saturday evenings Moore gave open-air gramophone recitals on the small verandah beside his chemist's shop – these events were grandiloquently advertised in the newspaper as 'promenade concerts on the Boulevard d'Apothicaire'. Informal concerts were held in the Court House where there was, for some

reason, a piano. Dances in aid of the church building fund took place at the Boat Club (headquarters of the Northwestern Rhodesia Rowing Association) and at Government House. Recitals, given by the band of the Barotse Native Police, were not invariably appreciated. On the rare occasions when a touring overseas entertainment visited the Victoria Falls Hotel special trains were organised to take the Livingstonians to the show. In 1906 Leopold Moore organised a lending library. Within three years it had accumulated some two hundred books, which were housed in the Court House.

Sporting facilities available by the end of 1908 included a golf course and a rifle range: cricket matches were held between the settlers and civil servants. Regattas were held annually on the Zambezi; that of 1905 was attended by Lewanika and the programme included a race for Lozi royal barges, which was won by Litia's crew. The 1910 regatta featured races for the World

Sculling Championship.

Good drainage and sanitation in the well-planned town, together with the regular use of quinine and mosquito nets, lead to a substantial and rapid reduction in the prevalence of malaria and blackwater fever. With the move to the new township the Chartered Company gradually assumed responsibility for the provision of other services to maintain the health of the community. In 1905-6 they erected a hospital consisting of three small wards and an operating theatre, the whole valued at one thousand seven hundred and fifty pounds, staffed by a doctor, two nurses and a dispenser. This hospital was for Europeans only and fees ranged from fifteen shillings to one pound per day. In a rare display of consideration for African welfare, Moore campaigned through the pages of the *Mail* for the provision of an African hospital. This was built in 1907 and fees were two shillings and sixpence per day. A dentist from Bulawayo paid occasional visits to the town.

With the suppression of malaria, dysentery became the main source of illness, particularly among the rapidly increasing European child population. The main cause of this was the water supply provided by the Railway Company. It was pumped from the Maramba River by a narrow pipe to two large tanks situated beside the main street. Since the pipe ran for over two kilometres on the surface of the sand the water was always very hot on arrival. Householders had to collect water from these tanks in buckets, and pay ten shillings a month for the privilege, in addition to the carrier's wages. Often the tanks ran dry. As Moore pointed out in his newspaper:

Complaint is worse than futile: the Acting Administrator is supplied from the same source and if the officials of the Chartered Company are content to bathe in thin mud, have their clothes washed in thin mud and drink, with the qualifying admixture, thin mud, who are we that we should complain?

In 1909, however, the water supply was taken over from the Railway by the newly constituted Livingstone Water Works Board, which spent two thousand pounds in laying a pipe from a new pump house near the Boat Club to three large tanks on the hill beside the hospital. From there water was piped by gravity to the various stands.

Sanitation was by bucket collected at night *via* the sanitary lanes. Employment of night-soil men continued in most parts of the town into the 1940s.

Electricity was available from the first years of the new settlement, but was extremely expensive. A generator owned by Paulings, the railway contractors, supplied the cold storage plant and the Northwestern Hotel. Few private houses were wired from this source as the cost of electricity was very high – fifteen shillings per month for each sixteen-candle-power lamp. Later the Administration took over the generator and by 1912 meters were installed in private houses and power was available from 6 pm to 11 pm at two shillings and sixpence per unit.

As early as 1901 the African Concessions Syndicate Ltd had obtained a seventy-five-year concession from the British South Africa Company to use the water power of the Victoria Falls for generating electricity. In 1906 rumours spread that work on this project was about to start, but at the end of that year the concession was ceded to the Victoria Falls and Transvaal Power Company. The Falls Power Station did not start production until 1938.

Transport in and around the town remained difficult for some years, due to the deep unconsolidated sand. Mules were the only practicable draft animals as horse-sickness was very frequent. The Northwestern Hotel's 'carriage' which 'met all trains' was in fact an old Zeederberg stage coach drawn by a team of mules. Paul Graetz brought a motor car through Livingstone in 1908 but it was the only one for many years. The Administrator, Robert Codrington, had a motor cycle, but there appears to have been no other motorised transport at that time. Rickshaws were used for a short period, but were not popular. Light trolleys consisting of two benches back to back and running on rails were installed in 1907–8 between the Northwestern Hotel and the Boat Club. They had a hand-brake but no motor, being pushed uphill by four Africans. Similar trolleys were later installed between the Falls Hotel and the Victoria Falls. They were popular among those passengers who were not involved in the occasional derailments. Examples of these trolleys are preserved today at the Railway Museum in Livingstone and in the courtyard of the Victoria Falls Hotel. By 1907 there were, twice daily on three days of the week, return trains between Livingstone and the Falls. Road development was slow and expensive: in the dry season the roads were little more than a strip of deep soft sand. In 1907 a hard road was laid from the Railway Station to Government House and similar work was carried out on a small scale in most years thereafter, but it was ten years before a road was built linking Livingstone and the Victoria Falls.

In 1907 arose a dispute between the Livingstone residents and the Chartered Company over the control of the town services. In March of that year Village Management Board regulations were promulgated, establishing a rudimentary council. Under these regulations, the Company, which paid no rates on its property, retained the right to nominate the chairman and two members, ensuring that control would remain in their hands. As a result of this, the ratepayers refused to co-operate and the Company had to nominate all the board members. In 1911 the constitution of the board was altered and Leopold Moore became the first elected member.

This last episode was but one phase in Moore's continuous battle with the Administration in the interests of the taxpayer, that is settler, for Moore does not seem to have considered it relevant that Africans also paid taxes. The following quotations from the *Livingstone Mail* between 1907 and 1910 amply illustrate Moore's views:

The management and control of the territory has been acquired by a company of financiers. . . . possessing neither knowledge of the country nor sympathy with the people whose destinies are in their hands, their aim being apparently first and foremost to wring profit and advantage from their position without effort or the expenditure of money.

What do we want? An Administration run in the interest of the settler. Cheap land and easily obtainable.

The form of government we are under is dictatorship – a benevolent despotism.

The exaction of taxation without the consent of the taxed is an unlawful, unconstitutional and impudent violation of the acknowledged rights of all British subjects.

We shall consistently oppose the employment of natives where they compete with or are substituted for white men.

It was characteristic of Moore's stubborn refusal to see anything but evil in the actions of the Administration or to acknowledge the rights or aspirations of any but his own small settler community that, even at the time of the town's greatest burst of development in 1907, he was still campaigning for the town to be moved closer to the Falls. A banner headline in the *Livingstone Mail* to the effect that the move had been approved turned out to be a false alarm. The campaign continued and eventually a group of British South Africa Company Directors visited Livingstone to enquire into the matter. They approved the plan to move the capital of Northwestern Rhodesia from Kalomo to Livingstone 'until such a time as the development of the territory necessitates its removal to a more central position' and promised further improvements to the town and its services. They also announced that a township would be established on the Southern Rhodesian bank of the river near the Victoria Falls railway station and that any Livingstone standholder who chose to move to the new township would receive compensation for his old stand. It does not appear that many Livingstonians took advantage of this offer and, with the transfer of the capital, the clamour for the removal of the township subsided. The Victoria Falls township, founded at this time, has remained a small settlement, catering almost exclusively for the tourist trade.

The movement of the capital from Kalomo to Livingstone further increased the latter town's prosperity. All the civil servants (numbering about thirty-five) and their personal and office equipment travelled in a single special train in October 1907. The Administrator moved into the former Northwestern Hotel as Government House. Due to the shortage of offices, many rooms in Government House were used as offices and staff-quarters combined. B. L. Hunt recorded that his bed and office desk were in the same room. Three months later the problem had been alleviated by the erection of a row of offices adjacent to Government House. Bachelor civil servants were housed in a mess known as the United Services Club.

A major event in the early history of the town was the visit of the Duke and Duchess of Connaught in 1910. They came to South Africa to open the first session of the Union Parliament and then proceeded on a tour of Southern and Northern Rhodesia. Lewanika and other Barotse royalty came to Livingstone for the occasion and were accommodated in the town. Lewanika arranged an exhibition and demonstration of traditional Lozi crafts in the Barotse Centre, of which he took the visitors on a conducted tour. As usual, Lewanika made an excellent impression on the visitors and the settlers.

In 1911 the amalgamation of the two territories of Northwestern and Northeastern Rhodesia came into effect and Livingstone became the capital of the whole of Northern Rhodesia. This involved the transfer of a substantial amount of equipment from Fort Jameson (Chipata) to Livingstone. At that time there was no road communication from Fort Jameson to the line of rail and all the equipment, including the presses of the Government Printer, had to be dismantled and transported by carriers over some five hundred and fifty kilometres of footpaths through rough country from Fort Jameson to Broken Hill (Kabwe) whence it was brought to Livingstone by train.

Fig. 13 The visit to Livingstone of the Duke and Duchess of Connaught, 1910.

buildings and other memories of its early history.

By 1911 the population of Livingstone and its immediate environs exceeded two thousand, including more than three hundred Europeans. At that time over one fifth of the Europeans in Northern Rhodesia lived in Livingstone. The town's 'pioneer days' were clearly over. Since that time its prosperity has been maintained but its importance has declined, first as a result of the removal of the capital to Lusaka in 1935 and, more recently, with the reduction in Zambia's trade links with the south. Largely because of the fact that Livingstone did not share in the great expansion of the country's urban areas which has taken place since the 1950s, the town still retains a large number of early

Select Bibliography
CLARK, P. M. *The Autobiography of an Old Drifter,* London, 1936.
The Livingstone Mail (1906–1966).
RANGELEY, H. 'Memoirs', *Northern Rhodesia Journal,* vi, 1965, pp. 35–52, 170–186, 351–363.
TRAYNER, W. 'The *Livingstone Pioneer', Northern Rhodesia Journal,* v, 1964, pp. 361–366.
WATT, D. Unpublished MS on the History of Livingstone, Livingstone Museum, n.d.
Many other articles in the *Northern Rhodesia Journal* (1950–1965) contain useful information on the history of Livingstone.

CHAPTER 9

Traditional Carving and the Livingstone Curio Trade

Per B. Rekdal

What is a 'curio'? According to Webster's Dictionary it is 'something arousing interest as being novel, rare or bizarre'. What is novel, rare or bizarre in Africa? To the early European colonisers it was the Africans' customs, their objects, and the Africans themselves. The word 'curio' was applied to those parts of the African material cultures that were of a reasonable size to be bought and taken home for souvenirs and house decoration.

The construction of the railway to the Victoria Falls and Livingstone brought tourists to the area. Africans and settled European businessmen soon realised that profit could be gained from selling curios to the tourists. As early as 1905, it is recorded that King Lewanika obtained an annual income in the region of two hundred pounds from his 'curio shop in Livingstone'. The first issues of the *Livingstone Mail* in 1906 contained advertisements for curios; and in the following year there is a description of curio trade with tourists:

> Three special trains arrived at the Falls on Saturday evening, carrying nearly four hundred excursionists from the Cape Colony. . . . On Monday 150 of them arrived, per special train, at Livingstone, and 62 followed in the afternoon. Livingstone, during the two hours of their visit, was a sight to be remembered. Every store displaying curios did a roaring trade and the visitors were surrounded by an odoriferous crowd of assorted natives, offering for sale anything between a spear and a handful of kaffir oranges; the prices they demanded were enough to take one's breath away, but in many cases they got them.

Most likely, the objects sold as curios in the first years were objects of the same kind as the Africans used themselves. After a few years – probably around the time of the First World War or earlier – Africans started regularly making sculptures with the sole intention of selling them to Europeans. This more specialised category of objects is that known today as curios.

To what extent, then, are modern curios similar to, or related to, traditional sculpture? To answer this question we must first find out who the carvers are and what the traditional sculpture of their tribes looks like. Research carried out by B. Keller in 1962, and by the author in 1969–70, has found that the majority of the curio producers in Livingstone are Luvale, Luchazi, Mbunda, Lozi and Leya. The first three peoples traditionally live in Zambia's North-western Province and are commonly termed the Lunda-Luvale peoples. The Lozi inhabit parts of the Western Province, and the Leya are the traditional inhabitants of the Livingstone area.

The traditional sculpture of these peoples shows considerable formal and functional differences. The Lunda-Luvale have an extremely rich and varied sculptural tradition, both profane and religious. Painted masks of barkcloth and wood were used at different stages of the boys' initiation ceremonies. Walking sticks, stools, musical instruments and calabashes were decorated showing animals, scenes from village life, inanimate objects and geometric designs.

Lozi traditional sculpture was largely confined to animal carvings and geometric decoration on the lids of wooden dishes, on stools and other utilitarian objects. Both animals and geometric decoration were very simple, though not unrefined, with few details and large, unbroken surfaces. Very little has been published about Lozi carving, but Holỳ (1967) illustrates a few examples.

Leya traditional sculpture was even more restricted than that of the Lozi. Geometric decoration was applied to stools and other utilitarian objects, with sporadic use of animal carvings of a nature very similar to Lozi examples.

Most older carvers of today agree that the Lozi were the first curio producers, and this is confirmed by the reference to Lewanika's curio shop of 1905, noted above. The objects made in the beginning were primarily animal sculptures. This corresponds well with what is known about Lozi traditional carving. Even as late as 1969 the author's research showed that, out of forty-six animal carvers, twenty-eight were Lozi, eleven Leya and only seven Lunda-Luvale. This is all the more remarkable considering that one hundred and six carvers were interviewed, of whom forty-one were Lozi, fourteen Leya and fifty-one Lunda-Luvale. Animal carving is still a Lozi, and now even a Leya, speciality.

The traditional sculpture of the Victoria Falls area is discussed above by K. Mubitana. Here, we only show a typical Lozi wooden dish (Fig. 1), with the characteristic carving on the lid, and Fig. 2, which is a traditional stool of Leya origin. From these traditional objects we turn to some modern curios, like the hippo (Fig. 3) and the buck (Fig. 4). The modern forms are more life-like, the surfaces more shiny, and the materials are selected hardwoods with beautiful colours and grains. Traditional objects were made of a lighter and slightly softer wood, perhaps not so beautiful, but more practical because it did not crack as easily as the hardwoods. Parts or the whole of the objects were usually blackened by burning.

Fig. 1 (top, left) Traditional Kwangwa wooden dish. Ht. 13·5 cm.

Fig. 2 (centre, left) Traditional Leya stool. Ht. 26·6 cm.

Fig. 3 (bottom, left) Hardwood hippo (Leya, curio). Length 30 cm.

Fig. 4 (top, right) Hardwood buck (Lozi, curio). Ht. 26 cm.

Fig. 5 (bottom, right) Hardwood elephant table (Lozi, curio). Ht. 42 cm.

Although the relationships with traditional forms are not always obvious, hippos, rhinoceroses, crocodiles, tortoises and elephants among the curios seem to be traceable to traditional sources. Buck and giraffes have a more uncertain origin, at least in their present shape; and a relationship with Kenyan curios is not unlikely. Tables carried by animals, usually elephants (Fig. 5), have a relatively clear traditional origin, but their traditional counterparts had a different function – they were stools (Fig. 2).

Occasionally one may still find wooden dishes with carvings on their lids, almost completely traditional in form; the only difference being the material (now a beautiful hardwood) and a slight 'modernisation' of the sculpture (Fig. 6). Unfortunately, this is a product nearly vanished from the curio markets in the Livingstone area.

In the 1930s, according to the carvers, masks and drums were regularly produced as curios. Carvers from the other two groups had taken to curio production, but Lozi carvers were still dominant for another ten to twenty years. Masks were simpler than modern ones and generally smaller. The common type was an almost undecorated face, with a large 'hair-top' above. Fig. 7 shows a modern mask very similar to those produced in the 1930s. The source is probably a simplified version of a certain Lunda-Luvale initiation ceremony mask called Nalindele (also called Mwana Pwo) (Fig. 8). Most later curio masks have developed from this basic form, adding all kinds of decorations.

At this stage, a distinction has to be drawn between softwood and the different kinds of hardwoods. Softwood is used in the production of masks, drums and shields. Masks are also made in hardwoods. Softwood is

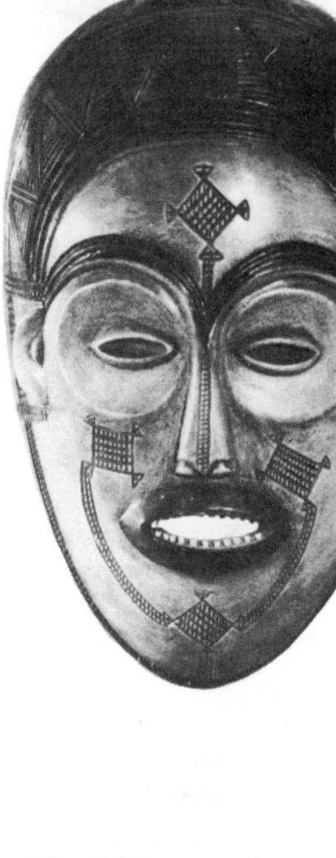

Fig. 6 (above, top) Hardwood dish (curio). Ht. 12 cm.
Fig. 7 (bottom, left) Hardwood mask (Lozi, curio). Ht. 49 cm.
Fig. 8 (above, right) Copy of traditional Nalindele mask. Ht. 25 cm.

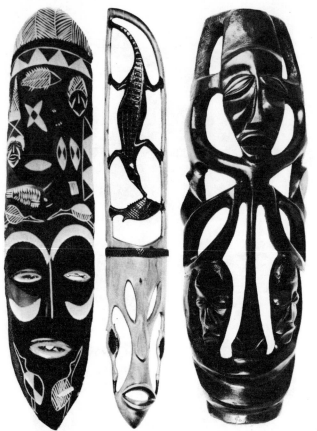

Fig. 9 (left) Softwood mask (curio). Ht. 90 cm.
Fig. 10 (centre) Hardwood mask (Lozi, curio).
Ht. 98 cm.
Fig. 11 (right) Hardwood mask (Lozi, curio). Ht.
60 cm.

from colouring and surface decorations. Besides, their light weight is very convenient for air-borne customers!

Softwood masks were probably the first to develop from the simple mask of the 1930s. In the 1950s, geometric decorations were peeled out with a knife from the surface of the mask, after it had been blackened by burning and polished with black shoe-polish. These geometric designs were largely similar to traditional Lunda-Luvale ornamentation, but were applied in much greater quantities and in untraditional places. In the 1960s the carvers added new colours to the masks – red, brown and green. The designs became increasingly three-dimensional and figurative, showing animals, human faces and hunting scenes, bird eating fish, crocodile eating fish, man hunting buck, etc. Geometric designs continued in use alongside the figurative ones (Fig. 9).

Hardwood masks are very seldom decorated with any amount of surface elaboration except for stripes filed into the surface, and some blackening with shoe-polish. The most important aim of the carver of hardwoods is to create a smooth, glossy surface so as to emphasise the natural beauty of the wood. Too much surface decoration would ruin this. A formal richness comparable with the softwood masks is, however, achieved through an extensive use of holes. Three-dimensional decoration surrounded by holes right through the mask does not disturb the shiny surface, and gives an elegant appearance (Fig. 10). In more extreme examples, the substantive parts of the mask are reduced to a suggestive framework round a series of holes (Fig. 11).

The conclusion must be that most modern curio masks are far developed from their point of departure, the simplified Nalindele

soft, whitish-yellow, and very light when dried. Softwood grows fast into large branches and consequently the carver may make large objects. Products of hardwoods are usually long and narrow due to the corresponding narrow branches of the trees. This explains why wide objects like drums and shields are very seldom made of hardwoods.

Softwood is not beautiful in itself; objects made of this material gain their attraction mask. The geometric decorations are now the only forms more or less similar to traditional ones. However, now and then masks with some resemblance to a variety of traditional masks like Samahongo and Chikuza (both Lunda-Luvale initiation ceremony masks) turn up, only to disappear again.

Drums are, with few exceptions, made of softwood. The most common type (Fig. 12) is closely related to traditional drums of the Lunda-Luvale (Fig. 13). Both are decorated with a face, and a band of geometric decoration stretching horizontally around the drum from the face. The shape of the base is essentially the same. Modern drums are however shorter and wider, the decorative parts are enlarged so that they nearly cover the body of the drum; all proportions are distorted. Colours are used in an untraditional fashion. Additionally, harder wood was used for traditional drums.

Other kinds of modern curio drums are more difficult to relate to traditional drums. Drum-making is a Lunda-Luvale speciality. Out of twenty carvers of drums, I found that nineteen were Lunda-Luvale, one Lozi.

Small musical instruments, metal-pointed spears, axes and walking sticks are also curios which are usually derived from the traditional cultures of the carvers. But then the list of what might be termed 'traditionalistic' items is exhausted. Most other products are inventions of the carvers themselves, copies of Kenyan curios, types introduced by European curio dealers, and mixtures of all categories.

The very common hardwood busts seem to be the carvers' own invention. According to the carvers, they were introduced at the end of the 1940s and are meant to be naturalistic representations of individual people (Fig. 14). A recent type (produced since the

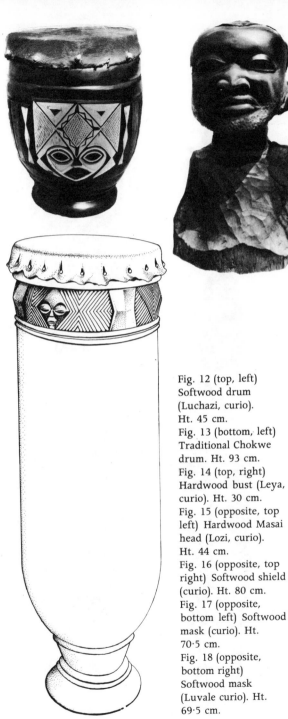

Fig. 12 (top, left) Softwood drum (Luchazi, curio). Ht. 45 cm.
Fig. 13 (bottom, left) Traditional Chokwe drum. Ht. 93 cm.
Fig. 14 (top, right) Hardwood bust (Leya, curio). Ht. 30 cm.
Fig. 15 (opposite, top left) Hardwood Masai head (Lozi, curio). Ht. 44 cm.
Fig. 16 (opposite, top right) Softwood shield (curio). Ht. 80 cm.
Fig. 17 (opposite, bottom left) Softwood mask (curio). Ht. 70·5 cm.
Fig. 18 (opposite, bottom right) Softwood mask (Luvale curio). Ht. 69·5 cm.

113

end of the 1960s) has faces carved out of an otherwise crude branch of hardwood.

Salad-servers and Masai heads (Fig. 15) are copies of Kenyan curios. Wooden shields (Fig. 16) were unknown in the traditional cultures of the carvers. The present type was introduced by an enterprising European curio dealer in the 1950s. That is also the case with masks called 'Congo' masks by the carvers, or 'Spirit of the Fish' by some European curio dealers (Fig. 17). The ancestry of this type is found in southern Zaïre. Shields and 'Congo' masks have, over the years, acquired decorative elements from other products, and traditionally derived geometric decorations are now applied to them. (Fig. 18).

Some very popular rough-hewn figures, often of considerable size, can be traced back through the teacher of the present carver to a European curio dealer, who let the first carver copy sculptures from the BaSuku people in Zaïre. The figures have changed considerably, but connections are easily established through older carvings and carvers' statements.

As has been shown above, present-day curios have a variety of sources. Several types are in some way related to the traditional carvings of the curio producers' home areas, but over a period of seventy-five years of specialised curio production, connections are growing faint. Still, products that are almost similar to traditional ones do appear occasionally. Furthermore, the Lozi, Leya and Lunda-Luvale prefer to make those curios which are most related to their own traditional sculpture. This is especially the case with the Lunda-Luvale carvers who prefer the softwood which enables them to use a variety of traditional forms. Lozi and Leya carvers, who have also borrowed forms from the Lunda-Luvale (e.g. masks), execute their products in hardwoods in a fashion much farther removed from traditional origins, although the smooth, unbroken surfaces of hardwood objects have much in common with the simple, traditional Lozi carving.

Traditional shapes, then, are not far below the surface. Most carvers, especially the Lunda-Luvale, have some knowledge of them. Their traditional sculpture was to a great extent made for ritual purposes and is today far from extinct in the Lunda-Luvale homelands. Lozi and Leya carving was mostly devoted to utilitarian objects and, as such, was readily replaced by enamel pans and other products of industrialisation.

This discussion of traditionalism may lead some to the conclusion that judgement of the quality of a curio should be based on its relative proximity to some traditional origin. This is of course a matter of personal taste, but the prospective buyer should remember that none of the curios is made in order to serve a traditional function, and that they are practically never wholly traditional in shape. They are made to satisfy a market of strangers; and the carver will use any saleable form that he knows and can execute with some skill.

Thus, one of the most successful curio carvers, and one of the most inventive of them, has specialised in making the rough-hewn figures that originally stem from the BaSuku people in Zaïre, and were introduced by a European curio dealer. He probably does not know the origin of the type he is making, but that really does not matter to him. Also, curios being what they are – a complete mixture of forms, most of them not even mentioned in this short article – it need not matter to the customer either.

What does matter is the highly misleading names occasionally found on curios in curio shops, such as 'The Spirit of the Wind'. This may give customers the impression that these special curios are traditional objects made to serve traditional functions, which is not true. It may further give the customer a distorted picture of traditional African cultures, which is all too similar to the one held by the early European colonisers.

Select Bibliography

BASTIN, M.-L. *Art Decoratif Tshokwe*, Lisbon (Museu do Dundo, Publicações Culturais no. 55), 2 vols, 1961.

BRELSFORD, W. V. *The Tribes of Zambia* (2nd. edn.), Lusaka, 1965.

HOLÝ, L. and D. DARBOIS *Masks and Figures of Eastern and Southern Africa*, London, 1967.

KELLER, B. *Wood Carvers of Zambia*, Livingstone, (National Museums of Zambia, Special Paper), 1967.

MUBITANA, K. 'Zambian sculptural art: its essence and development,' *Zambia Museum Journal,* i, 1970, pp. 16–21.

MUBITANA, K. 'Form and significance in the art of the Lunda, Luvale, Luchazi and Chokwe of Zambia,' *Zambia Museum Journal,* i, 1970, pp. 22–27.

CHAPTER 10

The Flora

D. B. Fanshawe

For more than a hundred years botanists have been accumulating a considerable mass of information bearing on the flora of the Victoria Falls and of the immediately surrounding country. The first scientific botanist in the field was Sir John Kirk, who accompanied Livingstone's second expedition to the Falls in 1860. Most of his collecting, in what must have been extremely arduous conditions, was carried out lower down the Zambezi, but he did make a few gatherings at the Falls themselves and he is responsible for the original description of that most striking feature of the vegetation, the Vegetable Ivory or Fan Palm (*Hyphaene ventricosa*). This expedition was also accompanied on the lower Zambezi by Thomas Baines who, apart from his fame as a traveller and artist, was one of the very early botanical collectors in south tropical Africa. Next we have Frank Oates who visited the Falls in 1875, but who stayed a very short time and, as a result of fever contracted there, died very shortly afterwards.

Systematic collecting can be said to have begun in 1904, when the two Southern Rhodesian botanists, Eyles and Allen, spent more extended periods here, but the opening of the rail bridge in 1905 was to provide the real impetus for travellers of all kinds. In this year the great German botanist Engler collected here, and wrote the first short botanical account of the vegetation. The well-known South African botanist, Burtt Davy, also visited the Falls in 1905. Then followed Miss Gibbs in 1906, who also published a short account of the vegetation, with photographs. In 1910, the most active collector of all at the Falls – Archdeacon Rogers – first arrived and greatly extended the number of recorded species. The next botanical visitor of note was R. E. Fries in 1912, who began his great Swedish-Rhodesian-Congo expedition there. The beautifully published account of this expedition also contains a short description of the flora and some magnificent photographs.

Now follows a considerable gap until Dr Hutchinson of Kew, in 1930, gave us a short impression of the flora of this district in his account of his botanical travels with Field-Marshal Smuts in south and central Africa.

With the possible exception of Rogers all these collectors spent very short periods at the Falls, and so, in spite of the voluminous records built up of species occurring here, there are still many gaps in our knowledge of the flora. Future collectors can still hope to find unrecorded species for a long time to come, and need not fear that they are working an exhausted field.

The Falls lie at an altitude of 915 metres above sea-level. The climate is rather hot with a mean annual maximum temperature of 15 degrees Centigrade. The rainfall is a low 600 to 700 millimetres per annum but the humidity during the rainy season of November to March is very high, producing four or five months of muggy weather.

Climatically, one would expect the area to support an open deciduous or semi-deciduous woodland but the effect of climate is offset by the geological formations. The Zambezi flows, in the region of the Falls, over a bed of dull, red-brown basalt. North and south of the Falls, however, one very soon strikes beds of the overlying reddish Kalahari Sand. The edges of these deposits are irregular in outline, and outliers of varying size form islands of Kalahari Sand on the basalt near the Falls. This is particularly noticeable near the Victoria Falls Hotel on the Zimbabwean side.

The basalt soils are shallow and stony, often with a wash of Kalahari Sand over them, and they carry either pure mopane woodland or a very mixed mopane scrub. The Kalahari Sands are deep and well-drained and carry Miombo/Kalahari woodland dominated by mukushi, (*Baikiaea plurijuga*), various species of *Brachystegia*, museshe (*Burkea africana*), mubako (*Erythrophleum africanum*) and muzauli (*Guibourtia coleosperma*). Mukushi produces a valuable timber commercially exploited in both Zambia and Zimbabwe for railway sleepers, mining timber and parquet flooring.

Mopane and Kalahari woodlands are independent of the Zambezi. In common with all rivers in tropical Africa, the Zambezi has a distinct fringing vegetation of gallery or riparian woodland. This is normally a very narrow belt, often only one tree wide, never more than a hundred metres wide. The much-publicised 'Rain Forest' at the Falls is merely an unusually extensive area of riverine forest (rather than woodland) made possible by the continuous spray from the Falls.

The riparian woodland trees are in the main the same as those found along most rivers in south central Africa. Many of the species, however, are found throughout tropical Africa suggesting that riverine vegetation is a remnant of a once much more extensive forest of higher rainfall vegetation which during wetter periods of fairly recent geological time may have covered much wider areas in Africa. This would explain the strange uniformity of species found fringing so many rivers separated by large tracts of lower rainfall vegetation now incapable of harbouring these riverine species.

The riparian woodland and 'Rain Forest' between them contain some one hundred and forty species equally distributed between trees and tall shrubs, plus fifty sub-shrubs and one hundred and fifty herbs. If grasses,

117

sedges, ferns and climbers are included the total is over four hundred species. The constant spray and mist from the Falls is particularly favourable to many small moisture-loving plants and among these *Lythraceae*, *Lentibulariaceae* and ferns are well represented.

An analysis of the 'Rain Forest' herb flora also reveals an unusually high proportion of apparently endemic species *i.e.* species that have never been recorded from anywhere else. The term 'apparently endemic' is used because the majority of such species probably occur in the spray zones of other waterfalls in Zambia and Zimbabwe but have not been collected or recorded from these other areas. Species such as *Rotala cataractae* may have evolved as distinct species or be the last survivors of once more widely distributed species, under the highly specialised conditions provided by the 'Rain Forest'. In other words the 'Rain Forest' contains a highly specialised flora of an island character with some endemic species, widely separated from other areas with similar ecological conditions.

Below the Falls the fringing forest is interrupted by the precipitous nature of the gorges and is replaced on the gorge sides by a deciduous woodland characterised by paper bark trees. Above Katombora the river is much more slow-flowing and winds through seasonally flooded plains which carry a swamp vegetation of reeds (*Phragmites mauritianus*), Papyrus (*Cyperus papyrus*) and other moisture-loving grasses and sedges.

The islands above the Falls, owing to their relatively small size, are covered mainly by riverine woodland and are fairly uniform in this respect. Some, such as Livingstone and Cataract Islands, are· basaltic while those further upstream, such as Palm Island, are

Fig. 1 Kalahari woodland.

large sandbanks. This naturally produces some minor differences – the Baobab (*Adansonia digitata*), for instance, does not occur on the sand islands. King George VI, or Long Island, is also exceptional in that it is more low-lying than other sand islands and has long, seasonally flooded, depressions running down its length. These carry swamp grasses and sedges with scattered trees and palms on the intervening ridges. Where sand spits run out into the river from this and other islands they bear dense masses of Reedgrass as soon as they become settled.

Some nine hundred species have been recorded from this very small area – a number approaching that of the flora of Ireland. In the following pages it will be possible only to mention the more dominant and showy species*. Where possible, com-

* Unfortunately, for reasons of space, a check-list cannot be included in this chapter. For such a list, see D. B. Fanshawe, 'Vegetation of the Victoria Falls', *Forest Research Pamphlets*, XLV.

mon English names have been given and also the Silozi names as this is the African language most widely spoken in the Falls area. The various localities of interest will now be taken in turn and, as the 'Rain Forest' will no doubt be the first spot visited by the botanist, this will be given pride of place.

The 'Rain Forest'

The so-called 'Rain Forest' is merely an extensive piece of riparian forest. Among the more striking tall trees are the African Ebony or muchenja (*Diospyros mespiliformis*), with black bark, straight bole, alternate oblong leaves and an oval yellow fruit the size of a small plum, fleshy within and edible but with a hardish skin. Another rather similar black-barked tree is the muchiningi (*Mimusops zeyheri*) whose elliptic yellow fruit has a milky edible pulp.

Four species of large fig are present, two of which are readily recognisable. The hairy-leaved Cape fig or mukuyu (*Ficus capensis*) has softly hairy fruit the size of edible figs borne in large woody panicles on the main stem. The other common fig, mututa (*Ficus ingens*), is a strangler which eventually kills the tree which supports it in its younger stages. It has smooth, silvery grey bark and small figs one centimetre in diameter, borne in the axils of the glabrous, ovate-cordate leaves.

Equally common are the two Waterbooms or mutoya (*Syzygium guineense ssp. barotsense* and *S. cordatum*). They both have opposite, leathery leaves, cordate in the latter and elliptic in the former, and masses of white Eucalyptus-like flowers. Another common tree is the musikili (*Trichilia emetica*), widely planted as a street tree, with pinnate leaves and velvety red fruiting capsules splitting to reveal the three to six bright red and black seeds. The mulombelombe (*Strychnos potatorum*) is not so common but readily recognised by its opposite, three-veined leaves and round, black, fleshy, edible, plum-sized fruit.

One of the commoner small trees is the African Olive (*Olea africana*) with olive-like fruit and alternate, narrow, lanceolate leaves with silvery-scaly undersides. The graceful wild date palm or nzalu (*Phoenix reclinata*) is common in the Rain Forest as well as in Palm Grove. The fruits actually have a very faint date flavour but the flesh is exceedingly thin.

The shrub layer of the 'Rain Forest' is well developed. Of the seventy species recorded, three of the commoner ones are particularly attractive. *Feretia aeruginescens,* a rather straggling shrub of the forest margin, produces masses of delicate pink flowers clustered along the leafless stems, followed by red fleshy fruit. *Pavetta cataractarum,* named in honour of the Falls, occurs in the wetter parts and produces globose masses, about ten centimetres in diameter, of tubular white flowers. *Hibiscus calyphyllus,* which can grow to a small tree, has the typical large yellow Hibiscus flower which opens out flat to show off the chocolate centre.

For attractiveness and rarity however, we must turn to the herbaceous flora of the 'Rain Forest'. Here is a wealth of species (about one hundred and fifty) from which to choose. In the early rains the Fireballs (*Haemanthus filiflorus* and *H. multiflorus*), with their large red globes of many slender tubular flowers, shine brightly among the dark green undergrowth. In December, a ground orchid, *Calanthe corymbosa,* with broad leaves and racemes of large white flowers, adds to the beauty of the forest floor. Other attractive rains species include the wild Gentian, *Chironia palustris,* with beautiful pink flowers on long stalks, and the well-known

119

Flame Lily, *Gloriosa superba,* with its large showy red and yellow flowers. Before the rains the rare Black Arum, *Amorphophallus abyssinicus,* with its large purple-black hood, can be found in shady places. The ferns of the 'Rain Forest' may be found at any time of the year. The well-known Maiden Hair *Adiantum capillus-veneris)* is quite common and one most unusual fern, *Cheilanthes farinosa,* the undersurface of whose fronds is a striking sulphur-yellow, is only known from here, the Zambezi rapids in Mwinilunga district and Kitwe.

Along the lip of the gorge next to the 'Rain Forest' there is a narrow treeless strip which receives a constant drenching spray and which, through most of the year, carries a large number of pretty and often rare herbaceous species. Among these are a bright yellow-flowered little Gentian (*Sebaea pentandra*), a straggling little blue-flowered Lobelia with ovate leaves (*Lobelia kirkii*) and a showy mauve-flowered Gladiolus (*G. unguiculatus*). The Lythraceae are represented by *Nesaea radicans,* with small capitate clusters of bright mauve flowers, and by two species of *Rotala* with straggling stems and tiny crowded decussate leaves almost hiding the minute axillary mauve flowers. *Scrophulariaceae* are represented by a pretty little Nemesia-like herb, *Diclis petiolaris,* with delicate white brownish-purple-blotched flowers furnished with a short spur, and the *Compositae* by the straggling *Emilia protracta,* a Senecio-like plant with brick-red florets and purple undersides to its glabrous leaves.

Palm Grove
Lianes are common throughout the fringing forest and are well represented and more easily visible in Palm Grove than elsewhere.

There used to be one spot where you could swing on a liane as thick as your thigh. The commoner large climbers with stems twenty to thirty centimetres in diameter include sikoka (*Cocculus hirsutus*) with hairy ovate leaves and small blue-black, fleshy fruit; the Flame Creeper or kachingamwezi (*Combretum paniculatum*) with unilateral spikes of brilliant red flowers and mukutinga (*Hippocratea africana*) which has greenish flowers and fruiting capsules shaped like a flattened money-bag, light brown in colour and splitting into two halves to release the membranous winged seeds.

There are more kinds of small liane, with stems one half to five centimetres in diameter, like the Wild Grape, (*Cissus quadrangularis*) with its fleshy, four-sided, jointed stems; Old Man's Beard or koti (*Clematis brachiata*) with its dissected leaves and fluffy heads of seeds with long white silky awns; silutombolwa (*Combretum mossambicense*) with short creamy flower-spikes; a Morning Glory (*Ipomoea rubens*) with showy mauve-pink flowers as its name implies and, finally, *Tacazzea apiculata* with its drooping panicles of reddish flowers and brownish velvety fruit composed of two divergent fusiform follicles.

Two other occasional climbers can soon be recognised: the mwiya (*Tiliacora funifera*) because it bears its greenish flowers and fleshy yellow fruits on the stem, often quite near the ground, and the Timbo (*Paullinia pinnata*), a tendril climber with a winged leaf rachis and small white flowers, the older stems three or four-sided or apparently made up of three or four fused and slightly twisted stems.

At the bottom of Palm Grove, the Wild Date palm or nzalu (*Phoenix reclinata*) is much more common than in the 'Rain Forest'. Its trunks are slender and often leaning, topped by the crown of feather-like leaves. The understorey vegetation is very dense in gaps, the path in places cutting its way through dense rambling masses of a white-flowered Plumbago-like creeper (*Commicarpus plantagineus*) mixed here and there with a prickly, scrambling Hibiscus (*H. surattensis*) which has large yellow flowers with a red centre, and the Potato Creeper (*Solanum seaforthianum*), with pale blue potato-like flowers and tiny dark red berries, introduced from the West Indies or Central America. The invasive *Lantana camara* is becoming prevalent in the lower part of Palm Grove and the exotic Jessamine (*Cestrum laevigatum*) has established itself at the foot.

The Fringing Forest of the River Banks
The fringing forest tends to vary in density and depth, so let us look at a couple of representative stretches.

(a) *Palm Grove to the Sprayview Restaurant on the northern bank*
The African Ebony, Waterboom and Wild Date palms, all of which we have seen in the 'Rain Forest,' are well in evidence but there are several other interesting trees. Among the larger trees the mubaba (*Albizia versicolor*) with its umbrella-shaped crown, bipinnate leaves and round velvety leaflets, and the Sycomore Fig or mukuyu (*Ficus sycomorus*) with ochreous bark and rounded leaves, sandpapery to the touch, stand out. The Zambezi Wattle or munyele (*Peltophorum africanum*) may also catch our eye at the beginning of the rains with its racemes of bright yellow flowers.

One of the more striking of the smaller trees is the African Mangosteen or mukwananga (*Garcinia livingstonei*). It begins to branch low down on the main stem at a narrow angle to the main axis. The main branches carry many short, stiff, erect, secondary branches which carry the small white or pale green flowers and later the orange-yellow, ovoid, fleshy, edible fruits which are the size of a small plum and have a delightful flavour. Another attractive small tree is the Zambezi Bird Cherry, Ebony or mukelete (*Dalbergia melanoxylon*) with pinnate leaves and small white pea flowers. The heartwood is black and very hard and is used for carving local curios. The mubaba (*Piliostigma thonningii*) with its bi-lobed Bauhinia-like leaves, yellow flowers and large dark brown pods also likes this situation.

(b) *From Cataract Island to the launch landing stages on the southern bank*
Here the mixture is much the same as on the northern bank but some additional species are conspicuous. The Dum or Fan Palm, munganda (*Hyphaene ventricosa*) is frequent around here although not strictly on the water's edge, and the Knobthorn or mukwena (*Acacia nigrescens*) with blue-green rounded leaflets (unusual for an Acacia) is also quite common. Its creamy, catkin-like flower-spikes make a fine show in the spring and the thorn-tipped bosses on the trunk render it immediately recognisable.

The Rain tree or mupanda (*Lonchocarpus capassa*) has grey-green pinnate leaves of five leaflets and showy panicles of violet pea flowers in spring, while the Leadwood or muzwili (*Combretum imberbe*) can be recognised by the minute scales on its small grey-green leaves. *Homalium abdessammadii* with its crenate leaves and unpleasantly scented pale cream flowers is common at the water's edge.

Hereabouts there are signs of old flood banks which have now become pleasant tree-covered glades. In this shade at the beginning

Fig. 2 Dum Palms (*Hyphaene ventricosa*) in riparian woodland on the islands of the Zambezi.

of the rains the Wild Ginger (*Kaempferia rosea*) may be found. These plants are rather Canna-like in habit but bear short spikes of the most delicate pale mauve or pink flowers, blotched with yellow in the throat.

The Livingstone Statue and top of Palm Grove

These are two small areas of basalt on opposite sides of the river carrying a scrub mopane vegetation. Mopane (*Colophospermum mopane*) is present but not dominant. Mwangula (*Pterocarpus antunesii*) is by far the commonest tree and is extremely handsome with its yellow pea flowers produced when the tree is leafless, but it tends to flower erratically at long intervals. No timber can be obtained from the tree as it is deeply fluted to the core, but the flutes make good paddles and axe-handles. Besides mwangula, six species of mubwabwa occur of which the commonest is *Commiphora mollis*. The bark of each is thin, translucent and papery with reddish,

greenish or brownish tints showing through. The fruits are green, fleshy and one-seeded, the seed being clasped by an orange, basal, more or less dissected aril.

Colonies of the sword-leaved, succulent Mother-in-Law's Tongue or mukusa (*Sansevieria desertii*) occur here and there. The stiff erect cylindrical furrowed leaves with spiny tips provide a good fibre known as Bowstring Hemp used for making sacks. A pretty Gardenia bush or sulu (*Gardenia resiniflua*) is occasional. It has smooth grey bark, obovate leaves and produces scented white flowers in November.

The Fringing Forest at Katombora

The fringing forest remains fairly uniform as far as Katombora with musikili, mutoya, muchenja, mukwananga and mucheningi still among the commonest species. At Katombora there is a small stand of a most unusual Acacia (*A. kirkii*) with a papery, peeling, orange bark, globose heads of yellow or pinkish flowers and a flat pod with conical protuberances along its flat sides.

This is also a good spot to see a number of April-flowering herbs which are especially common here. These include *Melastomastrum segregatum* which has purple flowers and characteristic leaves whose main veins run longitudinally down the leaf, chavani (*Barleria rogersii*) with showy pale blue flowers and two species of *Ruspolia* (*R. decurrens* and *R. seticalyx*) with brick-red flowers. The former may be distinguished by the minute stalked glands on the inflorescence.

The Road to Kazungula

Beyond Katombora upstream towards Kazungula the river becomes much more slow-flowing and winds among low flood plains. The fringing forest disappears and the river and its backwaters are bordered by dense stands of reeds or matete (*Phragmites mauritianus*), tall sedges like *Cyperus alternifolius*, *C. denudatus* and *C. digitatus* and by semi-aquatic grasses such as Kazungula grass (*Setaria sphacelata*) which is proving such a valuable introduced fodder in South Africa and Zimbabwe.

Floating on the backwaters are masses of a most intriguing plant, the Water Lettuce (*Pistia stratiotes*). This is a floating Arum with a tiny green spathe hooding the inflorescence at the base of the cup formed by the broad yellow-green leaves. These leaves are covered with a dense mat of short hairs which trap the air so that when the plant is forcefully submerged, it bobs up to the surface again like a cork.

Along with the Water Lettuce are colonies of the aquatic fern *Azolla pinnata* forming dark red-brown floating carpets. Another aquatic fern, Kariba weed (*Salvinia sp.*) has become a menace especially on the Kariba dam lower down the Zambezi.

On the southern bank of the Zambezi at Kazungula there stands the historic Kazungula (*Kigelia africana*) tree under which Dr Livingstone spent a night on his way to the Falls in 1855. The tree stands more or less at the junction of Zambia, Zimbabwe, Botswana and the Caprivi Strip and has given its name to the nearby village.

The Flora of the Gorges

The gorge walls, where they are not too precipitous, carry a deciduous woodland vegetation characterised by paper bark trees belonging to three different genera. The commonest is the Fever tree, mubwabwa (*Commiphora marlothii*) which has velvety pinnate leaves and a bright yellow-green papery bark. Not so common is mtelele (*Albizia tanganyikensis*) with bipinnate leaves and yellowish bark with a white bloom. The third paper bark tree is mukosa (*Sterculia quinqueloba*) with large three to five-palmately lobed leaves and brown velvety ovoid pods filled with oblong dull black seeds. The mupumena (*Entandrophragma caudatum*), one of the African mahoganies, occurs here but is rare. On the gorge walls above Palm Grove is a small stand of a very rare deciduous tree mutubetube (*Gyrocarpus americanus*) with rounded leaves, three to five-nerved from base, and winged red-brown fruit.

A Barleria (*B. matopensis*) with attractive blue flowers is locally abundant on the upper slopes of the gorges. On rock outcrops can be found the rare *Hibiscus praeteritus* with small scarlet flowers, and the Everlasting Plant (*Myrothamnus flabellifolius*), so called because of its ability to revive in water when apparently dead. A very rare Euphorbia (*E. fortissima*) occurs by the lip of the gorge at the Candelabra Pool. It has thick, fleshy, spine-encrusted three or four-winged stems up to two or four metres high.

Tucked away in rock crevices are two

tiny plants of interest, one a tiny fern *Actiniopteris radiata*, with palmate fronds reminiscent of the Hyphaene palm on a minute scale, and the other a fern-like Selaginella (*S. imbricata*) with tiny, closely imbricate leaves. In dry weather the fronds curl up and present a silvery buff appearance. After a shower it expands to reveal a green upper surface. The more rocky portions of the gorge walls are covered with clumps of Aloes (*A. chabaudii* and *A. cryptopoda*) which make a brave show with their spikes of brick-red to scarlet flowers in July and August.

Islands in the Zambezi

The islands vary in size from a few square metres to several square kilometres and are either sandbanks, with or without one or more central depressions, or basalt-based rocky islands. Livingstone and Cataract for instance are basaltic islands, Palm and King George VI are sand islands. The smallest ones bear reeds (*Phragmites*) alone, the slightly larger islands have a cover of reeds and Willow trees (*Salix subserrata*), and even larger ones a cover of reeds and water-booms (*Syzygium guineense ssp. barotsense*). The final stage is riparian or gallery woodland basically identical with the gallery woodland of the north and south banks of the river. The details, however, vary from island to island.

The mukolwe (*Byrsocarpus orientalis*), a scandent shrub, makes a particularly fine show on some of the islands. It produces in November a profusion of scented, white

Fig. 3 (top) The famous Kazungula tree (*Kigelia africana*) at Kazungula, beneath which David Livingstone camped in 1855.
Fig. 4 (bottom) Deciduous forest clinging to the walls of the gorge above the Boiling Pot.

Fig. 5 *Euphorbia fortissima* at Candelabra Pool.

flowers reminiscent of may-blossom. The Lucky Bean or mupiti (*Abrus precatorius*) is frequent on the islands. Its glossy, red and black beans are very popular with the curio-makers and, incidentally, with anyone who wants to get rid of his mother-in-law un-

obtrusively! Wild date palms (*Phoenix*) are a feature of many of the islands. Characteristic of the sandbanks by the water's edge is the munga (*Acacia albida*) whose fruits are coiled and twisted like apple-peel rings. Also at the water's edge can be seen the Waxberry (*Myrica serrata*), a much-branched shrub resembling the English Bog-myrtle or Sweet-gale. Many of the trees and shrubs are parasitised by a peculiar, leafless, Dodder-like plant, luze (*Cassytha filiformis*), with yellowish, thread-like stems straggling over their foliage.

The central deep sandy ridges of some of the islands produce a non-riparian vegeta-tion, with affinities to Kalahari woodland. Here you can see the museselesele (*Dichro-stachys cinerea*), an Acacia-like small tree with solitary instead of paired thorns; the mukoto-koto (*Acacia polyacantha*) with white catkin-like inflorescences and hooked thorns; and the muhonono or Yellow-wood (*Terminalia sericea*) which has silvery green leaves and two-winged fruits.

On the basalt-based islands near the Falls there are usually wet rocky ledges on the side next to the Falls covered with some of the most unusual flowering plants known to botanists. These are members of the *Podo-stemonaceae*, an aquatic family adapted to life in fast-flowing water, which attach them-selves firmly by clasping organs to the rocks or river bed. Their flowers are much reduced and very inconspicuous. One of these, *Inversodicraea tenax*, is very common and has a moss-like appearance with very minute scale-like trifid leaves. Another, *Tristicha trifaria*, has reddish stems and minute leaves running along the rock surface and tightly clinging to it throughout the whole length of the sterile branches. When the water level falls and the rocks dry, these branches re-

main as a greyish reticulated encrustation on
the rock surface.

Aquatics in the Zambezi

Aquatic species often have an almost cosmopolitan distribution and in the slower-moving
and shallower parts of the Zambezi above
the Falls the visiting botanist will be able to
recognise a number of familiar aquatic genera
or even species. Two pond-weeds are quite
common. One, with largish floating leaves
and narrow submerged leaves, is *Potamoge-
ton schweinfurthii,* while *P. octandrus* has
elliptic floating leaves only one centimetre
long. The Water Gentian (*Nymphoides indica*),
with its floating water-lily-like leaves and
small yellow starlike ciliate flowers, is also
easily recognised.

Among the submerged species is a Water
Milfoil (*Myriophyllum spicatum*), familiar to
both the European and South African
botanist, and *Hydrilla verticillata,* a relative
of the well-known Canadian Pond-weed
(*Elodea canadensis*). In the sandy streambed
grows a Quillwort (*Isoetes alstonii*) with thirty
to forty linear leaves. The introduced Kariba
weed (*Salvinia sp.*) is an aquatic fern now
very common in the backwaters.

The Non-Riverine Basaltic Flora

A low open woodland dominated by mopane
(*Colophospermum mopane*) and muzumina
(*Kirkia acuminata*) and usually designated
Mopane scrub occurs on the shallow soil of
the basalt areas. It is seen at its best along the
Hubert Young drive and in the Mosi-oa-
Tunya Zoological Park in Zambia and in the
region of the Big Tree (a Baobab) in Zim-
babwe.

Mopane is readily recognised by its
characteristic butterfly leaf which consists of
two triangular glossy green leaflets. The

Fig. 6 *Phragmites* reed-beds fringing the islands in
the Zambezi.

inconspicuous flowers are prolific nectar
producers, much favoured by bees. The
leaves are the favourite browse of the elephant and other wild animals as well as
cattle. Large Baobabs (*Adansonia digitata*)

126

occur here and there and are immediately recognised by their grotesque appearance and huge size, traditionally explained as planted by God upside down. The Knobthorn or mukwena (*Acacia nigrescens*) is a common associate as are the musheshe (*Burkea africana*), muzwili (*Combretum imberbe*), mubako (*Erythrophleum africanum*), muzumina (*Kirkia acuminata*) looking deceptively like the well-known marula (*Sclerocarya caffra*) which is also present but not common, mwangula (*Pterocarpus antunesii*), with its deeply fluted stem, and mukosa (*Sterculia quinqueloba*), one of the paper-bark trees also seen on the gorge slopes.

Among the shrubs and small trees one of the commonest is the mubwabwa (*Commiphora mollis*) with its smooth grey fluted and angular branches and sometimes boles, but the most showy are the Zambezi Wistaria (*Bolusanthus speciosus*) with its pendulous racemes of mauve purple pea flowers, mululwe (*Cassia abbreviata*) with yellow flowers and pods like long pendent rats' tails, and the Violet tree or mwinda (*Securidaca longepedunculata*) with its violet-scented mauve flowers and winged samaras.

The most breathtaking sight, however, is provided in the late dry or early rainy season by the flowering of a colony of Brooms and Brushes (*Vellozia equisetoides*). The ephemeral blue flowers appear in masses on the stiff and rather ugly fibrous stems and completely transform this small gaunt bush. The flowers are large but very delicate and nod in the breeze among the grass-like leaves. Another equally common attractive small shrub is *Turbina holubii* which produces masses of pale mauve Morning Glory flowers with a magenta centre in the late rains.

Particularly evident in mopane scrub is a showy Vlei lily (*Crinum macowanii*) with an umbel of large trumpet-shaped flowers, white except for the main vein of each perianth segment which is pink. One can find the little Adder's Tongue Fern (*Ophioglossum reticulatum*) under the Baobab trees. Its single, undivided, elliptic, sterile frond and the much modified fertile frond make it most unfernlike at first sight.

Most of the scrub mopane woodland is not on the level terraces by the Zambezi, but in broken country of low rocky hills and kopjes, the fringe of the escarpment country, a little way back from the river. Here can be seen the other mukosa (*Sterculia africana*) with its rather Baobab-like habit. The golden, velvety fruits are much larger than those of *Sterculia quinqueloba;* they are tipped with a horn and contain three to ten dull charcoal-grey, ellipsoid seeds. The golden acicular hairs are extremely irritant to the skin.

The Kalahari Sand Flora

A drive southwards along the Bulawayo road or westwards towards Katombora will soon take one into Kalahari sand vegetation. On the north bank at least this is Miombo/Kalahari woodland dominated by a mixture of miombo and Kalahari woodland species. At least three of the large trees produce fine timber and two of them are exploited commercially. The most important timber-producer is the Barotse Teak or mukusi (*Baikiaea plurijuga*), a handsome tree with dark green pinnate leaves, spikes of showy mauve flowers and velvety brown pods.

Almost as important is the Mukwa or Bloodwood (*Pterocarpus angolensis*), a deciduous tree whose yellow flowers appear before the leaves with flat, circular, winged fruit with a softly spiny centre, known to

children as monkeys' powder puffs. The muzauli (*Guibourtia coleosperma*) used to be highly esteemed for its burls but nearly all trees with burls have now been cut out. It is closely related to the mopane with dark green, paired, semilunar leaves and a glossy red-brown seed which dangles on a zigzag stalk from the open pod.

Fig. 7 (left) Mopani scrub on Pleistocene river-gravels west of Livingstone.

Other common trees include munyenye (*Amblygonocarpus andongensis*), one of the most attractive foliage trees with its grey-green bipinnate leaves and glossy brown

V   The view westwards
from the lip of the
Eastern Cataract,
Victoria Falls.

VI The Devil's Cataract,
  Victoria Falls.

VII View from the top of the
   Devil's Cataract.

VIII   The view eastwards from the Devil's Cataract;
Cataract Island is on the left.

Fig. 8 (centre) Baobab (*Adansonia digitata*) in mopane scrub.

Fig. 9 (right) Mukushi (*Baikiaea plurijuga*) in the Kalahari woodland.

or black four-sided pods; Zambezi Ash or museshe (*Burkea africana*) with bipinnate leaves and pendulous racemes of small white flowers; and mulamana (*Combretum collinum*) with simple oblong leaves and four-winged fruit. Also present is the mubako (*Erythrophleum africanum*), a close relative of the Ordeal Tree (*Erythrophleum suaveolens*) and containing the same mixture of poisonous alkaloids (the major one being cassaine) as that species, but in a less virulent form. (The poison was used by witch doctors in their

'Trials by Ordeal' and for murder.) Here too are the mulyambesu (*Crossopteryx febrifuga*) also called Ordeal Tree and used at one time in the Eastern Province of Zambia in the same way as *Erythrophleum*; the mungongo (*Ricinodendron rautanenii*) with its Balsa-weight wood, palmately divided leaves hoary below, and oily plum-like fruit; the mwande or Pod Mahogany (*Afzelia quanzensis*) with pinnate leaves, flowers with a single visible, broad pink petal and large black and red seeds used for curios in a thick black woody pod; and finally the muzwamaloa (*Xeroderris stuhlmannii*), resembling *Pterocarpus* but with white pea flowers and long flat grey pods with narrow marginal wings.

The miombo element is represented by three of the commoner *Brachystegia* species, mubombo (two of them) and mutuya, together with mwanza (*Julbernardia globiflora*).

The deciduous thicket or mutemwa which still occurs in places at the shrub level is composed largely of three of the more attractive shrubs of Kalahari woodland, isunde (*Baphia massaiensis ssp. obovata*) with creamy pea flowers and simple leaves; mupondopondo (*Bauhinia macrantha*) with large white flowers with crinkled petals and bifoliate leaves; and mulyanzovu (*Dalbergia martinii*), a scrambler or even a climber with pinnate leaves and small white pea flowers.

The attractive Crinum lily (*Crinum macowanii*) is dotted about beneath the trees and one may be lucky enough to see that other most surprising Amaryllid, *Pancratium trianthum*. Soon after the start of the rains, its large erect bell-shaped flowers pop open almost explosively and in rapid succession, dotting the veld with shining white. Unfortunately they wither in less than a day and one may consider oneself very fortunate to see them.

The remaining representatives of these most intriguing floras must be left to the visiting botanist to investigate. His search will not be a disappointing one and could easily be rewarded by the discovery of a species new to science.

Select Bibliography

BOUGHEY, A. S. 'The vegetation types of the Federation', *Proceedings Rhodesia Scientific Association,* xlv, 1957.

FANSHAWE, D. B. 'The vegetation of Zambia', *Forest Dept. Bulletin,* vii, 1969.

FANSHAWE, D. B. 'The vegetation of Kalomo District', *Forest Research Pamphlets,* xxxi, 1970.

FANSHAWE, D. B. 'The vegetation of Livingstone', *Forest Research Pamphlets,* xlii, 1972.

GIBBS, L. S. 'A contribution to the botany of Southern Rhodesia', *Journal Linnaean Society Botany,* xxxvii, 161, 1906.

HENKEL, J. S. 'Types of vegetation in Southern Rhodesia', *Proceedings Rhodesia Scientific Association,* xxx, 1930.

HUTCHINSON, J. *A Botanist in Southern Africa,* London, 1946.

MARTIN, J. D. 'The Baikiaea forests of Northern Rhodesia', *Empire Forestry Review,* xix, 1940.

OATES, F. *Matabeleland and the Victoria Falls,* London, 1881.

RATTRAY, J. M. 'Vegetation types of Southern Rhodesia', *Kirkia,* ii, 1961.

RENDLE, A. B. 'African notes II', *Journal Botany,* March–April–May, 1931.

TRAPNELL, C. G., MARTIN, J. D. and ALLAN W. *Memoir to the Vegetation Soil Map of Northern Rhodesia,* Lusaka, 1947.

WILD, H. 'A guide to the flora of the Victoria Falls' *in* B. M. Fagan (ed.), *The Victoria Falls,* Livingstone, 1964.

CHAPTER 11

The Mammals

Reay H. N. Smithers
revised by W. F. H. Ansell

Since the publication of the first edition of this guide there has arisen in Africa a growing realisation of the value of wildlife as a natural resource. Many more National Parks, Game Reserves and other areas have been specifically set aside where, with proper control and management, wildlife should continue to flourish. There are heartening signs that, with the recognition of wildlife's economic value in controlled hunting and as a source of protein, its future survival in at least some other areas is also assured.

From the tourist's point of view, it is fortunate that it has been possible to set aside areas in the immediate vicinity of the Victoria Falls where may be seen a substantial cross-section of the wildlife that occurs in this part of Africa. On the Zambian side of the Zambezi the Mosi-oa-Tunya National Park was created primarily to preserve as intact as possible the Falls and their environs, the gorges below and the riverine area above. Within the Mosi-oa-Tunya National Park there is an enclosed zoological park of approximately 10 square kilometres where the visitor can see a variety of large mammals, some of which, while occurring naturally in other parts of Zambia, are not indigenous to the vicinity of the Falls but have been imported from elsewhere. Among these have been wildebeest, puku, lechwe and giraffe. The giraffe, which in 1988 numbered about twenty, represent neither of the Zambian subspecies but are descended from animals imported from Zimbabwe many years ago. Some species, such as common duiker and bushbuck, were already in the area when it was fenced. For several years there were some White rhinoceros descended from animals imported from South Africa in 1963 but all but one were killed for their horns by a poacher in 1986, and the survivor subsequently also fell victim. The species may have been present at one time in south-western Zambia between the Zambezi and Mashi rivers, though this has never been definitely established, and it certainly never occurred in the rest of Zambia within the historical period. There were formerly enclosures inside the zoological park for lion, hyaena and other Carnivora but these have now been abandoned.

On the Zimbabwean side a similar situation prevails. The Victoria Falls National Park is a fine game viewing area, well worth a visit. Here, picnic and fishing sites have been opened and day camping is permitted. It is proposed in due course to consolidate the whole area including the Victoria Falls National Park through to the Hwange National park and west to the Botswana border as a single wildlife area, the long-term aim being eventually to upgrade this to National Parks standard.

In the country surrounding the Falls on both sides of the Zambezi many species of wildlife are found and even today wandering animals make their way to the immediate vicinity of the townships. There are elephant here which cross freely between the two banks of the river and to the islands above the Falls.

As a general rule, wild animals make off when approached but under certain circumstances they can become aggressive, and the visitor is warned not to interfere or provoke them in any way. The normally docile elephant, browsing peacefully by the roadside, may, without warning, become a screaming monster bent on destruction. Care should therefore be taken not to approach too closely. Accidents that have occurred have undoubtedly been due to the liberties taken by the visitor, and could easily have been avoided by the exercise of discretion.

African elephant (*Loxodonta africana*)

The elephant is probably the most imposing of all Africa's wonderful assemblage of animals. African elephants are larger than their Indian counterparts, averaging 3·2 metres high at the shoulder, compared with the Indian's at 2·8 metres; they have sloping foreheads, two-fingered tips to their trunks, much larger ears and saddle-like backs. Their poor eyesight and mediocre hearing is compensated for by their very keen sense of smell.

Elephant are regular visitors to the Victoria Falls on both sides of the river, small herds being resident. On the Zimbabwean side they have, in the past, penetrated as far as the Livingstone statue and the Rain Forest but today, with the growth of the Victoria Falls township and the greatly increased numbers of visitors, precautions are taken to prevent them penetrating so near to the Falls. They freely cross from either bank to the islands to feed on the fresh island vegetation, being particularly fond of the fruits of the vegetable ivory palm (*Hyphaene ventricosa*).

As the north-eastern parts of Botswana dry up, elephant seasonally move towards the Zambezi River west of the Falls and into the Hwange National Park further south, returning with the break of the rains. Comparison with the observations of F. C. Selous and other hunters and traders who visited the area in the second half of the nineteenth century leaves no doubt that, at least south of the Zambezi, there has been an increase in the numbers of elephant, and there is little danger that the elephant will be exterminated in this part of Africa. Control measures have in fact had to be exercised to retain numbers within the carrying capacity of their habitat.

Today the visitor is unlikely to see bulls carrying ivory over 30 kilograms in weight, the record for the Hwange area being 74·3 kilograms for a pair of tusks. Individuals with damaged tusks are sometimes encountered. They tend to be bad-tempered and should therefore be avoided.

The age to which elephants live in the wild is unknown. The period of gestation is approximately twenty-two months and a single birth is normal, though very rarely twins have been recorded. Calves may be born at intervals of between three and five years. The female has two teats which lie between the forelegs, and the calf suckles with its mouth like other mammals — not with the trunk as is sometimes supposed. Cows are more suspicious than bulls, probably owing to their responsibilities for protection of the calves, and cow herds with young may become aggressive with little provocation.

The size of the herd varies with the environment but, in the Victoria Falls area, the usual numbers are between six and thirty. Herds have a peculiar smell recognisable at a distance; the rumbling of their stomachs and the flapping of their ears are often audible over considerable distances. When moving and feeding, herds can be very noisy and at such times loud trumpeting and the squealing of the calves can frequently be heard. This cacophony ceases immediately the herd becomes suspicious, restarting again in unison, as if at a given signal, when the tension is relaxed. On the other hand they can move almost noiselessly and, in spite of their huge size, it is surprising how they can remain unseen in woodland areas, even at close range.

Elephant feed on a wide range of vegetation, but are discriminating feeders and will push over large trees for a few mouthfuls of succulent young leaves and twigs. In the Falls area they are fond of the fruit of the vegetable

Fig. 1 Elephant.

ivory palm and the mungongo (*Ricinodendron rautanenii*); the kernels of these fruits with their undigestible cover can commonly be seen in their droppings. From July to September they are often seen under camelthorn trees (*Acacia giraffae*) feeding on the nutritive grey seed pods. When they cannot reach the pods they may either shake or break off branches in order to bring them down. Elephant are also great diggers, uprooting certain trees for their roots, which probably supply them with essential nutrients. Overpopulation of elephants can have a devastating affect on their habitat. Within recent years the riverine forests of the Chobe and Zambezi rivers west of the Falls have suffered severely in this respect.

Elephant move and feed at night and in the cooler hours of the day; during the hottest midday hours they stand under shady trees. While they dislike negotiating steep downward slopes they will, without hesitation, struggle up steep rising banks. Their feet are very elastic and expand on being placed on the ground, contracting again when lifted. This enables them to cross muddy areas with ease. The under-surfaces of the feet are cracked and fresh spoor shows this feature very clearly. Elephant are rarely seen to lie down, although they wallow freely in mud. They also make great use of dust-baths, blowing the fine dust with their trunks over their backs and between their legs, just as they will spray themselves with water while drinking. It is estimated that a thirsty elephant drinks between 180 and 250 litres at a time.

If you meet elephant while motoring, keep inside your car and they will probably take little notice of you. If they do become inquisitive and approach unpleasantly close, move away or, if you get hemmed in, bang lustily on the outside panel of the door and shout. Do not blow your horn or unduly race the engine as this is apt to annoy them. If you are on foot, keep down-wind and well away from them.

Hippopotamus (*Hippopotamus amphibius*)

Hippopotamus are becoming increasingly scarce in the Zambezi between the Falls and Kazungula. They may still be seen in the vicinity of Princess Christian, King George VI and Kandahar Islands and as near the brink of the Falls as Cataract and Livingstone Islands. Normally they are careful not to approach too close to the edge of the Falls, but there are records of occasional individuals being swept over, *post mortem* examination of which showed no signs of previous wounding or disease. Hippopotamus are not recorded from the Gorge area below the Falls, no doubt because of the absence from the banks of the grasses which form their favourite food, and

also because of their dislike of the strong rush of water.

Hippo feed at night and are rarely seen out of the water during the day. They may be seen after dark on the main road near the measuring post on the Zambian side of the river. In drier areas they are capable of long journeys overland in search of food which, in the absence of the more succulent types found along river banks, consists of drier grasses. They are great raiders of mealie lands, and clear evidence of their maraudings are their large four-toed spoor and the remains of vegetation torn up by the roots.

The male hippo is darker than the female and broader in the forehead. When seen in the water their bodies are a rich brown or dark brownish-grey colour with a distinct pinkish tinge. As they emerge from the water the surface glands may be clearly seen standing out as dark spots on the surface of the skin. Although capable of long submersion, they must come to the surface to breathe. When they break surface, the blast accompanying the expulsion of air from their lungs is audible over long distances, as is their mooing grunt which is frequently heard along the river towards evening or in the early morning.

Few visitors see more of the hippopotamus than its nostrils, eyes and ears protruding from the water, the ears pricked well forward in the direction of the disturbance, and the swirling ripple that follows their submergence. During the day, however, they may be seen huddled together, usually on a sand bank in the middle of a large pool, sunning themselves half submerged, when their vast bulk may better be appreciated.

Normally docile, though inquisitive, hippopotamus may become aggressive, males especially at the mating period (about August or September) and females when they have calves, and they have been known to attack river craft without provocation. This is no doubt often due to previous wounding or interference or to their having young. Their inquisitiveness often leads to their investigating camp fires situated near their river haunts at night, but they are normally easily dissuaded from this unpleasant habit by loud noises.

Adult hippopotamus grow to over 3·6 metres from the tip of their nostrils to the base of their tail, up to 1·8 metres high at the shoulder, and they can weigh at least 3 tonnes. Shooting of these animals cannot be considered sporting as they may be approached very closely from the bank, but their palatable meat is eagerly sought after, and the hide, which is up to 45 millimetres thick on the back and shoulders, is in demand for the manufacture of *sjamboks*.

Giraffe (*Giraffa camelopardalis*)

Attaining a height of up to 5 metres, the giraffe is the tallest of all mammals. With its peculiar body-shape and gait it is a favourite subject for the animal photographer. There are a few in the Victoria Falls National Park on the south bank and in the Mosi-oa-Tunya Zoological Park, although they do not occur naturally in the Falls area on the Zambian side. Old bulls have chocolate-brown or almost black patches on their coats, whereas the females and young are lighter, the latter almost light brown. On breaking into a run, giraffe have a curious habit of swinging their tails in a rotary movement.

Despite their size, giraffe, with their dazzle camouflage, are difficult to pick out among the *Acacia* trees, on the tender shoots of which they feed. Both sexes have horns covered with skin, with a bony cap at the extremity.

Formerly much sought after by hunters for their skins which furnished the requisite length of hide for the lash of wagon whips, they were ridden down on horseback and shot from the saddle. Apart from man the lion is the only significant predator on giraffe, but their range of vision and ability to defend themselves with their powerful forelimbs affords a good degree of protection for adults.

Buffalo (*Syncerus caffer*)

Buffalo may be seen in the Victoria Falls National Park on the Zimbabwean bank and in the Mosi-oa-Tunya Zoological Park, and there are still a few to be seen in the country around the Falls. Thomas Baines, who visited the Victoria Falls in 1862, reported large herds and one of his paintings (reproduced as colour plate XII of this book) depicts a herd driven by hunters right to the edge of the Rain Forest. Buffalo are like cattle in their habits, being grazers never found far from water, which they drink twice or more during the day. They enjoy mud-baths, which help them to get rid of ticks and other parasites. In colour generally reddish or brown, buffalo darken with age, old bulls and some females being almost entirely black. Buffalo are frequently preyed on by lions, though this would not apply today in the immediate vicinity of the Falls where lions are only infrequent visitors.

Buffalo are naturally inquisitive and will approach the object of their curiosity with nose well forward and head raised, but they rarely attack unless wounded, when they become aggressive and clever adversaries. An inquisitive herd may approach a car at a fast trot, but they stop dead a few metres away, turn off and continue out of the way, or stand

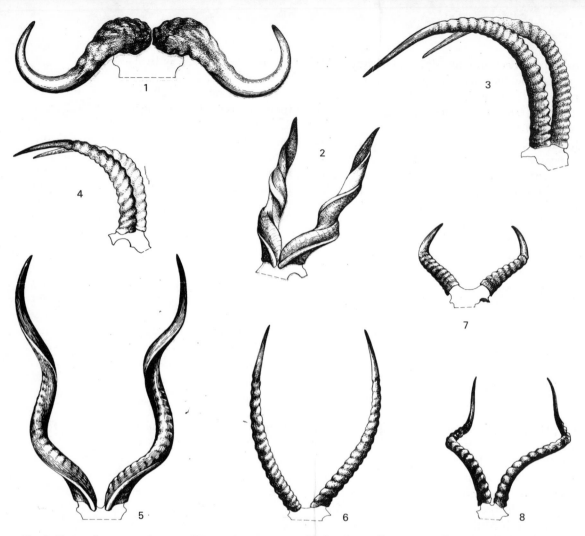

Fig. 2 Horns of game species: 1 Buffalo. 2 Eland.
3 Sable. 4 Roan. 5 Kudu. 6 Waterbuck. 7 Tsessebe.
8 Impala.

and stare with their heads raised, nostrils
testing the air.

Eland (*Taurotragus oryx*)

Eland, like buffalo, are now scarce in the
immediate vicinity of the Falls, not being
recorded within recent years on the Zambian
side except in the Mosi-oa-Tunya Zoological
Park, but there is still a small herd near
Kazungula and Westwood on the Zimbabwean side of the river. Eland are the largest of
the African antelopes, standing up to 1·8
metres high at the shoulders, and were much
sought after by the early hunters on account
of their palatable meat and useful fat. The
subspecies *Taurotragus oryx livingstonei* was
first described from Sikosi village on the
Zambian side of the Zambezi River approximately 200 kilometres above Livingstone.
Eland are not so inclined to stampede as other

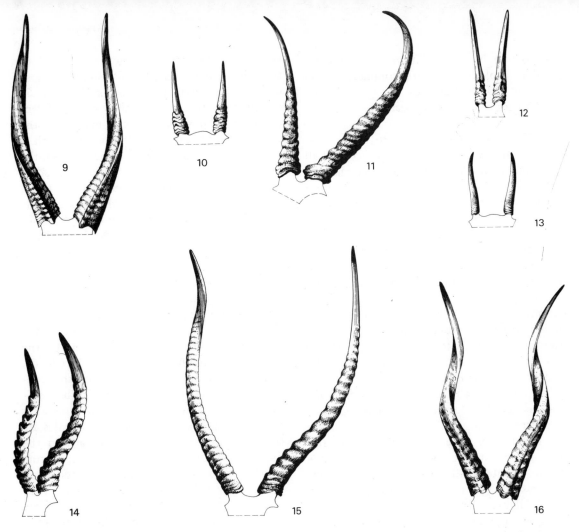

Fig. 3 Horns of game species: 9 Bushbuck.
10 Klipspringer. 11 Reedbuck. 12 Common Duiker.
13 Steenbok. 14 Puku. 15 Lechwe. 16 Sitatunga.

antelopes but move off, first with a series of bounds and later at a lumbering trot.

Both males and females are horned, the female's horns being lighter and longer than the male's and usually not as straight and even in shape. The horns are used with twisting motion to break down the branches of the browse on which they feed. Both sexes are tawny in colour and have a large dewlap. Adult bulls have a large tuft of dark hair on the forehead between the horns. The tufted tail reaches to the hocks.

Eland prefer bush or thinly wooded country and shun open plains. Herds, which in some places may be very large, are made up of males, females and young, though smaller groups are also found as well as solitary animals. Their senses are acute and they can detect slight movements at a great distance. While they are docile animals who rarely

137

show the slightest inclination to become aggressive, broken horns are common among the bulls, no doubt relics of fights among them during the breeding season.

Sable antelope (*Hippotragus niger*)

Very fine herds of this most magnificent of all our antelope may be seen in the Victoria Falls National Park but, although they were found in the Livingstone District until a few years ago, they are rarely seen there today except in the Mosi-oa-Tunya Zoological Park. The scimitar-shaped horns of the adult bulls sweep to their shoulders and attain lengths of up to about 130 centimetres, the world record being 154 centimetres. The jet-black colour of the adult males and their stately bearing are in harmony with their courageous nature. The visitor who is fortunate enough to see this keen and wary animal cannot but be struck by its noble bearing.

The adult sable is one of the few antelope that can stand up to and, with some certainty of success, fight a full-grown lion; they are also a match for a leopard. There is normally one adult bull to the herd and this position is bloodily contested. Immature bulls and cows, who also carry horns, are a rich brown in colour, lighter than the adults. Cows darken with age and in some cases their colouring approaches the dark brown or black of the adult bulls. Adults stand about 1·3 metres high at the shoulder, the back apparently sloping steeply to the hind-quarters – an illusion caused by the pronounced and vertically standing mane. Bulls may be in small groups, or solitary.

Roan antelope (*Hippotragus equinus*)

A close relative of the sable, the roan antelope, although slightly larger, cannot compare with it in beauty, its rufous grey colour being less striking and its horns, although of the same general scimitar-like shape as those of the sable, seldom reaching a length of 60 centimetres. It is nevertheless a magnificent antelope with striking facial markings, the whole of the muzzle being white, with a white eye tuft and a dark bridge between the muzzle and the eyes. They move in small herds, adult bulls often being found alone. They are no longer found on the Zambian side but the visitor may be lucky enough to see them in the Victoria Falls National Park, although they are now rare.

Kudu (*Tragelaphus strepsiceros*)

Kudu are very common in the area and in the early morning or late evening may be seen feeding in the vicinity of the Big Tree on the Zimbabwean side of the Zambezi and on the immediate outskirts of the township lands. They are now infrequently seen on the Zambian side. The males alone carry the well-known corkscrew-like horns. In the alert position noticeable features of the females are the large ears which point forward in the direction of the disturbance and twitch from side to side trying to pick up its exact location. Grey-brown in colour, washed with a bluish grey, and with nine or ten narrow vertical stripes on the back, kudu are relatively large antelopes, adults standing up to 1·5 metres at the shoulders.

Kudu flourish in a wide variety of habitats, from well-watered country to semi-desert, but in general they are seldom found far from water. They wander in small herds; bulls, without females, frequently congregate in herds of up to five or more individuals.

Waterbuck (*Kobus ellipsiprymnus*)

Until recently waterbuck were common visitors to the Rain Forest, but they have not been seen there for some time. They are, however, present within approximately eight kilometres of the Falls on both banks of the Zambezi. Only the males carry horns, which sweep back at the base and then curve forwards to their smooth tips. When brought to bay the waterbuck can be a desperate adversary which sweeps and lunges with its horns.

As their name implies, waterbuck are partial to the neighbourhood of water, but they resort at will to the stony hills and thick coverts up to 2 kilometres or so away. They feed entirely on grass and run in small herds. At a distance they look dark in colour, but closer examination shows that the shaggy coat is grizzled brown or grey-black with a distinct white elliptical ring on the rump.

Tsessebe (*Damaliscus lunatus*)

While these antelope have not been recorded recently from the Falls area they probably make their way into it on the Zimbabwean side from time to time. Standing about 1·2 metres at the shoulder, they appear at a distance to be dark in colour but they actually have a rich chestnut coat which, when seen at close quarters, has a distinct sheen. The horns are small for the size of the animal and are carried by both sexes. They incline obliquely upwards and outwards then bend upwards and further outwards in a smooth curve, the short smooth points inclining inwards at the tips. With their pronouncedly high humped shoulders and low hindquarters, tsessebe are relatively easy to distinguish. Fleet of foot and possessing great endurance, tsessebe are inquisitive, which probably explains why they have been largely shot out in certain districts.

Impala (*Aepyceros melampus*)

Impala can be seen both in the Victoria Falls

Fig. 4 Waterbuck.

National Park and in the Mosi-oa-Tunya Zoological Park. They move in troops of from a few individuals to upwards of two hundred. The males alone carry the slender lyre-shaped horns. The short glossy hair is uniformly foxy red on the upper parts, white on the belly, with black tips to the ears, a black stripe down the tail and crescentic black stripes on the buttocks and thighs. The name *melampus* refers to the black-haired glandular tufts situated above their hind hoofs.

Standing some 90 centimetres at the shoulder, the slender-legged impala is a particularly graceful antelope and it is a wonderful sight to see a troop streaking through the bush in a red line, individuals bounding over low bushes or imaginary obstacles in their path. Of the medium-sized antelopes they are the fleetest of foot over a short distance and, when thoroughly alarmed, they crouch low in their tracks and perform astonishing feats of leaping. They water several times a day and are partial to *mopane* woodland and sandy bush country.

Bushbuck (*Tragelaphus scriptus*)

Bushbuck are common in the Falls area on both sides of the river, occurring in the Rain Forest and in the riverine underbush; the visitor who does not see one can count himself unlucky. The males are generally darker in colour than the females, which are reddish brown with three or four narrow vertical white body stripes interspersed with white spots. Only the males carry horns which are roughly parallel and each has a spiral half twist. During the day bushbuck lie up in the dense bush, coming into the open to feed in the evening and early morning. If disturbed they dive, with a loud warning bark, for the cover of the bush. Bushbuck are usually solitary but may associate in loose groups of up to six. The bushbuck is a medium-sized antelope, the adults standing some 90 centimetres at the shoulder.

Klipspringer (*Oreotragus oreotragus*)

Klipspringer are found in the rock kopjes downstream of the Falls and come out on to the grassy areas in the vicinity of these in the evening and early morning to feed. They are, however, seldom seen. The horns, present only in the male, rise vertically to a height of about 10 centimetres above the eyes and are short and spike-shaped with a slight forward curvature.

Klipspringer differ from other antelopes in their coarse pithy hair and their very narrow

cylindrical hoofs, only the tips of which touch the ground. They are quite at ease leaping from pinnacle to pinnacle of the rocks and, with their four feet closely together, can stand balanced on an area not much larger than the palm of one's hand.

Their characteristic speckled appearance at close range is due to the colour of the hair, which is white at the base, grading to olive grey tipped with golden yellow. Standing 60 centimetres high at the shoulder, the klipspringer is a small antelope, the females being smaller than the males.

Zebra (*Equus burchelli*)

Zebra are uncommon in the area but may be seen on the southern bank upriver from the Falls and in the area of the gorges below them, particularly near the Masui-Zambezi confluence.

Reedbuck (*Redunca arundinum*)

Reedbuck may be seen in the vlei areas of the Victoria Falls National Park but have not been seen on the Zambian side in recent years. Ashy brown in colour with light belly and throat and with an ochre-brown head, they stand about 90 centimetres at the shoulder. The horns, carried only by the males, are up to 40 centimetres in length in adults and curl regularly forward from the head. When disturbed, reedbuck whistle loudly, march boldly off a few steps, whistle again looking in the direction of the cause of alarm, then bound away. While they usually associate in pairs, small herds of four to six are sometimes seen.

Duiker (*Sylvicapra grimmia*)

This small antelope, standing some 60 centimetres at the shoulder, is an even reddish brown or greyish fawn in colour; the males

alone carry straight horns which rise at an obtuse angle to the face. Duiker are still common around the Victoria Falls and may sometimes be seen in the vicinity of the Rain Forest where, in the early morning, pairs are usually found feeding on leaves of shrubs or annual plants.

Steenbok (*Raphicerus campestris*)

Slightly smaller than the duiker, the steenbok stands 50 centimetres at the shoulder. The males alone carry the short, straight, nearly parallel horns which, rising from close behind the eyes, are much more widely spaced and more slender than those of the duiker. The horns seldom attain a length of more than 10

Fig. 5 Zebra.

centimetres. The steenbok of the Falls area is an even rich reddish colour with white underparts; its legs lack the black frontal markings of the duiker.

Steenbok are grazers, partial to open flat country and thin forest. They appear to be independent of water. They lie tightly in thick grass, springing up at one's feet and running swiftly for a few hundred metres before stopping to look round at the cause of the disturbance. When on the run they may often be brought to a standstill by a sharp whistle. They have a habit of scratching up the ground with their hoofs, especially in the

141

spot where they deposit their droppings. Though occurring in south-western Zambia, the steenbok has not been recorded from the north bank anywhere near the Victoria Falls.

Sharpe's grysbok (*Raphicerus sharpei*)

This species and the steenbok are very often confused. Sharpe's grysbok occurs on both sides of the Zambezi and is indeed commoner in the area than the steenbok. It has shorter legs and an arched back; the hindquarters are 'tucked in' and appear higher than the forequarters. Only the males carry horns, which are straight and widely spaced, but shorter and blunter than the steenbok's. The coat is grizzled reddish with an admixture of white hairs.

When disturbed, grysbok crouch low to race off through the grass or underbush in a smooth run without bounding. They are often flushed from the dry thickets bordering the riverine forest.

Warthog (*Phacochoerus aethiopicus*)

This quaint animal is invariably a source of amusement to visitors, rushing off when disturbed with its tail firmly held in a vertical position, the brush of bristles at the end waving bravely like a small flag. Warthogs live in deserted antbear holes which they enter backwards, a feat which they can perform at a high rate of speed. They love a mudbath and are seldom found far from water.

It is unfortunate that there are not more in the vicinity of the Falls, but they are still common on the southern bank between the Falls and Kazungula and may often be seen between the Rest Camp and the entrance to the Victoria Falls National Park. They have not recently been recorded on the Zambian side outside the Mosi-oa-Tunya Zoological Park.

The general colour of the warthog is brownish grey. It is armed with two pairs of tusks, the larger of which, rising from the upper jaw, is coated with enamel at the tips only. An upward slash from these tusks can inflict an ugly wound.

Bushpig (*Potamocherus porcus*)

The bushpig is relatively common in the Falls area, occurring on both banks as well as on the islands, but it is rarely seen as it is a nocturnal animal and lies up during the day in thick grass and other dense cover. They are most destructive animals in cultivated lands, trampling down more than they eat.

In colour dark reddish grey, with a distinct ridge of long hair along the top of the shoulders, the bushpig lacks the prominent tusks of the warthog. Their ears terminate in tufts of long hair. They are generally found in 'sounders' of four to six and stand approximately 75 centimetres at the shoulder. Fleet of foot and expert swimmers, bushpig are reputed to be among the pluckiest of animals; even the leopard will hesitate to attack an adult.

Lion (*Panthera leo*)

Lion may be seen in the Victoria Falls National Park on the southern side of the river and occasionally wander into the Falls area on the Zambian side; they have even been reported fairly recently from the outskirts of Livingstone. They are too well known to require description, yet while many have heard their impressive roaring, fewer have seen these animals which dislike man's presence and normally make off on his approach. They are, however, quite unafraid of motor cars, probably unaware that their traditional enemies are inside. If care is exercised to keep downwind, they can be approached and observed from cars at quite close range. Two, three or four lions are more frequently met than single individuals, and they often band together in larger prides for mutual assistance in hunting. They drink at least once daily, more frequently in hot weather, and when a kill is made near water they may drink frequently during the meal.

Lions occasionally climb trees and they can move great distances, up to thirty kilometres and more, in the hours of darkness. During the heat of the day they lie up in a shady spot.

Leopard (*Panthera pardus*)

Occasionally seen at night in the lights of the car, leopards are quite common in the Falls gorges and along the southern river bank upstream of the Big Tree; they roam at night over a large area in search of food. Two to three metres in overall length and weighing upwards of 40 kilograms, leopards are predators on wild pig and baboons, both of which can be very destructive to growing crops. Their normal food consists of small antelope, baboons, monkeys, wild pig and rock rabbits.

Cheetah (*Acinonyx jubatus*)

Even at a distance, the cheetah is easily distinguished from the leopard by its longer legs and smaller head. It has a tawny coat covered with black spots varying in size from one to three centimetres across and a very distinct black 'tear' mark from the eye to the back of the lips. Although comparatively rare in the vicinity of the Victoria Falls, they are occasionally seen in the Victoria Falls National Park on the southern side of the river.

Cheetah are not strictly nocturnal and may be found on the move during the hottest hours of the day. They live mainly on small antelope but have been known to tackle and kill kudu. Cheetah are very fleet of foot but have no great stamina and are not aggressive. Unlike other members of the cat family, they are unable to withdraw their claws completely into the protecting sheaths.

Chacma baboon (*Papio ursinus*)

Baboons abound in the area, where they have become very tame. They move in troops, each controlled by an old male who forages rather apart from them, but always with a watchful eye for their welfare. These animals will be seen by all visitors to the Victoria Falls. It has been necessary to exercise control measures on the adults as they have become increasingly familiar and will snatch parcels or other accoutrements from visitors in the hope that they contain something to eat. They will clamber on to cars in the carparks and poke their heads and hands through the windows for titbits. The amusing and human-like antics of the troops are entertaining to watch, but care should be exercised not to give them too much encouragement as they quickly become an unmitigated nuisance. Provided the pedestrian is not carrying anything that looks as if it might contain foodstuffs he is unlikely to be troubled. Their barking may be heard any morning or evening in the Falls area.

Vervet monkey (*Cercopithecus aethiops*)

The vervet, or black-faced monkey as it is sometimes called, is more timid than the baboon and may be seen in the trees along the river, especially in the gorges and along Riverside Drive on the Zambian bank, swinging from one tree to another or peering inquisitively at the visitor from a safe retreat on a high branch. These monkeys go in troops like the baboon and may be heard chattering among themselves as they search for food,

Fig. 6 Vervet monkey, male (right) and female.

which consists predominantly of wild fruits and berries.

Nightape (*Galago moholi*)

The nightape is a beautiful little grey lemur, about 15 centimetres in body length, with a bushy tail slightly longer than its body. It is nocturnal and only becomes active after sundown. Common in the trees on the river banks, nightapes sleep during the day in holes in tree trunks or in forked branches. Although largely insectivorous, they also feed on vegetable matter, fruit and berries. They are unlikely to be seen by many visitors.

Clawless otter (*Aonyx capensis*)

The clawless otter is common in the area and, although predominantly nocturnal, may sometimes be seen during the day near Prin-

cess Christian Island and the Maramba River mouth. It feeds mainly on fish and crabs, but occasionally takes wild duck and other water birds. About 1·2 metres long and brown in colour with a pure white chin and throat, the streamlined shape of the otter is well adapted to its aquatic environment, and it swims both on the surface and underwater with remarkable speed.

Spottednecked otter (*Lutra maculicollis*)

Although this species has not been recorded in the immediate vicinity of the Falls, it does occur up-river and may possibly be present here. It is smaller than the clawless otter, up to about 1 metre in overall length, more slimly built, and has webbed back feet which are equipped with claws. The spotted underparts of the neck are a characteristic feature.

Other mammals

There are many other species in the Victoria

IX   The Third Gorge, looking eastwards.

X   David Livingstone's water-colour view,
     with measurements, of the Victoria Falls
     and Gorges, executed in August 1860.

XI   'The Falls at sunrise, with the ''Spray Cloud''
rising 1200 feet' by Thomas Baines (1863).

XII 'Herd of buffaloes driven
to the edge of the chasm'
by Thomas Baines (1863).

Falls area which the visitor may be fortunate enough to see. Many of these are, however, small in size or nocturnal and not normally seen. Some, such as the springhare (*Pedetes capensis*) whose eyes brilliantly reflect the lights of the car at night, one eye only being seen at a time like a lantern bobbing up and down as its kangaroo-like owner hops for cover, are nocturnal and seldom if ever seen during the day. Others, such as the yellow-spotted dassie (*Heterohyrax brucei*) may be seen in the hottest hours sunning themselves on the top of the rocks in the gorges or on the kopjes further downstream.

Among other nocturnal animals the ant-bear, *Orycteropus afer*, with its large hind-quarters and tapering snout; the porcupine (*Hystrix africaeaustralis*), which the visitor will have no difficulty in recognising by its armour of black and white quills; and the honey badger or ratel (*Mellivora capensis*), are worthy of note. It is possible that the night traveller may meet with a spotted hyaena (*Crocuta crocuta*); a sidestriped jackal (*Canis adustus*), about the size of a small dog with a bushy white-tipped tail; or the rusty-spotted genet (*Genetta rubignosa*), a small cat-like animal with a pointed muzzle and long ringed tail, which preys on small mammals and birds. The civet (*Viverra civetta*), which is less common and much larger than the genet, reaching a body length of some 90 centimetres, has a bushy tail and a black coat with indistinct white spots. It and the serval (*Felis serval*), are quite common in the area. The bat-eared fox (*Otocyon megalotis*) is a recent arrival in the Falls area on the southern side of the Zambezi, being first recorded at the Airport in 1970. It is now resident in the area but is unlikely to be seen except at night.

While rarely seen, the wild dog (*Lycaon pictus*), which roams in packs of some six to thirty individuals, occasionally visits the Victoria Falls area. Wild dog packs have a very large home range, though this is necessarily restricted when the females have young. Litters may number up to ten and more than one bitch may litter together, usually in deserted antbear holes. Wild dogs are not tolerated in cattle raising areas because of the damage they do to stock. They have traditionally also been looked upon as a menace to wild game, but in recent times have been accepted as a natural predator with a proper place in the ecosystem and accordingly are now protected in game reserves and national parks. Impala, reedbuck, and common duiker are among their favoured prey, but they may also kill larger species including wildebeest and rarely even sable antelope.

In the late evening the scrub hare (*Lepus saxatilis*) may be seen by the roadside. If the visitor is very fortunate he may see a caracal (*Felis caracal*) with its tufted ears, or a striped polecat (*Ictonyx striatus*) a small animal about 65 centimetres long with a very distinct long black and white coat and a bushy tail. When irritated, the striped polecat emits a most disgusting and penetrating odour from glands situated at the base of its tail, an act which can be performed at will. The African striped weasel (*Poecilogale albinucha*), a small, slender-bodied, short-legged and very uncommon species, has recently been recorded from the Falls area.

The slender mongoose (*Herpestes sanguineus*) is reddish grey with a black tuft on the end of its slender tail which it may erect when excited. It and the larger grey mongoose (*Herpestes ichneumon*) may frequently be seen scurrying across the road or through the undergrowth during daylight hours; but more commonly in the early morning or evening. The white-tailed mongoose (*Ichneumia albicauda) grey with a bushy tail and long-haired coat, and Selous' mongoose (*Paracynictus selousi*), similar to the white-tailed but smaller, rarely over 60 centimetres long, may both be seen after dark. The dwarf mongoose (*Helogale parvula*), a small dark brown animal barely 35 centimetres overall, which lives in troops of eight or more in deserted termite mounds, may be seen during the day, as may the bush squirrel (*Paraxerus cepapi*), which lives among rocks or on the larger trees, scampering about seeking the seeds, berries and insects on which it lives.

The area abounds in small rodents a few of which are worthy of mention, such as the red veld rat (*Aethomys chrysophilus*), a reddish coloured rat about 10 centimetres in body length with a tail of nearly equal length, and the gerbil (*Tatera leucogaster*), a reddish brown kangaroo-like rat with long hind and short front legs easily recognised from other small rats by the way it sits erect with its front legs extended horizontally. These gerbils live in families of up to twenty in extended warrens with many entrances, dug in the sandy soil which is common in the Falls area.

Neither of these rodents normally enter houses, the common household form in this area being the multimammate mouse (*Mastomys natalensis*), which breeds at a tremendous rate under favourable conditions. The pouched mouse (*Saccostomus campestris*), silky grey with a pure white belly, is met with in the sandy soil near the river. This beautiful mouse has cheek pouches and a very short tail, only a quarter the length of its body. The dwarf mouse (*Mus minutoides*) is, as the name implies, a very small form, the adults being barely 5 centimetres in body length. They are found under logs or in grain lands and are certainly one of the smallest known mammals. Another interesting rodent common in parts of the Falls area is the spiny mouse (*Acomys spinosissimus*) with its rich reddish-coloured coat composed of small spines instead of the soft fur normally associated with members of this group.

The aardwolf (*Proteles cristatus*), about the size of a large terrier dog, cream-coloured with side stripes and long hair, is occasionally seen by motorists on the roads south of the river in the vicinity of the Victoria Falls. This most interesting creature, in spite of its likeness to the jackal, feeds principally on termites. While it is equipped with formidable canine teeth, the molars are vestigial and it is doubtful if it could manage any more substantial diet. It is much less common on the Zambian side and has not so far been recorded in the vicinity of the Falls.

Select Bibliography

ANSELL, W. F. H. *The Mammals of Zambia*, Chilanga, 1978.
SMITHERS, R. H. N. *Land Mammals of Southern Africa*, Johannesburg, 1986.
STUART, C. and T. *Field Guide to the Mammals of Southern Africa*, London, 1988.

CHAPTER 12

The Birds

R. J. Dowsett

The aim of this chapter is first to describe the vegetation of the Victoria Falls area as it affects the distribution of birds, and then to list all the species known to occur, with some indication of where and when the bird-watcher is likely to find them. It is not possible to describe here what the birds themselves look like, and there are in fact several books available which will be useful for field identification, notably *Roberts' Birds of South Africa* by McLachlan and Liversidge (1970).

The area covered by this account consists of the Victoria Falls National Park in Zimbabwe (which covers about five hundred and fifty square kilometres) and the Mosi-oa-Tunya National Park in Zambia (about seventy square kilometres). I also include the town of Livingstone and Dambwa Forest Reserve on its northern edge, as being areas in which the visitor is likely to see birds. These areas are shown in maps on pp. 220–1.

Previous accounts of the birds of the Victoria Falls area have been given by Holliday (1964) and Winterbottom (1952) – full details of the books and papers referred to will be found in the bibliography at the end of this chapter. In addition, the birds of the Victoria Falls National Park in Zimbabwe have been catalogued provisionally by Jensen (1966). Both Mr C. W. Benson and I have lived in Livingstone, and have been able to collect or catch for ringing a large number of birds in the area. Mr M. P. Stuart Irwin and others have similarly studied the birds of the Zimbabwean side of the Zambezi, although much of their information is at present unpublished and not used here.

Thus it is now possible to present a far more complete and accurate account of the birds of the Victoria Falls area than hitherto. Doubtless some other species remain to be found, especially migrants, and I would welcome details from visitors of interesting species seen. There are specimens at Livingstone Museum of most of the species which occur in the area.

In this chapter frequent mention is made of the rains and the dry season. The rains in this area last mainly from December to March, and at this time grass is long, foliage luxuriant and there is much insect life. Although a few ground-nesting birds are forced to leave the area during the rains, this is more than compensated for by the arrival of many Eurasian migrants (notably swallows and warblers) and many intra-African migrants (most conspicuous being the cuckoos). In the dry season on the other hand most of the grass is burnt by fires and water levels drop considerably. Many of the trees, particularly the mopane, drop their leaves. The number of bird species present in the area in the dry season is considerably less than in the rains.

In the accounts that follow I have attempted to give an idea of the habitat in which a species is most likely to be found; for a more detailed ecological discussion of Zambian birds one should see *The Birds of Zambia* by Benson *et al.* (1971). Similarly, such terms as 'common' or 'uncommon' cannot cover all eventualities. 'Common' implies that a species is numerous in a suitable habitat and likely to be seen by a visitor. 'Uncommon' means that a bird is usually thin on the ground, and may or may not be found. In addition many birds may be 'local', that is to say that they occur in only a few areas and not necessarily wherever there is a suitable habitat.

The Bird Habitats

The occurrence of most species of bird is determined by the *structure* of the habitat,

rarely by the species of vegetation that are present. Some birds, such as the Palm Swift (*Cypsiurus parvus*), are often confined to one kind of tree, but this is very much the exception rather than the rule. Where a bird feeds in the mid-storey, for example, of trees with a canopy, it usually matters little whether it is in miombo woodland or *Baikiaea* (Teak) forest, although botanically there are some striking differences between the two habitats. An ornithologist does not usually need to know the species of plant which occur in an area, to know what birds to expect – a glance at the structure of the habitat is sufficient.

So although there are detailed chapters in this book on the vegetation and geology of the Falls area, the habitats must be explained in rather different terms for the person interested in birds. I therefore feel we should recognise here seven types of bird habitat:

1 Rocks.
2 Water.
3 Grassland.
4 Riparian.
5 Miombo woodland.
6 Mopane woodland.
7 Scrub.

I will describe these habitats, and the more common or interesting birds likely to be found in them.

Rocks

The rocks in the Zambezi above and below the Falls, the basalt gorges and their rocky surrounds, are important to few birds, but those that do occur are interesting.

In the gorges the rare Taita Falcon (*Falco fasciinucha*) breeds on precipitous rock faces, as may do the Black Stork (*Ciconia nigra*), Black Eagle (*Aquila verreauxi*), Augur

Buzzard (*Buteo rufofuscus*) and Peregrine Falcon (*Falco peregrinus*). The Taita Falcon is now known to occur widely in eastern Africa in rocky areas. Although it is listed in the *Red Data Book* of endangered species it is in fact merely thin on the ground by the specialised nature of its habitat and, except in the Victoria Falls area, rarely seen. A bird which is confined to cliff faces is the beautiful Mocking Chat (*Thamnolaea cinnamomeiventris*), which is most readily seen at Fifth Gorge on the Zambian side. Two species of swift nest in holes in the cliff faces – the African Black (*Apus barbatus*) and the Little Swift (*A. affinis*) – as do numerous Rock Martins (*Hirundo fuligula*).

On rocks in water one may see the Long-tailed Wagtail (*Motacilla clara*) – often right in the spray of the Falls. In the dry season large numbers of White-collared Pratincoles (*Glareola nuchalis*) may be seen nesting on rocks on the lip of the Falls, uncovered by the low water level.

Water

The Zambezi River in the Victoria Falls area does not support large numbers of water birds, mainly because the extensive and secluded marshes needed by ducks, geese, herons and egrets are generally lacking. The visitor is most likely to see a few Egyptian Geese (*Alopochen aegyptiaca*), White-crowned Plover (*Vanellus albiceps*), White-fronted Sandplover (*Charadrius marginatus*), Water Dikkop (*Burhinus vermiculatus*), Skimmer (*Rynchops flavirostris*), Reed Cormorant (*Phalacrocorax africanus*) and Pied Kingfisher (*Ceryle rudis*). On the quieter backwaters of the Zambezi and its tributaries the skulking Peters's Finfoot (*Podica senegalensis*) may be seen, and there White-fronted Bee-eaters (*Merops bullockoides*) are common.

Grassland

Open grasslands are rather lacking in the area, although there are a few along streams in the Victoria Falls National Park, and in the Mosi-oa-Tunya Zoological Park. *Dambos*, vleis and pans (usually all called *dambos* in this chapter) are drainage lines in woodland, grasslands through which a stream flows. Here can be found Pink-breasted Longclaws (*Macronyx ameliae*), Quail Finches (*Ortygospiza atricollis*) and several species of weaver, and one should look out for the Black Coucal (*Centropus grillii*) during the rains. Such grassland, on the edge of woodland, is often very profitable for the bird watcher, with a great number of species occurring.

Riparian

Riparian or riverine forest simply means the tall trees and thick undergrowth that occur along the banks of the Zambezi and its tributaries. A number of interesting birds can be found here, although many are skulking and patience is needed to obtain good views. Especially interesting are the Morning Warbler (*Cichladusa arquata*), the Nicator (*Nicator chloris*) and the Coppery Sunbird (*Nectarinia cuprea*), all birds that are very local in distribution in southern Africa. Look carefully too for the Blue-mantled Flycatcher (*Trochocercus cyanomelas*) which has recently been reported seen on the south bank of the Zambezi.

Especially conspicuous in this habitat are the noisy Trumpeter Hornbill (*Bycanistes bucinator*) and the Knysna Loerie (*Tauraco persa*), both of which are likely to be seen in the forest and palm grove around the Falls. In some areas large trees of *Acacia albida* occur near the Zambezi, and here one should look for Burnt-necked Eremomelas (*Ere-*

momela usticollis) and Black-cheeked Love-birds (*Agapornis lilianae*).

Miombo Woodland

This is a local name which refers to the *Brachystegia* deciduous woodlands of central Africa. In the Victoria Falls area much of such woodland is the result of Teak trees in the *Baikiaea* forests being cut down, and the undergrowth thinning out. But even the *Baikiaea* forests contain much the same species of bird as miombo woodland, and so for our purposes can be considered under this same heading. Perhaps the best area for birds is Dambwa Forest Reserve on the northern edge of Livingstone, which is partly *Baikiaea* and partly miombo woodland. Specialities to look out for here include the Red-crested Korhaan (*Eupodotis ruficrista*), Bradfield's Hornbill (*Tockus bradfieldi*), two closely related species of Pied Barbet (*Lybius frontatus* and *leucomelas*), the northern Grey Tit (*Parus griseiventris*), the Red-eyed Bulbul (*Pycnonotus nigricans*) (which occurs nowhere else in Zambia or Zimbabwe) and the Black-bellied Sunbird (*Nectarinia shelleyi*). During the rains Dambwa is the home of small numbers of the scarce Eurasian migrant the White-collared Flycatcher (*Muscicapa albicollis*).

Mopane Woodland

In the Victoria Falls area the mopane trees are generally of very small stature, and are to be found on rocky slopes and poorly-drained soils. There is a slight difference in the birds found in the two types of mopane; for example the Rock Bunting (*Emberiza tahapisi*) is abundant where there are rocks, but almost absent from mopane where rocks are lacking. There are a few species of bird which are confined to mopane woodland of some kind, such as the Double-banded Sand-grouse (*Pterocles bicinctus*), the Monotonous Lark (*Mirafra javanica*) and White-browed Sparrow-weaver (*Plocepasser mahali*). Some species, like the Black-cheeked Lovebird mentioned under the section on riparian forest, are confined to either mopane or *Acacia* woodland, being quite absent from miombo; but on the whole the birds of mopane woodland, especially those that make up the bird parties (mixed feeding flocks of several species), are the same species as can be found in miombo.

Scrub

Scrub is usually the result of degraded woodland, caused by axe and fire, but in some areas low *Acacia* bushes and in others fragmented dry thickets will be structurally similar. These habitats are often very rich in bird species and numbers, especially seed-eating birds. Species which are rather local in this part of Africa and which some bird watchers will be anxious to find include the Brown Firefinch (*Lagonosticta nitidula*), and the Shaft-tailed Whydah (*Vidua regia*) and its host the Violet-eared Waxbill (*Uraeginthus granatina*).

The list that follows documents the 385 species known to occur in the Victoria Falls area. A few species listed by Holliday (1964) and others, for which there is no definite proof that they occur in the area, are included in the list in parentheses.

In general, the Zambezi River above the Falls is not a barrier to bird distribution, and it may be assumed that the great majority of species listed below occur on both the Zambian (northern) and Zimbabwean (southern) sides of the river. As M. P. Stuart Irwin (*in litt.*) has pointed out, there are a number of striking differences in the bird populations of the north and south banks, but these are caused by vegetational differences and not by the river as a barrier. These differences warrant more detailed study, and in general are not discussed here.

Systematic List of the Birds of the Victoria Falls Area

Previous lists of the birds of all or part of the area of the Victoria Falls have been published by Winterbottom (1952), Holliday (1964) and Jensen (1966). The present list is based primarily on the records of C. W. Benson and myself during our residence in Livingstone, supplemented by the observations of some Zimbabwean ornithologists. As a result of our increased knowledge of the birds of this area, some of the records appearing in earlier lists are considered erroneous, and are here relegated to square brackets. Most of our identifications are based on specimens in the National Museum of Zambia at Livingstone and the Natural History Museum of Zimbabwe at Bulawayo, or on reliable sight records.

The English names in this list follow McLachlan and Liversidge (1970), while the Latin names follow Benson et al. (1971). Unless stated to the contrary a species may be assumed to occur in all months of the year. All the birds known from the area are described in various books, notably that by McLachlan and Liversidge, and so no attempt is made to describe them here.

Grebes: Podicipedidae
Dabchick (*Tachybaptus ruficollis*). Occasional on dams and pools.

Cormorants: Phalacrocoracidae
[White-breasted Cormorant (*Phalacrocorax carbo*). There have been a number of unconfirmed reports, most doubtless through confusion with the next species.]
Reed Cormorant (*P. africanus*). Common on any water.

Darters: Anhingidae
Darter (*Anhinga rufa*). Occasional on any water.

Herons, Egrets etc.: Ardeidae
[Bittern (*Botaurus stellaris*). Sound records mentioned by Holliday (1964) require confirmation.]
Little Bittern (*Ixobrychus minutus*). Occasional in reed beds.
Dwarf Bittern (*I. sturmii*). Occasional at pools and in *dambos* from December to April.
Night Heron (*Nycticorax nycticorax*). Occasional in reed beds.
White-backed Night Heron (*N. leuconotus*). Scarce, in forest along rivers.
Squacco Heron (*Ardeola ralloides*). Quite common in reeds by any water.
Cattle Egret (*A. ibis*). Quite common, especially with game animals or cattle. Most numerous during the rains.
Green-backed Heron (*Butorides striatus*). Common by any water with timbered banks, less often on *dambos*.
Rufous-bellied Heron (*B. rufiventris*). Rarely recorded, on *dambos*.
Black Heron (*Egretta ardesiaca*). Rarely recorded, by any water.
Great White Egret (*E. alba*). Frequent, by any water.
Yellow-billed Egret (*E. intermedia*). Occasional, by any water.
Little Egret (*E. garzetta*). Frequent, by any water.

Grey Heron (*Ardea cinerea*). Occasional, by any water.

Black-headed Heron (*A. melanocephala*). Occasional during the rains (once during the dry season), usually on dry land near water.

Goliath Heron (*A. goliath*). Occasional, usually on rivers.

Purple Heron (*A. purpurea*). Occasional, in reed beds.

Hamerkop: Scopidae

Hamerkop (*Scopus umbretta*). Quite common, by any water.

Storks: Ciconiidae

White Stork (*Ciconia ciconia*). Occasional on open grassland and fields, usually during the rains.

Black Stork (*C. nigra*). One or two occasional in the gorges, where they breed, notwithstanding the suggestion by Jensen (1966) that records may be in error.

White-bellied Stork (*C. abdimii*). Occasional, locally common, in open country during the rains.

Saddlebill (*Ephippiorhynchus senegalensis*). Occasional, usually in *dambos*.

Openbill (*Anastomus lamelligerus*). Frequent, by any water.

Marabou (*Leptoptilos crumeniferus*). Occasional, by any water.

Wood Stork (*Ibis ibis*). Occasional, usually on sand beaches on the Zambezi.

Ibises: Threskiornithidae

Sacred Ibis (*Threskiornis aethiopica*). Occasional, by any water.

Hadeda (*Bostrychia hagedash*). Quite common along wooded river banks.

Glossy Ibis (*Plegadis falcinellus*). According to Holliday (1964) this is a rare visitor to the area.

Spoonbill (*Platalea alba*). Occasional, usually on sand beaches on the Zambezi.

Ducks and Geese: Anatidae

Fulvous Whistling Duck (*Dendrocygna bicolor*). A few records during the rains.

White-faced Whistling Duck (*D. viduata*). Locally quite common by any water.

Egyptian Goose (*Alopochen aegyptiaca*). Not uncommon on the Zambezi.

Spurwing Goose (*Plectropterus gambensis*). Occasional by any water.

Knob-billed Duck (*Sarkidiornis melanotos*). Occasional by any water.

Pygmy Goose (*Nettapus auritus*). Locally quite common, especially in the rains, on lagoons and pools.

Black Duck (*Anas sparsa*). Scarce, confined usually to streams with wooded banks.

Yellow-billed Duck (*A. undulata*). Recorded in December in Victoria Falls National Park by Jensen (1965).

Red-bill Teal (*A. erythrorhynchos*). Occasional on dams and lagoons.

Hottentot Teal (*A. hottentota*). Occasional on dams and lagoons.

Red-eyed Pochard (*Netta erythrophthalma*). According to Holliday this species occurs rarely, and Jensen (1966) gives a December record from the Victoria Falls National Park.

White-backed Duck (*Thalassornis leuconotus*). Scarce, on lagoons.

Vultures, Eagles, Hawks etc.: Accipitridae

Lappet-faced Vulture (*Aegypius tracheliotus*). Not common, over open country.

White-headed Vulture (*Trigonoceps occipitalis*). Occasional, usually singly, over any country.

White-backed Vulture (*Gyps bengalensis*). Locally quite common on game or cattle carcasses.

Hooded Vulture (*Neophron monachus*). Local, in small numbers, at carcasses.

[Palm-nut Vulture (*Gypohierax angolensis*). Unlike Jensen (1966) I cannot accept the sight record by Mrs Alston, pending further substantiation.]

Pallid Harrier (*Circus macrourus*). Occasional over open grassland. A Eurasian migrant, present only during the rains.

Marsh Harrier (*C. aeruginosus*). Recorded over *dambo* and reed beds by Holliday (1964).

Gymnogene (*Polyboroides radiatus*). Occasional, usually in open woodland.

Bateleur (*Terathopius ecaudatus*). Quite common over any country.

Black-breasted Snake-eagle (*Circaetus pectoralis*). Occasional over rather open country, especially during the dry season.

Brown Snake-eagle (*C. cinereus*). Occasional in any woodland.

Banded Snake-eagle (*C. cinerascens*). Occasional, usually in trees near the Zambezi.

Black Sparrowhawk (*Accipiter melanoleucus*). Apparently sparse in Dambwa Forest Reserve.

[Ovambo Sparrowhawk (*A. ovampensis*). Reported by Holliday (1964) but requires confirmation, although likely to occur in woodland.]

African Goshawk (*A. tachiro*). Occasional, mainly in riparian woodland.

Little Banded Goshawk (*A. badius*). Quite common in any country, even within Livingstone.

Little Sparrowhawk (*A. minullus*). Occasional, in any woodland.

Dark Chanting Goshawk (*Melierax meta-*

Fig. 1 (top) Hamerkop.
Fig. 2 (centre) Saddlebill.
Fig. 3 (bottom) Egyptian Goose.

153

bates). Occasional in tree savanna.

Gabar Goshawk (*M. gabar*). Quite common in any woodland.

Lizard Buzzard (*Kaupifalco monogrammicus*). Quite common in woodland.

Augur (Jackal) Buzzard (*Buteo rufofuscus*). Regular in small numbers in the gorges, where it presumably breeds.

Steppe Buzzard (*B. buteo*). This Eurasian migrant occurs in small numbers in open country and on the edge of woodland during the rains.

Long-crested Eagle (*Lophaetus occipitalis*). Not uncommon in trees near water.

Martial Eagle (*Polemaetus bellicosus*). Occasional over rather open country.

African Hawk Eagle (*Hieraaetus spilogaster*). Rarely recorded, in open woodland.

Black Eagle (*Aquila verreauxi*). One or two seen occasionally in the gorges, where it may perhaps nest.

Tawny Eagle (*A. rapax*). Sparsely recorded in open country.

Lesser Spotted Eagle (*A. pomarina*). This Eurasian migrant passes over in small numbers during November.

Wahlberg's Eagle (*A. wahlbergi*). Quite common in woodland, but present only from September to March.

Fish Eagle (*Haliaeetus vocifer*). Common along the Zambezi and by other large areas of water.

Black Kite (*Milvus migrans migrans*). This Eurasian migrant is present in small numbers during the rains, often on roads.

Yellow-billed Kite (*M. migrans parasitus*). This intra-African migrant is common in woodland and near habitation between late July and early March.

Cuckoo Falcon (*Aviceda cuculoides*). Recorded from dry woodland near Livingstone (once breeding) and Victoria Falls, but apparently sparse.

Black-shouldered Kite (*Elanus caeruleus*). Occasional in tree savanna, especially during the dry season.

Bat Hawk (*Macheirhamphus alcinus*). Occasionally seen, but perhaps sparse, though easily overlooked.

Osprey: Pandionidae

Osprey (*Pandion haliaetus*). Single birds are seen from time to time on the Zambezi, and it may be expected to occur in any month.

Falcons: Falconidae

Lanner (*Falco biarmicus*). Occasional, over any country.

Peregrine (*F. peregrinus*). Sparsely recorded in the gorges, where it may perhaps nest.

Taita Falcon (*F. fasciinucha*). A few pairs breed in the gorges, and feeding birds wander as far as Livingstone on occasion.

African Hobby (*F. cuvierii*). A single specimen has been obtained in Dambwa Forest Reserve.

Hobby (*F. subbuteo*). This migrant from Eurasia is not uncommon in the rains, in light woodland or over open country.

Red-necked Falcon (*F. chicquera*). Sparse, usually near palms or in *Acacia*.

Dickinson's Kestrel (*F. dickinsoni*). Small numbers in the vicinity of palms, occasionally in woodland.

Western Red-footed Kestrel (*F. vespertinus*). Small numbers of this Eurasian migrant occur during the rains, as with the other migrant falcons often feeding on flying ants.

Eastern Red-footed Kestrel (*F. amurensis*). Similar to the last species, but usually more common.

Lesser Kestrel (*F. naumanni*). Another Eurasian falcon present in small numbers during the rains.

Francolins and Quails: Phasianidae
Coqui Francolin (*Francolinus coqui*). Locally quite common, usually in miombo woodland.
Crested Francolin (*F. sephaena*). Small numbers occur locally in riparian thicket.
Shelley's Francolin (*F. shelleyi*). Rather scarce, in rocky woodland.
Natal Francolin (*F. natalensis*). Small numbers, usually in riparian thicket.
Swainson's Francolin (*F. swainsonii*). Common in bush and scrub.
Harlequin Quail (*Coturnix delegorguei*). Not uncommon in damp grassland during the rains.
Blue Quail (*C. chinensis*). Sparse during the rains, usually in grassland in woodland.

Guinea-fowl: Numididae
Crowned Guinea-fowl (*Numida meleagris*). Locally common, especially along the Zambezi.

Button-quails: Turnicidae
Kurrichane Button-quail (*Turnix sylvatica*). Small numbers locally in rank grass.
Hottentot Button-quail (*T, hottentotta*). Occasional in wet grassland during the rains, when specimens have flown into buildings in Livingstone.

Cranes: Gruidae
Crowned Crane (*Balearica pavonina*). Occasionally seen, according to Holliday (1964).

Rails etc.: Rallidae
Corncrake (*Crex crex*). Small numbers in grassland during the rains. A migrant from

Fig. 4 (top) Fish Eagle.
Fig. 5 (bottom) Swainson's Francolin.

Eurasia.

African Crake (*C. egregia*). Locally common during the rains in wet grassland.

Black Crake (*Limnocorax flavirostris*). Quite common locally in reeds by water.

Buff-spotted Flufftail (*Sarothrura elegans*). Benson (1962) mentions one heard by Mitchell in forest by the Zambezi in March.

Lesser Moorhen (*Gallinula angulata*). Locally not uncommon during the rains by lagoons and pans.

Moorhen (*G. chloropus*). Very seldom seen, according to Holliday.

Purple Gallinule (*Porphyrio porphyrio*). According to Holliday (1964) quite common in reed beds in the area.

Lesser Gallinule (*P. alleni*). Holliday (1964) says that this species occurs in reeds and papyrus but, as with a number of other species, it is possible that his records are from towards Kazungula, and not therefore from the area of the Victoria Falls as considered in this list.

Finfoots: Heliornithidae

Finfoot (*Podica senegalensis*). Small numbers are present on wooded stretches of the Zambezi and its tributaries, but this bird is easily overlooked.

Bustards: Otididae

Stanley Bustard (*Otis denhami*). There is a single record from Livingstone airfield, perhaps merely a straggler.

Red-crested Korhaan (*Eupodotis ruficrista*). Small numbers around Livingstone, mostly in light woodland.

Black-bellied Korhaan (*E. Melanogaster*). Small numbers in open woodland, locally not uncommon in Victoria Falls National Park (Jensen, 1966).

Jacanas: Jacanidae

African Jacana (*Actophilornis africanus*). Quite common on most areas of water.

Lesser Jacana (*Microparra capensis*). Rather rare, and found only where there is plenty of floating vegetation on water.

Painted Snipes: Rostratulidae

Painted Snipe (*Rostratula benghalensis*). Sparse, and easily overlooked, by lagoons and pans.

Plovers: Charadriidae

Blacksmith Plover (*Vanellus armatus*). Quite common, by any water, especially in the dry season.

Crowned Plover (*V. coronatus*). Occasional over Livingstone during the dry season, when it presumably occurs on the airfield.

White-crowned Plover (*V. albiceps*). Quite common on the Zambezi sand beaches, moving to drier ground during floods.

Senegal Plover (*V. senegallus*). Small numbers locally by pans.

Three-banded Sandplover (*Charadrius tricollaris*). Small numbers, especially by lagoons and dams.

[Kittlitz's Sandplover (*C. pecuarius*). Occasional, according to Holliday, but requires confirmation.]

White-fronted Sandplover (*C. marginatus*). Small numbers breed on the Zambezi sand beaches, and apparently leave the area during high water.

Waders: Scolopacidae

Apart from the Ethiopian Snipe, all the following waders are Eurasian migrants, and present normally only between August and April.

Greenshank (*Tringa nebularia*). Small numbers on the Zambezi in all months.

Marsh Sandpiper (*T. stagnatilis*). Occasional, by any water.

Wood Sandpiper (*T. glareola*). Locally common, especially in marsh.

Green Sandpiper (*T. ochropus*). Rare, singly by pools or dams.

Common Sandpiper (*T. hypoleucos*). Common, especially along the Zambezi between August and December.

[Turnstone (*Arenaria interpres*). Occurs rarely according to Holliday (1964), but no details are available. May be expected very rarely at the most, between September and November.]

Great Snipe (*Gallinago media*). One seen in December in a flooded meadow in Victoria Falls National Park (Jensen, 1966). According to Holliday 'uncommon'.

Ethiopian Snipe (*G. nigripennis*). Holliday reports it as uncommon, during floods.

Curlew Sandpiper (*Calidris ferruginea*). Very sparse, on the Zambezi sand beaches, in September and October.

Little Stint (*C. minuta*). Small numbers between September and November by any water.

Ruff (*Philomachus pugnax*). Very sparse, usually by lagoons.

Stilts and Avocets: Recurvirostridae

Stilt (*Himantopus himantopus*). Occasional, usually by sand beaches.

Avocet (*Recurvirostra avosetta*). According to Holliday individuals have been seen at low water. Smithers *et al.* (1957) report one collected on the Zambezi some 10 kilometres west of Victoria Falls; according to *Ostrich* 1952: 101, this was one of a party of three on 26 December.

Fig. 6 (top) White-crowned Plover.
Fig. 7 (bottom) Water Dikkop.

Dikkops: Burhinidae

Cape Dikkop (*Burhinus capensis*). Occasional in light woodland away from the Zambezi.

Water Dikkop (*B. vermiculatus*). Common on sand beaches along the Zambezi.

Coursers and Pratincoles: Glareolidae

Temminck's Courser (*Cursorius temminckii*). Small numbers occasional during the dry season on open or burnt ground.

Bronze-wing Courser (*Rhinoptilus chalcopterus*). Small numbers in light woodland, especially during May and June.

White-collared Pratincole (*Glareola nuchalis*). Present during July to December, when large numbers nest on rocks in the Zambezi, especially on the lip of the Falls. At the end of the breeding season, in October and November, groups feed regularly over Livingstone at dusk.

Gulls and Terns: Laridae

Grey-headed Gull (*Larus cirrocephalus*). Very sparse on the Zambezi.

White-winged Black Tern (*Chlidonias leucoptera*). Small numbers of this Eurasian migrant may be seen on the Zambezi between September and April.

Skimmers: Rynchopidae

Skimmer (*Rynchops flavirostris*). Small numbers along the Zambezi during the dry season, when they nest on sand beaches.

Sandgrouse: Pteroclidae

Yellow-throated Sandgrouse (*Pterocles gutturalis*). Holliday says it occurs rarely, presumably on passage.

Double-banded Sandgrouse (*P. bicinctus*). Widespread in small numbers in rocky mopane woodland, where it breeds.

Pigeons and Doves: Columbidae

Red-eyed Turtle Dove (*Streptopelia semitorquata*). Common in trees near water.

Turtle Dove (*S. capicola*). Common, especially in open woodland and scrub.

Laughing Dove (*S. senegalensis*). Locally not uncommon in the dry season, usually in mopane woodland.

Namaqua Dove (*Oena capensis*). Small numbers in open woodland or scrub, with increases in numbers through immigration in some dry seasons.

Emerald-spotted Wood Dove (*Turtur chalcospilos*). Common in any woodland or thicket.

Green Pigeon (*Treron australis*). Locally common at fruiting trees, especially figs.

Parrots: Psittacidae

Brown-necked Parrot (*Poicephalus robustus*). Small numbers in any woodland.

Meyer's Parrot (*P. meyeri*). Common in any woodland.

Nyasa (Black-cheeked) Lovebird (*Agapornis lilianae*). Small numbers in mopane and *Acacia* woodland along the Zambezi.

Loeries: Musophagidae

Knysna Loerie (*Tauraco persa*). Quite common in thick forest along rivers, especially in the Palm Grove below the Falls.

Grey Loerie (*Corythaixoides concolor*). Small numbers in dry, open woodland.

Cuckoos and Coucals: Cuculidae

Great Spotted Cuckoo (*Clamator glandarius*). According to Holliday this species occurs during the rains, but further information is lacking.

Jacobin Cuckoo (*C. jacobinus*). Small numbers during the rains in rather open woodland.

Striped Cuckoo (*C. levaillantii*). Not uncommon during the rains in woodland with thickets.

Red-chested Cuckoo (*Cuculus solitarius*). Locally common during the rains, especially near water.

Black Cuckoo (*C. clamosus*). Small numbers during the rains in woodland, often near water.

Cuckoo (*C. canorus*). Both the Eurasian and African races are present in small numbers in woodland during the rains.

Klaas's Cuckoo (*Chrysococcyx klaas*). Probably resident in woodland in small numbers.

Diederik Cuckoo (*C. caprius*). Common during the rains in open country or light woodland.

Emerald Cuckoo (*C. cupreus*). Locally present in small numbers in thick woodland, usually near water.

Black Coucal (*Centropus grillii*). Seen twice in December on *dambos* in Victoria Falls National Park (Jensen, 1965).

Coppery-tailed Coucal (*C. cupreicaudus*). According to Benson *et al.* (1971) this species occasionally wanders to within about 3 kilometres above the Falls, although the large reed beds that it usually inhabits are generally lacking in the Victoria Falls area.

Senegal Coucal (*C. senegalensis*). Small numbers occur locally in thicket, often near water.

White-browed Coucal (*C. superciliosus*). Very sparse, in similar habitat to the last species.

Barn Owls: Tytonidae

Barn Owl (*Tyto alba*). Common in buildings, sometimes in woodland.

Fig. 8 (top) African Skimmer.
Fig. 9 (bottom) White-collared Pratincole.

Owls: Strigidae

Scops Owl (*Otus scops*). Occasional in any woodland.

Spotted Eagle Owl (*Bubo africanus*). Quite common on roads at night in any woodland.

Fishing Owl (*Scotopelia peli*). Small numbers occur in forest along the Zambezi, even in the gorges below the Falls.

Wood Owl (*Ciccaba woodfordii*). Small numbers in woodland and thicket, usually near water.

Nightjars: Caprimulgidae

European Nightjar (*Caprimulgus europaeus*). There are specimens from Livingstone, and this Eurasian migrant may be regular during the rains in very small numbers.

Rufous-cheeked Nightjar (*C. rufigena*). There are specimens of this African migrant from Livingstone and it may be regular on passage between September and December and again in April. Surprisingly, Jensen (1966) calls this the commonest nightjar throughout the Victoria Falls National Park, occurring on rocky outcrops, during December.

Fiery-necked Nightjar (*C. pectoralis*). Common in any woodland in all months, but most in evidence when calling during the dry season.

Freckled Nightjar (*C. tristigma*). Small numbers present on rocks in the area around the gorges.

Moçambique Nightjar (*C. fossii*). Small numbers present in any woodland, probably throughout the year.

Pennant-wing Nightjar (*Macrodipteryx vexillarius*). Very common in any woodland between September and February.

Swifts: Apodidae

Palm Swift (*Cypsiurus parvus*). Locally common near palm trees.

Black Swift (*Apus barbatus*). Common in the gorges, where it breeds.

European Swift (*A. apus*). This Eurasian migrant is quite common during the rains, especially in November.

Little Swift (*A. affinis*). Small numbers are resident in the gorges.

Horus Swift (*A. horus*). According to Holliday it breeds in sand banks above the Falls.

White-rumped Swift (*A. caffer*). Jensen (1966) records this swift on one occasion in Victoria Falls National Park, but although common not far north of Livingstone it does not otherwise seem to occur in the Victoria Falls area.

Mousebirds: Coliidae

Red-faced Mousebird (*Colius indicus*). Present in small numbers in dry thicket areas.

Trogons: Trogonidae

Narina Trogon (*Apaloderma narina*). There is a January specimen from the north bank of the Zambezi and this species may be present in small numbers during the rains in rich woodland, but it is easily overlooked.

Kingfishers: Alcedinidae

Giant Kingfisher (*Ceryle maxima*). Small numbers occur on well-wooded parts of the Zambezi and its tributaries.

Pied Kingfisher (*C. rudis*). Common on any water.

Half-collared Kingfisher (*Alcedo semitorquata*). A few occur locally on wooded stretches of the Zambezi and its backwaters.

Malachite Kingfisher (*A. cristata*). Small numbers on most streams and lagoons, and often on the Zambezi.

Natal Kingfisher (*Ispidina picta*). Locally common in woodland during the rains.

Woodland Kingfisher (*Halcyon senegalensis*). Small numbers are present in woodland during the rains.

Striped Kingfisher (*H. chelicuti*). A common resident in dry, open woodland.

Brown-hooded Kingfisher (*H. albiventris*). A common resident in trees along rivers and streams.

Grey-hooded Kingfisher (*H. leucocephala*). Locally quite common during the rains in woodland.

Bee-eaters: Meropidae

European Bee-eater (*Merops apiaster*). This Eurasian migrant is locally common in woodland and scrub during the rains.

Blue-cheeked Bee-eater (*M. superciliosus*). The Malagasy race occurs occasionally on passage in September and April. According to Holliday the Eurasian *persicus* occurs too, but this floodplain bird may not do so within the Victoria Falls area.

Carmine Bee-eater (*M. nubicus*). Small numbers occur in any month, but it is most common in the dry season along parts of the Zambezi.

Little Bee-eater (*M. pusillus*). Locally common in scrub on the edge of woodland.

White-fronted Bee-eater (*M. bullockoides*). Common along the banks of the Zambezi and its backwaters.

Swallow-tailed Bee-eater (*M. hirundineus*). Small numbers occur in woodland during the dry season.

Rollers: Coraciidae

European Roller (*Coracias garrulus*). Small numbers of this Eurasian migrant occur in open woodland during the rains, especially on passage in November and March.

Lilac-breasted Roller (*C. caudata*). Small numbers are present in open woodland and scrub, being especially noticeable in the dry season.

Racquet-tailed Roller (*C. spatulata*). Occurs rather sparsely in thicker woodland than the last species.

Purple Roller (*C. naevia*). Very sparse in light woodland during the dry season, although recorded rarely in December too in Victoria Falls National Park (Jensen, 1966).

Broad-billed Roller (*Eurystomus glaucurus*). Not uncommon locally in woodland during the rains.

Hoopoes: Upupidae

Hoopoe (*Upupa epops*). Locally quite common in all months, but most noticeable in mopane woodland during the dry season.

Wood Hoopoes: Phoeniculidae

Red-billed Hoopoe (*Phoeniculus purpureus*). Quite common in woodland.

Scimitar-billed Hoopoe (*P. cyanomelas*). Small numbers in woodland.

Hornbills: Bucerotidae

Grey Hornbill (*Tockus nasutus*). Common, especially in the more open, drier woodlands.

Red-billed Hornbill (*T. erythrorhynchus*). Locally common in mopane woodland.

Bradfield's Hornbill (*T. bradfieldi*). Occasional, usually in *Baikiaea* forest.

Trumpeter Hornbill (*Bycanistes bucinator*). Common in forest along the Zambezi, especially about the Victoria Falls.

Ground Hornbill (*Bucorvus cafer*). Occasional in open woodland.

Barbets: Capitonidae

Black-collared Barbet (*Lybius torquatus*). Locally common in most types of woodland.

Acacia Pied Barbet (*L. leucomelas*). Small numbers in *Acacia* trees along the Zambezi, rarely in any other woodland.

Miombo Pied Barbet (*L. frontatus*). Locally not uncommon in *Baikiaea* forest at Livingstone, where it hybridises with the last species.

Yellow-fronted Tinker Barbet (*Pogoniulus chrysoconus*). Locally common in any woodland.

Crested Barbet (*Trachyphonus vaillantii*). Quite common in any woodland, especially mopane.

Honeyguides: Indicatoridae

Greater Honeyguide (*Indicator indicator*). Small numbers in any woodland.

Lesser Honeyguide (*I. minor*). Small numbers in woodland, and especially near water.

Slender-billed Honeyguide (*Prodotiscus zambesiae*). Occurs sparsely in richer woodlands around Livingstone.

Sharp-billed Honeyguide (*P. regulus*). Small numbers present in any woodland.

Woodpeckers: Picidae

Bennett's Woodpecker (*Campethera bennettii*). Quite common in any woodland.

Golden-tailed Woodpecker (*C. abingoni*). Small numbers, usually in woodland or forest along rivers.

Cardinal Woodpecker (*Dendropicos fuscescens*). Common in any woodland.

Bearded Woodpecker (*Thripias namaquus*). Sparse, in any woodland.

Larks: Alaudidae

Monotonous Lark (*Mirafra javanica*). Small numbers present in rocky mopane woodland.

Rufous-naped Lark (*M. africana*). Small numbers locally in open grassland or scrub.

Flappet Lark (*M. rufocinnamomea*). Quite common, especially on the edge of woodland, and locally very common in mopane.

Fawn-coloured Lark (*M. africanoides*). A specimen collected in mopane woodland near Livingstone in September was perhaps a vagrant.

Dusky Lark (*M. nigricans*). A very common passage migrant in mopane woodland in April and May.

[Spike-heeled Lark (*Certhilauda albofasciata*). This resident of south-western Africa is recorded visually from Victoria Falls National Park by Jensen (1965), but the record needs substantiation.]

Red-capped Lark (*Calandrella cinerea*). A few occur locally on dry, open ground.

Grey-backed Finch-Lark (*Eremopterix verticalis*). This species occurred in the Livingstone area during an influx into south-western Zambia between June and October 1964.

Chestnut-backed Finch-Lark (*E. leucotis*). Occasional on open ground, or on roads in light woodland, especially during the dry season.

Swallows and Martins: Hirundinidae

European Sand Martin (*Riparia riparia*). This Eurasian migrant occurs occasionally during the rains, over any water.

African Sand Martin (*R. paludicola*). Occasional on the Zambezi according to Holliday (1964), and apparently seen by Jensen (1966).

European Swallow (*Hirundo rustica*). This Eurasian migrant is by far the most numerous swallow during the rains.

Wire-tailed Swallow (*H. smithii*). Common along rivers, especially around the Falls.

White-throated Swallow (*H. albigularis*). Small numbers occur in the area on passage, especially in April and May.

Mosque Swallow (*H. senegalensis*). Occasional in woodland.

Greater Striped Swallow (*H. cucullata*). There are sight records of this African migrant in the area in July and December.

Lesser Striped Swallow (*H. abyssinica*). Common, especially along the Zambezi.

Grey-rumped Swallow (*H. griseopyga*). Locally not uncommon during the dry season over open ground, especially when freshly burnt.

Rock Martin (*H. fuligula*). Common in the gorges, where it breeds.

House Martin (*Delichon urbica*). This Eurasian migrant is seen on rare occasions during the rains.

Drongos: Dicruridae

Fork-tailed Drongo (*Dicrurus adsimilis*). Common in any woodland.

Orioles: Oriolidae

African Golden Oriole (*Oriolus auratus*). Locally quite common in the thicker woodlands.

Black-headed Oriole (*O. larvatus*). Common in any woodland.

Crows: Corvidae

Pied Crow (*Corvus albus*). Very common, especially near habitation.

Black Crow (*C. capensis*). A single one seen in Livingstone may have been an escape from captivity.

White-necked Raven (*C. albicollis*). Reported on rare occasions from the gorges.

Tits: Paridae

Northern Grey Tit (*Parus griseiventris*). Small numbers in miombo woodland.

Southern Black Tit (*P. niger*). Common, usually in the more open woodlands.

Penduline Tits: Remizidae

Grey Penduline Tit (*Remiz caroli*). Small numbers in thicker woodlands.

Babblers: Timaliidae

Arrow-marked Babbler (*Turdoides jardineii*). Quite common in thickets and scrub.

[White-rumped Babbler (*T. leucopygius*). Reported by Holliday (1964) to occur in small flocks, but there are to date no specimens from the Victoria Falls area.]

Cuckoo-Shrikes: Campephagidae

White-breasted Cuckoo-Shrike (*Coracina pectoralis*). Occasional in woodland.

Black Cuckoo-Shrike (*Campephaga phoenicea*). Small numbers in any woodland during the rains.

Bulbuls: Pycnonotidae

Black-eyed Bulbul (*Pycnonotus barbatus*). Numerous in any woodland.

Red-eyed Bulbul (*P. nigricans*). Resident alongside the last species, but much scarcer.

Yellow-bellied Bulbul (*Chlorocichla flaviventris*). Quite common especially in thicket along the rivers.

Terrestrial Bulbul (*Phyllastrephus terrestris*). Locally common in dry thickets.

Yellow-spotted Nicator (*Nicator chloris*). Occurs locally in small numbers in riparian forest and thicket upstream from the Falls, just within the area of the National Parks.

Thrushes, Robins and Chats: Turdidae

Familiar Chat (*Cercomela familiaris*). Small

numbers are present in the gorges and in rocky mopane woodland.

Arnot's Chat (*Thamnolaea arnoti*). Small numbers present in miombo woodland.

Mocking Chat (*T. cinnamomeiventris*). Very small numbers occur in the gorges.

Angola Thrush (*Monticola angolensis*). Small numbers occur in open *Baikiaea* forest near Livingstone.

White-browed Scrub Robin (*Erythropygia leucophrys*). Locally common in woodland and scrub.

Bearded Robin (*E. quadrivirgata*). Not uncommon, but easily overlooked, in thicket and forest along rivers.

Morning Warbler (*Cichladusa arquata*). Locally not uncommon in thickets and near palms.

Natal Robin (*Cossypha natalensis*). This skulking species has been heard in dense thickets near the Falls, and it may in fact be not uncommon in the area during the rains.

Heuglin's Robin (*C. heuglini*). Locally common in any thicket.

Thrush Nightingale (*Luscinia luscinia*). This Eurasian migrant is quite common in thickets from December to March, and several have been mist-netted for ringing. The birds reported by Jensen (1966) at the top of the gorges with Familiar Chats were not in suitable habitat and were perhaps not this species.

Kurrichane Thrush (*Turdus libonyana*). Locally common in rather open woodland.

Groundscraper Thrush (*T. litsipsirupa*). Occurs very sparsely in woodland.

Warblers: Sylviidae

African Sedge Warbler (*Bradypterus baboecalus*). According to both Holliday (1964) and Jensen (1966) this species is common in reed beds in the area.

River Warbler (*Locustella fluviatilis*). A single example of this scarce Eurasian migrant was caught for ringing near Livingstone in January. Small numbers may occur annually in December and January in deciduous thickets.

European Sedge Warbler (*Acrocephalus schoenobaenus*). A Eurasian migrant, locally common during the rains in rank grass, thickets and, less commonly, reed beds.

European Marsh Warbler (*A. palustris*). Small numbers of this Eurasian migrant occur during the rains, mainly in thickets.

European Great Reed Warbler (*A. arundinaceus*). Common during the rains, mainly in thicket and scrub.

African Marsh Warbler (*A. baeticatus*). Locally quite common in reed beds along the Zambezi, and also around pans.

Cape Reed Warbler (*A. gracilirostris*). Small numbers occur in dense reed beds, several kilometres upstream from the Falls.

Garden Warbler (*Sylvia borin*). Another Eurasian migrant, present only during the rains, when it is locally common, especially in thicket and scrub.

Whitethroat (*S. communis*). This Eurasian migrant occurs during the rains in small numbers in *Acacia* scrub.

Tit-babbler (*Parisoma subcaeruleum*). Two specimens have been collected in *Baikiaea* forest at Livingstone, but it is normally confined to dry *Acacia* thicket outside the Victoria Falls area.

Willow Warbler (*Phylloscopus trochilus*). A common Eurasian migrant, in any woodland, during the rains.

Tawny-flanked Prinia (*Prinia subflava*). Common in any scrub.

Yellow-breasted Apalis (*Apalis flavida*). Small numbers are to be found on the edge of

Fig. 10 Familiar Chat.

riverine forest or thick woodland.

Grey-backed Bush Warbler (*Camaroptera brachyura*). Locally quite common in thicket.

Barred Warbler (*C. stierlingi*). Small numbers occur in thicket inside woodland.

Yellow-bellied Eremomela (*Eremomela icteropygialis*). Small numbers occur in miombo woodland and *Baikiaea* forest, less often in thicket and scrub.

Greencap Eremomela (*E. scotops*). Quite common in miombo woodland and *Baikiaea* forest.

Burnt-necked Eremomela (*E. usticollis*). Small numbers occur in *Acacia* trees.

Crombec (*Sylvietta rufescens*). Locally quite common, especially in mopane woodland and scrub.

Red-faced Cisticola (*Cisticola erythrops*). Quite common in rank growth along streams.

Lazy Cisticola (*C. aberrans*). Small numbers occur in trees and bushes in the rocky gorges.

Rattling Cisticola (*C. chiniana*). Common in dry scrub.

Tinkling Cisticola (*C. rufilata*). Small numbers occur locally in scrub on the edge of woodland.

[Black-backed Cisticola (*C. galactotes*). Holliday (1964) mentions sight records from this area, but there are no specimens of this flood-plain warbler to support this.]

Croaking Cisticola (*C. natalensis*). Small numbers are to be found on *dambos*.

Neddicky (*C. fulvicapilla*). Quite common in any woodland.

Fantail Cisticola (*C. juncidis*). Small numbers locally in grassland.

Desert Cisticola (*C. aridula*). Very local, in dry grasslands.

Flycatchers: Muscicapidae

Spotted Flycatcher (*Muscicapa striata*). A Eurasian migrant, which is quite common in any woodland during the rains.

White-collared Flycatcher (*M. albicollis*). Another Eurasian migrant, which occurs in small numbers during the rains in *Baikiaea* forest at Livingstone.

Blue-grey Flycatcher (*M. caerulescens*). Quite common, especially in riparian forest.

Grey Tit-babbler (*Myioparus plumbeus*). Small numbers occur in woodland and thicket.

Black Flycatcher (*Melaenornis pammelaina*). Small numbers occur in any woodland.

Mouse-coloured Flycatcher (*Bradornis pallidus*). Locally quite common in any woodland.

Chin Spot Batis (*Batis molitor*). Common in any woodland.

[Blue-mantled Flycatcher (*Trochocercus cyanomelas*). There are sight records from riparian forest on the Zimbabwean bank of the Zambezi, which require confirmation (M. P. Stuart Irwin, *in litt.*).]

Paradise Flycatcher (*Terpsiphone viridis*). This African migrant is common in any woodland during the rains.

Bush Shrikes: Malaconotidae

Brubru Shrike (*Nilaus afer*). Small numbers are present in any woodland.

Puffback Shrike (*Dryoscopus cubla*). Common, especially in trees along rivers and streams.

Three-streaked Tchagra (*Tchagra australis*). Locally common, especially in *Acacia* trees and scrub.

Black-crowned Tchagra (*T. senegala*). Quite common, especially in bushes on the edge of woodland.

Boubou (*Laniarius ferrugineus*). Common in any thicket or scrub.

Orange-breasted Bush Shrike (*Malaconotus sulphureopectus*). Quite common in *Acacia* trees, scrub and thicket.

Grey-headed Bush Shrike (*M. blanchoti*). Locally not uncommon in riverine forest, and even at times in gardens.

Wagtails and Pipits: Motacillidae

Yellow Wagtail (*Motacilla flava*). Small numbers of this Eurasian migrant occur during the rains in grassland by water.

[Cape Wagtail (*M. capensis*). The comment by Holliday (1964) 'common in the gorges and above the Falls at low water' must surely refer to the next species, which he does not mention.]

Long-tailed Wagtail (*M. clara*). Small numbers occur on rocks in the Zambezi, from the lip of the Falls and throughout the gorges.

African Pied Wagtail (*M. aguimp*). Common by water, less often around habitation.

Richard's Pipit (*Anthus novaeseelandiae*). Locally quite common in any grassland.

Plain-backed Pipit (*A. leucophrys*). There is a single specimen from Livingstone in June (Benson and Irwin, 1967), and it can be no more than rare in grassland in this area.

Buffy Pipit (*A. vaalensis*). Small numbers occur on bare ground in the dry season.

Nicholson's Pipit (*A. similis*). Small numbers occur locally in miombo woodland.

Tree Pipit (*A. trivialis*). Small numbers of this Eurasian migrant occur during the rains in miombo woodland.

Striped Pipit (*A. lineiventris*). Small numbers occur in rocky woodland around the gorges.

Pink-throated Longclaw (*Macronyx ameliae*). Very local, in small numbers, in *dambos*.

Shrikes: Laniidae

Red-backed Shrike (*Lanius collurio*). Quite a common Eurasian visitor during the rains mainly in scrub.

Lesser Grey Shrike (*L. minor*). Another Eurasian migrant, but present in the area, in *Acacia* scrub usually, only on passage in October/November and March.

Long-tailed Shrike (*L. melanoleucus*). Occurs in open *Acacia* scrub, but rather sparse in the area.

Helmet Shrikes: Prionopidae

White Helmet Shrike (*Prionops plumata*). Common in any woodland.

Red-billed Helmet Shrike (*P. retzii*). Small numbers occur in woodland.

Starlings and Oxpeckers: Sturnidae

Red-winged Starling (*Onychognathus morio*). Numerous in the gorges and, in the dry season mainly, in Livingstone town.

Lesser Blue-eared Glossy Starling (*Lamprotornis chloropterus*). Small numbers occur in the area, mainly in miombo woodland.

Blue-eared Glossy Starling (*L. chalybaeus*). Locally common, in more open country than the last species.

Long-tailed Glossy Starling (*L. mevesii*). Small numbers occur locally in mopane woodland and *Acacia* trees.

Plum-coloured Starling (*Cinnyricinclus leucogaster*). At times numerous, in all months of the year, at fruiting trees.

Wattled Starling (*Creatophora cinerea*). Occurs in flocks in open country from time to time.

Yellow-billed Oxpecker (*Buphagus africanus*). Occurs occasionally on game animals in the Mosi-oa-Tunya Zoological Park.

Red-billed Oxpecker (*B. erythrorhynchus*). Quite common locally, especially on game animals in the Victoria Falls National Park and the Mosi-oa-Tunya Zoological Park.

Sunbirds: Nectariniidae

Collared Sunbird (*Anthreptes collaris*). Common, especially in riverine forest.

Black Sunbird (*Nectarinia amethystina*). Common at times in any woodland.

Scarlet-chested Sunbird (*N. senegalensis*). Common in any woodland.

White-bellied Sunbird (*N. talatala*). Locally common, especially in mopane and *Acacia* woodland.

Black-bellied Sunbird (*N. shelleyi*). Small numbers are to be found in *Baikiaea* forest at Livingstone.

[Marico Sunbird (*N. mariquensis*). Although recorded as 'not at all common' by Holliday (1964) there is as yet no evidence that this species occurs within the Victoria Falls area as considered here, although it should be watched for.]

Purple-banded Sunbird (*N. bifasciata*). Small numbers occur in riverine forest.

Coppery Sunbird (*N. cuprea*). Small numbers occur locally on the edge of forest and woodland.

White-eyes: Zosteropidae

Yellow White-eye (*Zosterops senegalensis*). Quite common in any woodland.

Weavers etc.: Ploceidae

Thick-billed Weaver (*Amblyospiza albifrons*). Has been seen in reed beds near the Falls, and small numbers may be widespread in suitable habitat.

Golden Weaver (*Ploceus xanthops*). Common near water.

[Lesser Masked Weaver (*P. intermedius*). According to Holliday (1964) there are sight records, but there seem to be no definite records from what we now consider as the Victoria Falls area, although it may well occur.]

Masked Weaver (*P. velatus*). Locally quite common, especially near water.

Spotted-backed Weaver (*P. cucullatus*). Small numbers occur locally near water.

Red-headed Weaver (*Malimbus rubriceps*). Small numbers occur in woodland.

Red-billed Quelea (*Quelea quelea*). Abundant at times, especially in more open, drier woodlands and reed beds (where it roosts).

Red Bishop (*Euplectes orix*). Numerous in grassland near water.

Cape Widow (*E. capensis*). Quite common in long grass and scrub.

Yellow-backed Widow (*E. macrourus*). Small numbers occur locally on *dambos*.

White-winged Widow (*E. albonotatus*). Locally common in rank grass and scrub.

Buffalo Weaver (*Bubalornis albirostris*). Benson *et al.* (1971) report it westwards along the north bank of the Zambezi in mopane and *Acacia*, but it must be sparse in the Victoria Falls area and it is unknown from the Victoria Falls National Park (Jensen, 1966).

White-browed Sparrow-weaver (*Plocepasser mahali*). Abundant in mopane, especially in rocky country around the gorges.

House Sparrow (*Passer domesticus*). Very common around habitation in Livingstone and Victoria Falls township.

Grey-headed Sparrow (*P. griseus*). Locally quite common in mopane woodland.

Yellow-throated Sparrow (*Petronia superciliaris*). Locally common in any woodland.

Pin-tailed Whydah (*Vidua macroura*). Quite common locally, especially on the edge of *dambos*.

Shaft-tailed Whydah (*V. regia*). Small numbers occur in the area in dry *Acacia* scrub.

Black Widow-finch (*V. purpurascens*). Small numbers occur on the edge of woodland.

Steel-blue Widow-finch (*V. chalybeata*). Locally common, especially in scrub near habitation.

Paradise Whydah (*V. paradisea*). Quite common in open woodland.

Broad-tailed Paradise-Whydah (*V. orientalis*). Less numerous than the last species and found in thicker woodland.

Waxbills: Estrildidae

Golden-backed Pytilia (*Pytilia afra*). Small numbers occur locally, mainly in miombo woodland.

Melba Finch (*P. melba*). Locally common, especially in thickets.

[Red-throated Twinspot (*Hypargos niveoguttatus*). Holliday (1964) says 'sight record only', but small numbers may be expected to occur locally in thickets, although Benson *et al.* (1971) give no record in this area above the middle Zambezi valley.]

Brown Firefinch (*Lagonosticta nitidula*). Small numbers occur in thickets, especially along the Zambezi.

Red-billed Firefinch (*L. senegala*). Common in scrub around habitation, less often in thickets.

Jameson's Firefinch (*L. rhodopareia*). Locally common, especially on the edge of thickets.

Fig. 11 (opposite, top) White-browed Sparrow-Weaver.

Fig. 12 (opposite, bottom) Rock Bunting (male on left).

Blue Waxbill (*Uraeginthus angolensis*). Common in any woodland or scrub.

Violet-eared Waxbill (*U. granatina*). Fairly common in *Acacia* scrub and the undergrowth on the edge of *Baikiaea* forest.

Common Waxbill (*Estrilda astrild*). Locally common in rank grass near water.

Quail Finch (*Ortygospiza atricollis*). Locally common in grassland.

Bronze Mannikin (*Lonchura cucullata*). Quite common, especially in scrub or on the edge of forest near water.

Cut-throat Finch (*Amadina fasciata*). Not uncommon in mopane woodland, but easily overlooked.

Buntings and Canaries: Fringillidae

Golden-breasted Bunting (*Emberiza flaviventris*). Quite common in most woodland.

Rock Bunting (*E. tahapisi*). Locally very numerous, especially in the rocky country around the gorges.

Lark-like Bunting (*E. impetuani*). A single bird was seen in mopane woodland near Livingstone in April 1965, at a time when this species apparently irrupted into Zambia from south-western Africa.

Yellow-eye Canary (*Serinus mozambicus*). Locally not uncommon, especially in rather open woodland.

Black-throated Canary (*S. atrogularis*). Small numbers are to be found locally on the edge of *dambos*.

Bully Seed-eater (*S. sulphuratus*). Small numbers occur locally, mainly in bushes on the edge of *dambos*.

Stripe-breasted Seed-eater (*S. reichardi*). Found in small numbers in *Baikiaea* forest and miombo woodland at Livingstone.

Black-eared Seed-eater (*S. mennelli*). Quite common in *Baikiaea* forest and miombo woodland.

Acknowledgements

I am most grateful to Messrs C. W. Benson and M. P. Stuart Irwin for their observations and for their comments on this chapter. I must thank too the many bird watchers who have passed on to me their records for this area.

Select Bibliography

BENSON, C. W. 'Some additions and corrections to a *Check List of the Birds of Northern Rhodesia*', Occ. Pap. Nat. Mus. S. Rhod. xxvi B, 1962, pp. 631–652.

BENSON, C. W., BROOKE, R. K., DOWSETT, R.J. and IRWIN, M. P. S. *The Birds of Zambia*, London, 1971.

BENSON, C. W. and IRWIN, M. P. S. *A Contribution to the Ornithology of Zambia*, Lusaka, (Zambia Museum Papers, no. 1), 1967.

HOLLIDAY, C. S. 'The birds' *in* B. M. Fagan (ed.), *The Victoria Falls* (2nd edn.), Livingstone, 1964, pp. 91–108.

JENSEN, R. A. C. 'Interesting sight records from the Victoria Falls National Park, Southern Rhodesia.' *Ostrich*, xxxvi, 1965, p. 95.

JENSEN, R. A. C. 'The birds of the Victoria Falls National Park, Rhodesia,' *S. Afr. Avi. Ser.* xxxiii, 1966, pp. 1–35.

McLACHLAN, G. R. and LIVERSIDGE, R. *Roberts' Birds of South Africa*, Johannesburg, 1970.

SMITHERS, R. H. N., IRWIN, M. P. S. and PATERSON, M. L. *A Check List of the Birds of Southern Rhodesia*, Salisbury, (Rhodesian Ornithological Society), 1957.

WINTERBOTTOM, J. M. 'The birds' *in* J. D. Clark (ed.), *The Victoria Falls* (1st edn.), Livingstone, 1952, pp. 94–105.

CHAPTER 13

The Reptiles and Amphibians

Donald G. Broadley

This account of the herpetofauna of the Victoria Falls area is based on material in the Natural History Museum of Zimbabwe which has been collected within ten kilometres of the Zambezi River between Kazungula and the Songwe Gorge. Most of the specimens from the Zambian side were collected by B. L. Mitchell during 1958–61. The author collected in the Victoria Falls area during 1961 and in the Kazungula-Katombora area during 1982. Additional material has been collected by the staff of the Victoria Falls National Park or the Victoria Falls Snake Park. A review of these collections indicates that the area under consideration is inhabited by a minimum of sixty-nine reptile and twenty-three amphibian species; these are listed in the Check List which forms an appendix to this chapter. A number of reptile species which occur in western Zambia may eventually be found along the Zambezi downstream from Kazungula, as they could be transported on rafts of floating vegetation. The absence of papyrus and reeds in the gorges below the Victoria Falls eliminates most semi-aquatic reptiles and amphibians from this stretch of the Zambezi.

Reptiles

Order CHELONIA (Terrapins, Tortoises and Turtles)

Family PELOMEDUSIDAE (Terrapins)
At least three species occur in the area. The African Marsh Terrapin (*Pelomedusa subrufa*) is the only one in which the anterior portion of the plastron (lower half of the shell) is not hinged in adults. This terrapin has a flattened shell, pale olive above and yellow below; few specimens exceed 15 centimetres in shell length. The Marsh Terrapin lives in tem-

porary pans and water holes, burying itself in the mud when they dry up. Terrapins devour a wide range of aquatic insects, tadpoles, frogs and small fishes.

The Okavango Terrapin (*Pelusios bechuanicus*) has a well-arched elongate shell which may exceed 30 centimetres in length. The most distinctive feature of this species is the enormous head with bright yellow markings; the shell is usually entirely black. The Okavango Terrapin inhabits the crystal-clear waters of the Upper Zambezi-Okavango system. It has not been recorded below the Falls.

The Serrated Terrapin (*Pelusios sinuatus*) is the common species in the Zambezi below the Victoria Falls, but I have also caught it in muddy backwaters above the Falls. It avoids the clear water favoured by the Okavango Terrapin. This species usually has a well-developed vertebral keel and the rear edge of the carapace (upper shell) is serrated. The carapace is black, the plastron yellow with a sharply defined black peripheral pattern. The head is small and is completely concealed when the hinged anterior portion of the plastron is raised like a drawbridge. Large specimens may attain more than 30 centimetres in length.

Family TESTUDINIDAE (*Tortoises*)
The Leopard Tortoise (*Geochelone pardalis*) has a high domed shell with attractive black and yellow markings; it may exceed 30 centimetres in length. This species feeds mainly on grass.

Bell's Hinged Tortoise (*Kinixys belliana*) has a flattened shell and rarely grows longer than 20 centimetres. Adults have the posterior portion of the carapace hinged, so that it can be drawn in to protect the hind legs and tail. This tortoise has a very catholic diet; the vegetation consumed includes succulents and fungi, while millipedes, snails and carrion are all eaten avidly.

Order CROCODYLIA (Crocodiles)

Family CROCODYLIDAE
The Nile Crocodile (*Crocodylus niloticus*) is no longer plentiful in the Upper Zambezi, due to the activities of commercial hunters. Marked juveniles from Zimbabwean Crocodile farms are being used to restock the Zambezi above the Falls. Although this reptile has been known to reach a length of 6 metres, specimens longer than 4 metres are very scarce today.

The female crocodile lays her eggs in sandy soil above flood level and the young are 30 centimetres long on hatching. They initially keep to weedy backwaters, where they feed on insects. Moderate-sized specimens feed largely on fish, while crocodiles over 3 metres in length prey upon mammals, water birds and terrapins.

Order SQUAMATA (Scaled reptiles)
Suborder SAURIA (Lizards)

Family GEKKONIDAE (*Geckos*)
The Tropical House Gecko (*Hemidactylus mabouia*) may be found on tree-trunks or in rock crevices, but it is one of the geckos which regularly frequents house walls, both exterior and interior. This gecko has a flattened head and body; the body is covered with keeled tubercles separated by smaller scales and the tail has six longitudinal rows of spines. The average length is 10 centimetres and the coloration varies from pale grey to grey-brown, depending on background and light intensity. This species emerges at dusk to hunt its insect prey.

The Cape Dwarf Gecko (*Lygodactylus*

capensis) is a small diurnal species which can be seen basking in the sun on house walls and trees. Averaging 7 centimetres in length, this gecko has a smooth grey-brown skin and the eye has a round pupil.

The Chobe Dwarf Gecko (*Lygodactylus chobiensis*) is slightly larger and more robust than the previous species. Above it is blue-grey with large pale dorsal spots; the belly is yellow and the throat black (or with two black chevrons) in adult males. This gecko is common on tree trunks.

O'Shaughnessy's Banded Gecko (*Pachydactylus oshaughnessyi*) is an attractive species which rarely exceeds 8 centimetres in length. During the daytime these geckos usually take cover beneath logs and stones.

Family AGAMIDAE (*Agamas*)

The Spiny Agama (*Agama aculeata*) is a common terrestrial species. Averaging 20 centimetres in length, this lizard has a short chunky head, squat body and slender tail. The scales on the back are rough, with rows of short spines. The coloration is usually some shade of red-brown to match the sandy ground on which it is most commonly found. The head becomes pale blue during the breeding season. Adult males have a pale vertebral band flanked by dark triangles; females have a vertebral row of pale spots. In females the tail is about as long as head and body together, but the tail is much longer in males. Spiny Agamas feed largely on ants.

Family CHAMAELEONIDAE (*Chameleons*)

The Common Flap-necked Chameleon (*Cha-*

Fig. 1 (top) Okavango Terrapin.
Fig. 2 (centre) Leopard Tortoise.
Fig. 3 (bottom) Nile Crocodile.

maeleo dilepis) is widespread in eastern and central Africa. Specimens from the Zambezi are larger than average, exceeding 30 centimetres in total length. This species has a pair of occipital flaps which cover the nape, but can be raised like an elephant's ears when the reptile is angry. There is a row of small conical scales along the spine and a similar one (of white scales) along the midline of the belly. The prehensile tail is usually a little shorter than head and body together. Chameleons include a wide variety of insects in their diet. The female lays thirty-five to sixty-five spherical, soft-shelled eggs in a hole which she digs after the ground has been softened by rain. The eggs do not hatch until the following rainy season.

Family SCINCIDAE (Skinks)

The Rainbow Skink (Mabuya quinquetaeniata) is a conspicuous species on rock outcrops. Females and juveniles have a dorsal pattern of three yellow stripes on a black background; the tail is bright blue. Adult males lose the striped pattern and become golden brown, each scale having a pale spot; the tail changes from blue to brown and finally to bright orange. A large specimen may attain a total length of 30 centimetres. Skinks have polished close-fitting scales, and in the Rainbow Skink the body scales show a rainbow iridescence as the lizard basks in the sun. The diet consists largely of grasshoppers. The female lays about ten eggs during the summer.

The Variable Skink (Mabuya varia) is a small, dark brown terrestrial skink. The dorsal markings are variable, but there is usually a well-defined white lateral stripe. Although mainly insectivorous, this species sometimes devours smaller lizards. The

female gives birth to about six young during the summer.

The Common Striped Skink (Mabuya striata) is a very common species which may be found basking on tree trunks or house walls. The top of the head is orange-brown, the back grey-brown with ill-defined pale dorso-lateral bands and there is a broad black lateral band extending from the eye to about midbody. The underside is white except for the throat, which is streaked with orange in males. A large specimen may attain 25 centimetres in length. This species breeds throughout the year, females giving birth to between five and ten live young.

Sundevall's Writhing Skink (Lygosoma sundevallii) is a common, but secretive species, usually found beneath logs, where it feeds largely on termites. The cylindrical body and tail are covered with smooth scales and the limbs are very small and little used, although five digits are present on each limb. The dorsal coloration is grey-brown, each scale darker at the base; the belly is white. The maximum length is about 17 centimetres, half of this being tail. Most adults have short regenerated tails, this appendage being shed very readily to distract a predator.

Wahlberg's Snake-eyed Skink (Panaspis wahlbergii) is another common species which feeds on termites, but it is frequently seen gliding through drifts of dead leaves. Its main distinguishing feature is the lack of movable eyelids, the eye being protected by a transparent 'watchglass' scale similar to that found in snakes. The limbs are small, but with five digits on each; the tail is long and slender. These little skinks are light grey-brown above, much darker on the flanks. The underside is white, except in breeding males, which are bright vermillion below. The maximum length is about 12 centimetres.

The Gracile Limbless Skink (*Typhlacontias gracilis*) is a common burrowing skink which is usually found under logs. In colour it is buff above, with an ill-defined dark median stripe and a broad grey-brown lateral band extending from the eye onto the tail. The maximum length is about 13 centimetres.

Family CORDYLIDAE (*Plated and Girdled Lizards*)

The Black-lined Plated Lizard (*Gerrhosaurus nigrolineatus*) is a handsome species which may be observed basking in the sun, but is more often already streaking for its burrow when first seen. This streamlined lizard has a pointed snout, well-developed limbs and a very long tail (which is often shed and regenerated). These lizards are protected by bony armour underlying the scales; a longitudinal groove of soft skin separates the dorsal armour from the belly shields and allows for expansion due to full stomach or ovaries. The back is red-brown, separated from the bright vermillion flanks by black-edged yellow dorso-lateral stripes. The diet consists largely of grasshoppers.

The Tawny Plated Lizard (*Gerrhosaurus major*) is a robust species averaging half a metre in length. It is yellow-brown, streaked with black posteriorly and with the tail largely black. It lives in termitaria, small rock outcrops and hollow logs. The diet consists largely of insects and millipedes, but some fruit and vegetation is eaten. Smaller lizards are sometimes preyed upon.

Family LACERTIDAE (*Sand Lizards*)

The Ornate Scrub-lizard (*Nucras taeniolata*) is a slender, long-tailed, fleet-footed species

Fig. 4 (top) O'Shaughnessy's Banded Gecko.
Fig. 5 (bottom) Tawny Plated Lizard.

which may be seen hunting grasshoppers in open terrain. The back is red-brown, the flanks darker and the tail red. Juveniles have three yellow dorsal stripes, but these fade out in adults; there are white vertical bars on the side of the neck, while the flanks are spotted or stippled with white.

The Moçambique Rough-scaled Sand Lizard (*Ichnotropis squamulosa*) is a species of moderate build, its rough appearance being due to strongly keeled dorsal scales.

Family VARANIDAE (*Monitor Lizards or Leguaans*)

The Nile Monitor or Water Leguaan (*Varanus niloticus*) is very common along the Zambezi. This is the largest African lizard, attaining a maximum length of nearly two and a half metres. The head is relatively small and is carried on a long neck, the limbs are powerful and armed with long claws; the long tail is vertically flattened and serves to propel the lizard rapidly through the water. Juveniles are dark olive-green with transverse rows of yellow spots on the back and bands on the tail, this pattern being suffused with scattered orange, yellow and black scales; the belly is yellow. The pale markings tend to fade out in adults.

The jaws of this species are equipped with powerful conical teeth, which are used to crush the crabs and snails which form an important part of the diet, supplemented by an assortment of small mammals, birds, reptiles, amphibians and invertebrates. When cornered, this big lizard can defend itself with powerful whip-lash blows from its tail. The Water Leguaan may be seen basking on rocks or tree trunks, but usually dashes for the water when disturbed. It is an accomplished swimmer and diver, but is preyed upon by crocodiles.

The Savanna Monitor or Tree Leguaan (*Varanus exanthematicus*) is a more heavily built reptile than the previous species, but rarely exceeds one and a half metres in length. It is dirty white with black markings, the principal ones being a dark stripe on the side of the neck, transverse rows of pale-centred ocelli on the back and broad transverse bands on the tail. This rather sluggish reptile feeds on carrion and slow-moving prey like snails and millipedes. It lives in hollow trees, ant-bear holes and rock crevices.

Suborder AMPHISBAENIA (Amphisbaenians)

Family AMPHISBAENIDAE

The Round-snouted Amphisbaenian (*Zygaspis quadrifrons*) is the commonest of the four species of amphisbaenian found in the Victoria Falls area. These limbless burrowing reptiles are covered with soft pink skin which is divided into rings of rectangular segments. The eyes are hidden under the head shields. Amphisbaenians may be encountered on the surface of the ground following heavy rain, but they are usually dug up in sandy ground or found under logs. They feed on beetle larvae and other invertebrates. This is a small species, which rarely exceeds 20 centimetres in length. The largest local species *Dalophia pistillum* may exceed 60 centimetres.

Suborder SERPENTES (Snakes)

Family TYPHLOPIDAE (*Blind Snakes*)

Schlegel's Blind Snake (*Typhlops schlegelii*) is covered with close-fitting, highly polished scales; the head is protected by a large shield like a finger nail and the mouth is set back from the snout like that of a shark. The stubby tail terminates in a sharp spine – the reptile's sole means of defence. The dorsal pattern may consist of narrow dark longitudinal stripes (becoming uniform brown in large adults), or irregular black blotches on a pale background. This species may reach a length of almost one metre. Blind snakes spend most of the time underground, where they feed on termites, but they may be found on the surface after heavy rain.

Family LEPTOTYPHLOPIDAE (Worm Snakes)

Peters' Worm Snake (*Leptotyphlops scutifrons*) is a tiny black species resembling a pencil lead in thickness. As in the Blind Snakes, the head is covered with a large shield, but the tail is much longer. The average length is about 20 centimetres. These snakes feed entirely on termites.

Family BOIDAE (Boas and Pythons)

The African Python (*Python sebae*) is the largest snake found on the continent, attaining a maximum length of about 7 metres. Its dorsal scales are smaller than in any other local snake. The colour pattern is complex, mainly light and dark brown above, black and white below; there is a prominent dark spear-shaped marking on the head.

Pythons are very much at home in the water, but are frequently preyed upon by crocodiles. These snakes prey upon a wide range of mammals and birds, which are seized by the jaws, rolled up in the python's coils and killed by constriction which results in suffocation. Even a small python should be treated with caution, as its numerous needle-sharp recurved teeth can inflict a nasty wound.

Fig. 6 (top) Savanna Monitor.
Fig. 7 (bottom) African Python.

Family COLUBRIDAE (Typical Snakes)

The Common House Snake (*Lamprophis fuliginosus*) is a common nocturnal species. Resembling a miniature python in build, it is a harmless constrictor which rarely exceeds one metre in length. Local specimens are red-brown above, mother-of-pearl white

177

below. Juveniles feed largely on lizards; adults prey upon rats.

The Cape File Snake (*Mehelya capensis*) is a powerful nocturnal constrictor which may exceed one and a half metres in length. It has a flat head with a square snout; the body is triangular in cross-section, with the prominent bicarinate dorsal scale row ivory white, in contrast to the rest of the dorsal scales, which are purple-brown and widely separated to expose the pinkish skin between them. The belly is ivory white. The File Snake preys upon other snakes, lizards and toads. It climbs trees to obtain boomslangs and arboreal lizards and has been reported from the Victoria Falls rain forest.

The Black File Snake (*Mehelya nyassae*) is a small species, rarely exceeding half a metre in length. It is uniform blackish above and brown below. Its diet consists largely of small lizards.

The Cape Wolf Snake (*Lycophidion capense*) is a small nocturnal constrictor which averages half a metre in length. It is dark brown to black above, the head stippled with white and each scale white-tipped; the belly is white, more or less blotched or infuscate with dark grey. This snake derives its name from the long teeth in the front of the jaw, which enable the snake to get a firm grip on the smooth-scaled skinks upon which it preys.

The Olive Marsh Snake (*Natriciteres olivacea*) is a semi-aquatic diurnal snake which averages less than half a metre in length. It is olive or slate-grey above with a darker vertebral stripe; the belly is bright yellow, edged with olive or grey. This snake is usually found near the water's edge and its diet consists of frogs, tadpoles and small fishes.

The Mole Snake (*Pseudaspis cana*) is a powerful constrictor with a small, pointed head. A Livingstone snake measuring 1410 millimetres is the largest recorded locally. Juvenile snakes are light red-brown with black and cream markings, often including a dark zig-zag down the back. Adults usually become pale grey above with dark-tipped scales, but the big Livingstone female retained the juvenile markings. These snakes spend most of the time in the burrows of the rodents upon which they prey.

The Angolan Green Snake (*Philothamnus angolensis*) is a common diurnal snake in reedbeds and bushes along the Zambezi. This is a handsome snake, slender in build with a long tail and averaging 75 centimetres in length. The coloration is emerald green above, paler below; the scales on the neck are bordered with black, and the eye has a golden iris. This snake preys largely on frogs and toads, but juvenile chameleons are sometimes eaten. When molested, this harmless species inflates its throat like the boomslang.

The Bush Snake (*Philothamnus semivariegatus*) is a slender snake which may exceed a metre in length. The head and anterior portion of the body is blue-green; the neck has irregular black transverse bars, becoming uniform bronze posteriorly. Below, the chin is white, throat white or bright yellow, belly cream or mauve. This agile tree snake is common in dry savanna, especially Mopane woodland and thornbush, where it preys largely on lizards. Although quite harmless, the Bush Snake inflates its throat and bites fiercely when handled.

The Black-templed Cat Snake or Herald Snake (*Crotaphopeltis hotamboeia*) is a common nocturnal species which averages half a metre in length. It has a broad head, the eye has a vertical pupil and the tail is short.

The dorsal coloration varies from olive to blackish, with conspicuous blue-black patches on the temples; the underside is white. This back-fanged species is not dangerous to man. Its diet consists of frogs and toads.

The Tiger snake (*Telescopus semiannulatus*) is another back-fanged nocturnal species. It is a handsome snake, bright orange or salmon-pink in colour, with a row of about twenty-five black blotches extending from nape to tail tip. The head is very broad, the slender, vertically compressed body tapering into a fairly long tail. This snake is semi-arboreal and preys largely on geckos and sleeping chameleons; small bats are sometimes caught and eaten.

The Rufous-beaked Snake (*Rhamphiophis oxyrhynchus*) is a rather secretive diurnal snake, which reaches a maximum length of one and a half metres. The best distinguishing feature is the distinctly hooked snout. The body is light pinkish-brown above, the scales dark-edged, pure white below. This back-fanged snake spends much of its time in rodent burrows. Its diet includes rodents, small birds, lizards and smaller snakes.

The Olive Grass Snake (*Psammophis phillipsii*) is a very common diurnal snake which sometimes exceeds one and a half metres in length. With a slender body and whip-like tail, this is one of the fastest moving local snakes. The body is olive or grey-brown above and yellow to white below; the head often has symmetrical chestnut markings, including rows of rings on the lips. In spite of its large size, this back-fanged snake is harmless to man. It feeds on rodents, lizards and amphibians, but small birds and other

Fig. 8 (top) Mole Snake.
Fig. 9 (centre) Black-templed Cat Snake.
Fig. 10 (bottom) Rufous Beaked Snake.

snakes are occasionally taken. This snake usually frequents long grass, reedbeds and riverine vegetation.

The Stripe-bellied Sand Snake (*Psammophis subtaeniatus*) is one of the most frequently encountered diurnal snakes in dry open situations. The very slender build of this species is accentuated by a pair of yellow dorso-lateral longitudinal stripes on the brown body. The ventral coloration is distinctive, a broad yellow median band being separated by black hairlines from white lateral bands. This swift-moving, back-fanged snake preys largely on lizards and frogs; rodents are occasionally taken.

The Boomslang (*Dispholidus typus*) is a common arboreal snake which averages nearly one and a half metres in length. The distinctive features are a short 'chunky' head with very large eyes, and the dorsal scales, which are narrow, strongly keeled and obliquely set. Males are usually green, often with black-edged scales; females are brown or grey. Juveniles are very distinctive, with bright green eyes, back blackish with paired blue spots on the tips of adjoining scales, throat bright yellow, belly stippled maroon. This is the only back-fanged snake with a venom powerful enough to make its bite really dangerous to man, due to defibrination of the blood and consequent haemorrhage. Fortunately the very good eyesight of the Boomslang enables it to give man a wide berth and bites are rare. The Boomslang feeds principally on chameleons, birds' eggs and fledgling birds. Its presence is often given away by the commotion caused by birds (especially bulbuls) mobbing it.

The Vine Snake (*Thelotornis capensis*) is another common back-fanged tree snake. It is extremely slender, with a lanceolate head. The top of the head is green with a stippled black and pink Y-shaped marking; the upper lips are white with a black streak extending diagonally backwards from the eye. The body is ash-grey with pink, black and white markings. With its body twined in a bush, the Vine Snake remains motionless and relies on its excellent camouflage to escape detection. This snake has excellent eyesight, apparently correlated with a peculiar horizontal dumbell-shaped pupil: it recognises prey at a distance and then stalks it, moving forward slowly with head raised, finally making a short dash to seize its victim. The diet consists of small snakes, lizards, frogs, birds' eggs and fledglings. The Vine Snake's venom resembles that of the Boomslang in causing haemorrhage, but is less potent.

The Common Egg-eating Snake (*Dasypeltis scabra*) is a nocturnal species which averages about half a metre in length. It is a rather slender snake with a small, blunt head. The dorsum is pale brown with dark brown markings, consisting of a forward-directed chevron on the neck (often one or two narrower chevrons on the head), a vertebral series of elongate blotches and a lateral series of vertical bars; the belly is white. This harmless snake is virtually toothless and feeds entirely on birds' eggs, which are taken into the throat and crushed against a series of projections from the neck vertebrae; the crumpled eggshell and any embryo is then ejected and the contents of the egg pass on to the stomach.

Family ATRACTASPIDIDAE (Stiletto Snakes)

Bibron's Stiletto Snake (*Atractaspis bibronii*) is an insignificant species which rarely exceeds half a metre in length. It is purple-brown to black above and brown or white below. The head is small and flat, the body rather slender, the tail very short and terminating in a sharp spine. This species is nocturnal and forages by investigation of holes in the ground and under logs and rocks. It preys upon lizards, small snakes, frogs and rodents. The fangs are very long and are brought down on each side of the compressed lower jaw with the mouth closed, an adaptation for killing prey in a confined space. This snake cannot safely be held behind the neck, as it can easily twist and stab a finger with one fang. The bite causes considerable local pain and swelling, often causing slight tissue destruction around the fang puncture.

Family ELAPIDAE (Cobras, Mambas, etc.)
The Half-banded Garter Snake (*Elapsoidea semiannulata*) is a primitive burrowing elapid which rarely exceeds half a metre in length. It is rather heavily built, with a short tail. The dorsal scales are large, in only thirteen longitudinal rows at midbody. Juveniles are black above, with a white marking on top of the head and a series of about ten white crossbands on the body, which are less than half the width of the black interspaces; the belly is grey. When the snake reaches a length of 20 centimetres, the white bands begin to darken from the centre and are quickly reduced to a pair of narrow white lines, which may persist for a long time. This snake feeds on other snakes, lizards and frogs.

The Egyptian Cobra (*Naja haje*) is a robust snake which attains a length of two and a half metres. When disturbed, it rears up and spreads a broad hood. Juveniles are yellow, adults dark brown or banded in black and yellow. The chin and anterior portion of the body are yellow below, with a broad dark

Fig. 11 (top) Vine Snake.
Fig. 12 (centre) Common Egg-eating Snake.
Fig. 13 (bottom) Half-banded Garter Snake.

Snake Bites

Snake bites in Africa are rare except where people go barefoot. If a bite does occur, keep the victim as calm as possible and avoid unnecessary movement of the affected limb. Remove the victim to a hospital or doctor as soon as possible; alternatively get a doctor to the patient. First-aid measures should be used as follows:

The first concern is to stop the spread of the venom. The latest research into snake-bite has shown that the application of a firm bandage (crepe or similar) along the length of the bitten limb slows down the progress of the venom *via* both the blood vessels and the lymphatics. Do not waste time by removing clothing; apply the bandage over it. Keep the limb immobilised by applying a splint. The pressure bandage may be kept in place for 2–3 hours. If swelling of the extremities occurs, loosen the bandage.

The Spitting Cobra can project venom into the eyes. This must be quickly washed out with water or any non-caustic liquid which is available, otherwise the eyesight may be permanently affected. If there is a delay in washing out the eyes, antivenene diluted 1:10 with water should be used as soon as possible.

a few hours.

The Moçambique Spitting Cobra (*Naja mossambica*) is a relatively small species, rarely exceeding one and a half metres in length. Above it is light grey or olive brown, the scales being dark-edged; below it is salmon pink with a series of irregular black bands and blotches on the throat. It spreads a much narrower hood than the Egyptian Cobra. The diet consists largely of toads, but rodents, birds and small snakes are also taken. Spitting Cobras will bite if handled, but normally defend themselves by projecting a spray of venom into the eyes of an enemy. The fangs are modified so that the venom canal turns forward. The effective range of a Spitting Cobra is about one and a half times its own length.

The Black Mamba (*Dendroaspis polylepis*) is Africa's largest venomous snake, averaging

brown band on the throat (*i.e.* face of the hood). This species is distinguished from other cobras by a series of subocular scales, which exclude the labial shields from the eye. The Egyptian Cobra preys upon toads, other snakes and rodents; it can also become a raider of poultry runs, where it swallows eggs and chicks. The venom of this snake is a powerful neurotoxin, which can kill a man in

Fig. 14 (left) Egyptian Cobra.
Fig. 15 (right) Black Mamba.

nearly two and a half metres in length. Despite its vernacular name, it is usually olive brown above and dirty white below, often with irregular dark blotching or cross-bands towards the tail, which is usually blackish. The head is long and almost coffin-shaped, with a square snout. The body is slender and the tail long. When disturbed, a Mamba may raise the anterior third of its body from the ground, open its mouth to reveal a blackish interior, and spread a narrow hood. When a nervous Mamba assumes this posture, it will strike at the slightest provocation. A full bite can kill a man within half an hour. Mambas are most plentiful in dense riverine forest and on bush-covered rock outcrops; they feed largely on rodents and fledgling birds.

Family VIPERIDAE (Adders and Vipers)

The Snouted Night-Adder (*Causus defilippii*) is a small snake rarely exceeding 40 centimetres in length. It has a triangular head, stubby body and very short tail. The dorsal markings consist of a black, forward-pointing chevron on the head and a series of black rhombic blotches along the spine; the ground colour is pinkish brown. This snake feeds on toads and if it bites a man the only results are local pain and swelling which subsides within twenty-four hours.

The Puffadder (*Bitis arietans*) is an obese, sluggish snake with a broad, flat head and a short tail. The dorsal pattern of forward-directed, black and yellow chevrons breaks up the outline and provides perfect camouflage against a background of dry vegetation. The snake ambushes its prey, which consists largely of rats. Puffadders do not get

183

out of the way when a man approaches and barefoot pedestrians are frequently bitten on the leg. The bite is rarely fatal, but often causes severe local tissue destruction, sometimes necessitating the amputation of a limb.

Amphibians

Order ANURA (Tail-less Amphibians)
Family PIPIDAE (Tongue-less Frogs)
The local race of the Temperate Platanna or Clawed Frog (*Xenopus laevis*) is *petersii* Bocage, described from Angola. In lagoons along the Zambezi I have taken both this species and the tropical form *X. muelleri*. Platannas are totally aquatic and have the eyes placed on the top of the head, so that they can watch for enemies or potential prey as they bask in shallow water. They have flat bodies and powerful hind legs with strongly webbed toes which enable them to move quickly through the water. The first three toes are armed with black claws. These frogs prey upon aquatic insects, tadpoles and small fish, which are pushed into the mouth with the long fingers. The translucent tadpoles have large flat heads with tentacles bordering the mouth; they float in the water head down, with the finely pointed tail vibrating. The larvae feed on algae.

Family BUFONIDAE (Toads)
The Gutteral Toad (*Bufo gutturalis*) is a common species which may exceed 75 millimetres in length. It is light brown with a dorsal pattern of paired dark rectangular blotches. During the summer months these toads emerge after dark and may be found around human habitations, where they feed on insects which are attracted to the lights; many are killed on tarred roads.

Family RANIDAE (Frogs)
The Plain Ridged Frog (*Ptychadena anchietae*) is the common species along the water's edge. It escapes by making great leaps rather than by taking to the water. Usually pale grey-brown in colour, this species has a paler triangle on the snout and there are longitudinal dark stripes on the inside of the thigh. The toes are extensively webbed.

The Natal Puddle Frog (*Phrynobatrachus natalensis*) is a common small frog with a rugose skin. It is olive-brown, often with a yellow or green vertebral stripe or band. This frog is usually common around small pools or backwaters.

The Grey Tree Frog (*Chiromantis xerampelina*) is a common species in Mopane woodland. It is a robust frog with large discs on the digits; the colour varies from greyish white to dark grey-brown. Large females may exceed 80 millimetres in length. The most remarkable feature of this frog is its breeding habits. When the rains break, the pair of frogs select a branch or rock which overhangs a pool of water and build a foam nest from a secretion discharged by the female. The small white eggs are laid in the mass of foam and the outer surface hardens so that the nest resembles a large meringue. The small tadpoles develop within the shelter of the nest until their activity reduces the interior to a liquid state and eventually the bottom of the nest collapses and the tadpoles fall into the pool below to complete their metamorphosis.

Systematic List of the Reptiles and Amphibians of the Victoria Falls Region
Reptilia

PELOMEDUSIDAE

Pelomedusa subrufa	African Marsh Terrapin
Pelusios bechuanicus	Okavango Hinged Terrapin
Pelusios sinuatus	Serrated Hinged Terrapin

TESTUDINIDAE
Geochelone pardalis — Leopard Tortoise
Kinixys belliana — Bell's Hinged Tortoise
CROCODYLIDAE
Crocodylus niloticus — Nile Crocodile
GEKKONIDAE
Hemidactylus mabouia — Tropical House Gecko
Lygodactylus capensis — Cape Dwarf Gecko
Lygodactylus chobiensis — Chobe Dwarf Gecko
Pachydactylus bibronii — Bibron's Gecko
Pachydactylus punctatus — Spotted Ground Gecko
Pachydactylus oshaughnessyi — O'Shaughnessy's Banded Gecko
AGAMIDAE
Agama aculeata — Spiny Agama
CHAMAELEONIDAE
Chamaeleo dilepis — Common Flap-necked Chameleon
SCINCIDAE
Mabuya quinquetaeniata — Rainbow Skink
Mabuya varia — Variable Skink
Mabuya striata — Common Striped Skink
Lygosoma sundevallii — Sundevall's Writing Skink
Panaspis wahlbergii — Wahlberg's Snake-eyed Skink
Typhlosaurus gracilis — Gracile Limbless Skink
CORDYLIDAE
Gerrhosaurus nigrolineatus — Black-lined Plated Lizard
Gerrhosaurus major — Tawny Plated Lizard
LACERTIDAE
Nucras taeniolata — Ornate Scrub Lizard
Ichnotropis squamulosa — Moçambique Rough-scaled Sand Lizard
Ichnotropis capensis — Cape Rough-scaled Sand Lizard
VARANIDAE
Varanus niloticus — Nile Monitor or Water Leguaan
Varanus exanthematicus — Savanna Monitor or Tree Leguaan
AMPHISBAENIDAE
Zygaspis quadrifrons — Round-snouted Amphisbaenian
Monopeltis mauricei — Maurice's Amphisbaenian
Dalophia pistillum — Zambezi Square-tailed Amphisbaenian
Dalphia longicauda — Long-tailed Amphisbaenian

TYPHLOPIDAE
Typhlops schlegelii — Schlegel's Blind Snake
LEPTOTYPHLOPIDAE
Leptotyphlops longicaudus — Long-tailed Worm Snake
Leptotyphlops scutifrons — Peters' Worm Snake
BOIDAE
Python sebae — African Python
COLUBRIDAE
Boaedon fuliginosus — Common House Snake
Mehelya capensis — Cape File Snake
Mehelya nyassae — Nyasa File Snake
Lycophidion capense — Cape Wolf Snake
Natriciteres olivacea — Olive Marsh Snake
Limnophis bicolor — Piscivorous Water Snake
Pseudaspis cana — Mole Snake
Meizodon semiornatus — Semiornate Snake
Philothamnus hoplogaster — Eastern Green Snake
Philothamus angolensis — Angolan Green Snake
Philothamnus semivariegatus — Variegated Bush Snake
Amblyodipsas polylepis — Purple-glossed Snake
Amblyodipsas ventrimaculata — Kalahari Purple-glossed Snake
Xenocalamus mechowii — Mechow's Quill-snouted Snake
Aparallactus lunulatus — Reticulated Centipede-eater
Aparallactus capensis — Cape Centipede-eater
Crotophopeltis hotamboeia — Black-templed Cat Snake
Telescopus semiannulatus — Tiger Snake
Hemirhagerrhis nototaenia — Bark Snake
Rhamphiophis oxyrhynchus — Rufous Beaked Snake
Dromophis lineatus — Lined Grass Snake
Psammophis phillipsii — Olive Grass Snake
Psammophis subtaeniatus — Stripe-bellied Sand Snake
Psammophis angolensis — Dwarf Sand Snake
Dispholidus typus — Boomslang
Thelotornis capensis — Savanna Vine Snake
Dasypeltis scabra — Common Egg-eater
ATRACTASPIDIDAE
Atractaspis bibronii — Bibron's Stiletto Snake
ELAPIDAE
Elapsoidea semiannulata — Half-banded Garter Snake
Naja haje — Egyptian Cobra
Naja mossambica — Moçambique Spitting Cobra
Dendroaspis polylepis — Black Mamba

VIPERIDAE

    Causus defilippii   Snouted Night Adder

    Bitis arietans   Puffadder

Amphibia

PIPIDAE

    Xenopus laevis   Temperate Platanna

    Xenopus muelleri   Tropical Platanna

BUFONIDAE

    Schismaderma carens   Red Toad

    Bufo gutturalis   Guttural Toad

    Bufo maculatus   Flat-backed Toad

    Bufo garmani   Olive Toad

    Bufo fenoulheti   Flat Toad

MICROHYLIDAE

    Phrynomerus bifasciatus   Banded Rubber Frog

RANIDAE

    Tomopterna cryptotis   Tremolo Sand Frog

    Tomopterna marmorata   Russet Sand Frog

    Ptychadena subpunctata   Spot-bellied Ridged Frog

    Ptychadena anchietae   Plain Ridged Frog

    Ptychadena porosissima   Three-striped Ridged Frog

    Ptychadena guibei   Guibe's Ridged Frog

    Ptychadena mossambica   Broad-banded Ridged Frog

    Phrynobatrachus natalensis Natal Puddle Frog

    Phrynobatrachus mababiensis   Dwarf Puddle Frog

HEMISIDAE

    Hemisus marmoratus   Marbled Pig-snouted Frog

RHACOPHORIDAE

    Chiromantis xerampelina   Grey Tree Frog

HYPEROLIIDAE

    Leptopelis bocagii   Bocage's Burrowing Frog

    Kassina senegalensis   Senegal Walking Frog

    Hyperolius nasutus   Long Reed Frog

    Hyperolius marmoratus   Painted Reed Frog

Select Bibliography

BROADLEY, D. G. 'The Reptiles and Amphibians of Zambia', *Puku*, vi, 1971, pp. 1–143.

BROADLEY, D. G. *'Fitzsimons' Snakes of Southern Africa*, Johannesburg, 1983.

FITZSIMONS, V. F. M. *The Lizards of South Africa*, Pretoria (Transvaal Museum Memoirs, no. 1), 1943.

FITZSIMONS, V. F. M. *Snakes of Southern Africa*, Cape Town, 1962.

POYNTON, J. C. 'The Amphibia of Southern Africa: a faunal study', *Annals Natal Museum*, xvii, 1964, pp. 1–134.

POYNTON, J. C. and BROADLEY, D. G. 'Amphibia Zambesiaca', *Annals Natal Museum*, xxvi (2), 1985, pp. 503–553; xxvii (1), 1985, pp. 115–181; xxviii (1), 1987, pp. 161–229.

CHAPTER 14

The Fishes

Graham Bell-Cross
revised by John Minshull

Probably the most interesting yet mystifying feature concerning the fishes of the Victoria Falls region is the appreciable difference in fish faunas above and below the Falls. Over eighty different species are known to occur in the Upper Zambezi system, and sixty-four species in the Kariba system. However, only thirty-odd species are common to both systems.

The Zambezi River

No glimpse of the fishes of the Victoria Falls would be complete without some background on the whole of the Zambezi drainage basin. The most recent fisheries work carried out indicates that over three hundred and sixty species of fish have been recorded from the entire river system. The fish faunas of various sub-systems differ markedly and this has resulted in a division of the Zambezi into six zoogeographical units. They are, from west to east, the Upper Zambezi, Kariba, Kafue, Middle Zambezi, Lake Malawi and the Lower Zambezi sub-systems. There are possibly only two river systems on the African continent with richer fish faunas than the Zambezi: the Congo with over six hundred species and the Nile with about the same number as the Zambezi.

The Victoria Falls separate the Upper Zambezi and Kariba sub-systems and we shall take a closer look at both these areas.

The Upper Zambezi

Rising in the Mwinilunga district of Zambia at approximately 1433 metres, very near to where the three territories of Angola, Zaïre and Zambia share a common border, the river flows some 1440 kilometres and drops nearly 520 metres before taking the big plunge at the Victoria Falls. Throughout its course the river flows strongly over the wide

187

Kalahari sands of the central and southern Barotse floodplains and over numerous stretches of rapids and small waterfalls. Only a single large waterfall, the Gonye at Sioma, interrupts canoe or barge traffic over most of its length. These beautiful semi-circular falls are some 21 metres in height and, though they interrupt fish movement during the dry season, they do not constitute a barrier during the flood period since, due to the restricting nature of the gorge below the falls, the water levels above and below the falls then tend to level off.

The river water of the Upper Zambezi is remarkably clear throughout the year. This is partly due to its long passage over the Kalahari sand beds – of great aesthetic value perhaps but resulting in little in the way of nutrient acquisition. Though the river can, and does, support a wide variety of fish species, the production in terms of commercial fisheries cannot compare with neighbouring rivers such as the Kafue.

In any river system the distribution of fishes conforms to a recognisable pattern. Near the source are found those species with particular adaptations to life in fast-flowing water, often at high altitudes. They are able to withstand low temperatures and often have sucker-like fins or mouths to ensure easy purchase on rocks or vegetation in a strong current. Their small size is also an important factor which enables them to escape predation by hiding under pebbles and vegetation in shallow water. As the stream becomes a river, additional habitats become available – deeper water allowing larger fish to move freely with little danger of predation. Lagoons and backwaters become the home of swamp-loving species. In tropical waters, the larger the river the greater the number of fish species to be found. This is

perhaps a rather long-winded way of explaining the distribution of fishes in the Upper Zambezi and, though eighty-four species are now recognised there, barely three-quarters of them will be found in the immediate neighbourhood of the Victoria Falls.

Lake Kariba
The old course of the Zambezi below the Victoria Falls was not a hospitable environment for many fish species, particularly those of small size. Due mainly to a lack of vegetation, very little shelter was available to prevent predation from fishes like the Tigerfish (*Hydrocynus vittatus*). It is possible that this part of the Zambezi might not always have been as unsympathetic to small fish species as it has been in recent times. Collections made recently in Moçambique rivers have turned up several Upper Zambezi species which have not been recorded in the intervening river, possible proof of their existence there at some time in the past.

The formation of Lake Kariba has vastly changed the habitat now available to fish. The old river shoreline with its sandbanks and rock outcrops and its fast-flowing water has given way to a far greater area of shoreline with steadily increasing stands of aquatic plants of many species. Quiet lagoons and tributary river mouths encourage invasion by the more sedentary species. Proof that the environment is now rather sympathetic to many species is the successful invasion and population build-up of at least nine Upper Zambezi species not previously recorded below the Victoria Falls. It must be realised, however, that many of the smaller species in the system only occur within the inflowing rivers and not in the actual lake.

Origin of Fish Faunas

It has been generally accepted that the Congo basin is possibly the ancestral home of African freshwater fishes. The evidence for this is not as conclusive as one might wish, but must serve for the purpose of this discussion. A glance at a map of central Africa shows that the Congo River system stretches from its delta on the West Coast, three-quarters of the way across the continent towards the Indian Ocean. Two of its largest southern tributaries, the Kasai and the Lualaba, share a common watershed with the Zambezi. It is basically because of the widely different faunas of these two Congo tributaries that we have such a variation in the fish species of the Upper Zambezi, Kariba and other sub-systems of the Zambezi River.

To understand the present distribution of fishes it is necessary to go back in time more than one million years, when the earliest discernible distribution pattern became evident. At that time the Upper Zambezi formed part of a large basin of internal drainage which included the present Cunene, Kafue and Okavango drainages. The watershed separating the Upper Zambezi and Kasai Rivers has gradually migrated southwards, involving the two systems in repeated river captures. Thus at one point in time, at the beginning of this story, the Upper Zambezi, Kafue and Cunene all had a common fish fauna. The Cunene was probably the first river to break away from the basin of internal drainage, followed by the Kafue. It was at this stage of events that the most recent Kasai/Zambezi capture occurred, resulting in the invasion of at least seventeen fish species, including the Tigerfish.

The Middle and Lower Zambezi story appears to be more complicated. It is obvious that when the Upper Zambezi was diverted from the internal drainage basin into the Batoka Gorge, thus presenting us with the picture we see today, a number of Upper Zambezi species gained access to that system. This does not, however, account for the thirty-odd species occurring below and not above the Victoria Falls. Just as the Kasai arm of the Congo was responsible for the Upper Zambezi fauna it would appear that the Lualaba arm contributed to the Zambezi river fauna below the Falls. That there was a direct exchange of fauna between the Lualaba and the Middle Zambezi seems unlikely. The Zambian Congo system – Lakes Bangweulu, Mweru and the intervening Luapula River, which constitutes part of the Upper Lualaba system – shares a common watershed with the Zambezi, but does not contain many species common to the Lualaba and Middle Zambezi systems. We must then look elsewhere for a Lualaba/Zambezi invasion route. Recent collections from the Rufiji and Ruvuma rivers in Tanzania, on the East Coast, indicate that the most likely route has been from the Lualaba *via* its tributaries, the Lukuga and Malagarasi, to the Rufiji and Ruvuma Rivers and down the East Coast to the Lower Zambezi. We have glibly talked of fishes moving between presently isolated river systems – what are the mechanics of fish distribution? We have already mentioned river capture (Kasai to Upper Zambezi), but several other courses are possible. Confluence between river systems across low-lying floodplains occurs today on the coastal plains of Moçambique, *e.g.* the Urema Depression, linking the Lower Pungwe and Lower Zambezi Rivers. It appears possible that rivers such as the Buzi and Pungwe might have been confluent during a time of ocean regression when the present coastline might have been more than ten kilometres further eastwards.

The Cahora Bassa Dam wall might today constitute a barrier to the movement of fish species from the Lower to the Middle Zambezi, but the original rapids are not considered to have inhibited the movement of most ex-Lualaba species upriver, before the dam was built.

Interesting Fishes from above and below the Victoria Falls

Family ANGUILLIDAE

Only one of the four central African freshwater Eels, the African Mottled Eel (*Anguilla bengalensis labiata*), has been recorded from above the Falls. In fact, to my knowledge, only a single specimen has been captured and that was taken in the water diversion channel *above* the Falls. Recent capture of the elvers of the Mottled Eel at the base of the Siengwazi Falls on the Kalomo River – above the Kariba dam wall – has ended speculation on whether elvers can successfully negotiate the wall. How they do it remains a mystery but it is suspected that they manage somehow to go through the turbines and up the penstock at some stage of hydro operations. Cahora Bassa Dam is now the main barrier to eels and very few are today found in the Kariba Dam turbine wells during maintenance. A large specimen will weigh 13·6 kilograms and measure all of 1·9 metres, and is a worthy opponent at the end of a fishing line. The spawning site of our eels is in the Indian Ocean, probably to the east of Madagascar.

Family MORMYRIDAE

This family, which is endemic to the African continent, is well represented by some seven species in our area.

Most species are large enough to be taken by the angler and the largest, the Cornish Jack (*Mormyrops deliciosus*), attains a known weight of 13·7 kilograms. Only two species, the Cornish Jack and the Eastern Bottlenose (*Mormyrus longirostris*), are restricted to the river below the Falls. Some members of this family are noted for their ability to give a slight electric shock. It appears unlikely that sufficient current is generated to aid in capturing prey, as with the Electric Catfish, but almost certainly it is used as a form of 'radar' to facilitate navigation.

The smallest Mormyrid of our region, the Dwarf Stonebasher (*Pollimyrus castelnaui*), is only found above the Falls. It inhabits aquatic weeds in quiet water and, as it attains a maximum length of only 8 centimetres, is an attractive little aquarium species.

Two closely related forms, the Eastern Bottlenose (below the Falls) and the Western Bottlenose (above the Falls), are well-known to the angler. Though extremely similar in general morphology – except for the longer snout in the Eastern Bottlenose – their maximum known sizes vary greatly. The current angling records stand at 9·9 kilograms and 2·3 kilograms respectively. If the Western Bottlenose invades Kariba from the Upper Zambezi it appears possible that hybridisation may take place as the two species are not sympatric (do not coexist) in any river system.

Family CHARACIDAE

The Tigerfish (*Hydrocynus forskablii*) needs no introduction. Four species are known from the African continent with the Goliath Tiger (*Hydrocynus goliath*) from the Congo system the grand-daddy of them all, achieving a total weight of 50 kilograms. Ours is the southernmost species and the second largest, and the current angling record stands at 15·5 kilo-

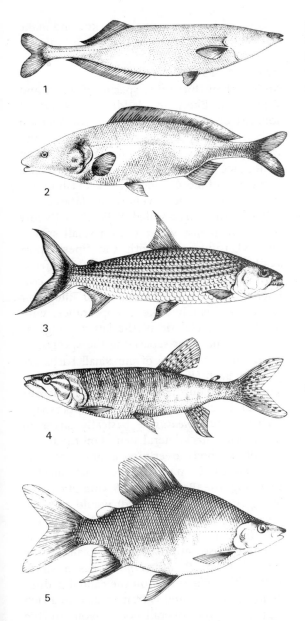

Fig. 1 1 Cornish Jack (*Mormyrops deliciosus*);
2 Western Bottlenose (*Mormyrus lacerda*); 3 Tigerfish
(*Hydrocynus forskablii*); 4 African Pike (*Hepsetus
odoe*); 5 Nkupe (*Distichodus mossambicus*).

grams. Of the many descriptions of its sporting qualities I favour the following quotation from a bygone era: '... I have stated heretofore in print and am still ready to maintain my pronouncement, that the Tiger Fish of Africa is the fiercest fish that swims. Let others hold forth as advocates for the Mako shark, the Barracuda, the Piranha of the Amazon, or the Blue Fish of the Atlantic. To them I say, "Pish and Tush"...'*

Though Tigerfish can be caught on bait or lure throughout the year, there appear to be two distinct angling seasons. At the end of the rainy season, when tributary rivers or flood-plains discharge small and juvenile fishes back into the main river – usually in May and June when the water is still quite warm – Tiger appear to be in peak condition. After winter, when temperatures start rising, the second angling season gets under way and lasts until January when the rivers come down in spate.

May is my favourite fishing month on the Upper Zambezi for many reasons. Terns, gulls and cormorants tend to concentrate in areas where the juvenile fishes are forced back into the main river, due to receding water levels on the floodplains. At these hot-spots shoals of small Tiger patrol inshore in the shallower water with larger shoals in the deep water. It appears more common, too, at this time of the year, for really large fish to attack and maul small specimens fighting at the end of a line. With a little experience 'Tiger water' can easily be recognised. Apart from bird indicators, rapidly deepening water below a sandbank is a favourite refuge. Look for shoals of small fishes and you will find small Tigerfish. Where you find small Tiger, with deep water close by, you will assuredly find the heavyweights.

* Leander J. McCormick, *Game Fish of the World*.

191

Three other species make up the complement of Characins; all are small species, referred to as robbers, and form part of the diet of the Pike and Tiger.

Family HEPSETIDAE

Not as well known as the preceding species, the African Pike (*Hepsetus odoe*) is a fine fighter and, in its efforts to escape the hook, will jump out of the water more frequently than the Tigerfish. It is present above but not below the Falls and, due to the dominant role of the Tiger in the open water, the Pike is restricted to lagoons and backwaters where it finds some measure of protection from large Tigerfish. Parent fish construct a surface bubble nest for eggs. The largest specimen from the Upper Zambezi was only 1·4 kilograms in weight but it is known to reach 2·0 kilograms in the neighbouring Kafue River where *Hydrocynus* is absent.

Family DISTICHODONTIDAE

The Nkupe (*Distichodus mossambicus*) and Chessa (*Distichodus schenga*) are two of the more popular bait-fishing species found below the Falls. Only Nkupe is illustrated here, but Chessa is similar in build and lighter in colour, with a shorter snout and underslung mouth. Like so many other species inhabiting Kariba, lacustrine conditions appear to have favoured the growth and survival of large specimens and the present angling record for Nkupe is 7·0 kilograms and for Chessa 6·35 kilograms.

Family CITHARINIDAE

A family that contains some large commercially important fish species in the east and central African lakes is represented in the Zambezi by three small species which seldom exceed 6 centimetres. Though rather dowdy in colour, they are strongly marked and make a welcome appearance in many fish tanks.

Family CYPRINIDAE

No less than thirty-five species of Barbs and Yellowfish, likely to gladden the heart of aquarist or angler, are found in the Victoria Falls area. Many anglers, who know the river well, prefer to bait-fish for Yellowfish in preference to Tiger as they maintain it is a stronger and more skilled fighter. Fishing for the Upper Zambezi Yellowfish (above the Falls) or the Large-scaled Yellowfish (below the Falls) in fast water with a small spoon, must, I think, rate with the finest sport available in freshwater anywhere in Africa. Both species, *Barbus marequensis* and *B. codringtoni*, are known to attain 3·0 kilograms and are extremely alike in appearance, with the higher dorsal fin of the latter being the principal character separating the species.

The most colourful of our small barbs are the Red Barb (*Barbus fasciolatus*) – a blood-red body colour interrupted by numerous vertical black bands; and the Copperstripe Barb (*B. multilineatus*) – basically silver in colour with black lateral stripes on the upper half of the body overlying a single copper-coloured band. Many of the other species, including the Beira Barb (*B. radiatus*) and Orangefin Barb (*B. eutaenia*) would not disgrace any aquarium. Like most species the colours of the adult fishes intensify as the breeding season approaches. For example, the Spottail Barb (*B. afrovernayi*) has a silver body with a black spot on the caudal peduncle in the winter and is transformed to a rich coppery-maroon overall body colour during the summer.

The Mudsuckers (*Labeo*) are a group of large Cyprinids similar in body configuration to the Yellowfish but generally with jaws

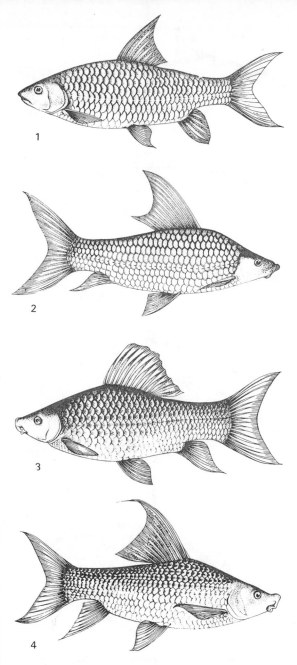

Fig. 2 1 Largescale Yellowfish (*Barbus marequensis*);
2 Manyame Labeo (*Labeo altivelis*); 3 Purple Labeo
(*Labeo congoro*); 4 Upper Zambezi Labeo (*Labeo
lunatus*).

situated underneath the snout. The Manyame
Labeo and the Purple Labeo are two of the
largest members of Zambezi Labeo; both
species are readily taken by anglers and
current records are both over 3·0 kilograms.
If you look at the submerged boulders in the
Gorge below the Falls you might well see
traces of their mouth scrape marks as they
remove the algae adhering to the rock face.

Family BAGRIDAE

Three species of Bagrids inhabit the Falls area.
The Spotted Sand Catlet (*Leptoglanis rotun-
diceps*), a little chap scarcely 4 centimetres in
length, is widely distributed throughout Zimbabwe wherever sandy river beds occur. The
smaller Chobe Sand Catlet (*L. dorae*) appears
to be restricted to the river above the Falls.
The Grunter (*Auchenoglanis ngamensis*) is another late invader from the Kasai/Congo into
the Upper Zambezi system. Never weighing
much more than 0·5 kilogram, it is seldom
taken by the angler and does not feature
much in commercial catches.

Family SCHILBEIDAE

The Silver Barbel (*Schilbe mystus mystus*) lives
above, and the Butter Barbel (*Eutropius de-
pressirostris*) below the Falls. There are few
morphological differences between the two
sub-species except that the Butter Barbel
possesses an additional fin – the adipose –
and herein lies an intriguing mystery. The
Silver Barbel populations of the Upper Zambezi occasionally produce a specimen *with* an
adipose fin, and the Butter Barbel populations
below the Falls, one *without* an adipose.
Examinations of Kafue River *Schilbe mystus*
populations over several years indicate that
the proportion of *Schilbe* with an adipose fin
is now higher than it was a decade ago. If this
proves to be true the big question is whether

193

unusual environmental conditions, *e.g.* temperature, are responsible for the appearance or disappearance of this characteristic. Both sub-species are easily caught on bait but the angler takes great care to avoid the sharp, serrated, dorsal spines which are covered with a toxic mucus and can inflict severe pain. Some little while ago I was asked to identify a small fish bone which had apparently lodged in the throat of an unfortunate man, and had gradually worked its way into the heart and killed him. It proved to be a pectoral spine of the Silver Barbel. Though neither sub-species attains a great size, the Butter Catfish appears to grow to twice the size of the Silver and specimens of 1·4 kilograms have been caught.

A most exciting recent addition to the Upper Zambezi fauna is *Schilbe yangambianus* – a smaller, darker relative of the Butter Catfish, which had only previously been known from the Kasai and its tributaries in Zaïre: further evidence of the affinity between Upper Zambezi and Kasai fish faunas! Reports by anglers of this *Schilbe* in the Zambezi in Barotseland preceded its capture by many years, and this is not the first time that anglers have beaten the scientists to a new discovery.

Family AMPHILIIDAE

A lover of small rocky streams, the Stargazer Mountain Catfish (*Amphilius uranoscopus*), has been found from an altitude of 2000 metres to less than 600 metres in central African waters. It is usually the first fish species encountered at the headwaters of streams in rocky areas and seldom appears to exceed 20 centimetres in length. A shy, secretive creature whose dark blotchy appearance blends in well with its habitat, it is seldom seen unless its habitat is disturbed.

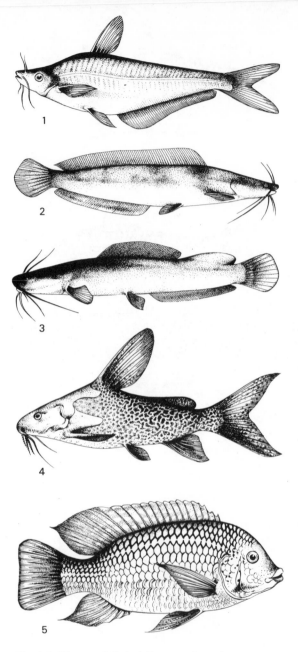

Fig. 3 1 Silver Catfish (*Schilbe mystus*); 2 Sharptoothed Catfish (*Clarias gariepinus*); 3 Vundu (*Heterobranchus longifilis*); 4 Upper Zambezi Squeaker (*Synodontis woosnami*); 5 Greenheaded Tilapia (*Oreochromis macrochir*).

194

Family CLARIIDAE

The heavyweights of the Zambezi fish fauna belong to this family with the Vundu (*Heterobranchus longifilis*) as the regional champion. The current angling record of 50 kilograms gives some indication of size but, judging by the number of stories about the bigger ones that got away, I suspect the record will soon be broken. The Vundu, another of the species found only below the Falls, will eat anything that moves and a lot that does not. Most anglers have a favourite bait for this fish which 'never fails'! Next in line for a shot at the title is the Sharp-toothed Catfish (*Clarias gariepinus*) with a record weight of 30·8 kilograms. This particular specimen was taken in 1947 and really is a whopper, but the usual weight for a big one is nearer 17 kilograms. Found both upstream and downstream of the Falls, it is a scavenger with the most incredible items recognised from gut contents, including small crocodiles, snails, birds, berries and other fishes. Its practice of quartering below heronries is well established and many an unwary young egret has fallen out of its nest virtually into the wide gape of this predator. The closely related Blunt-toothed Catfish (*C. ngamensis*) is similar in appearance but does not attain half the size of *C. gariepinus* and does not occur below the Victoria Falls.

Three other small species are known from the Falls, but they are small secretive animals seldom seen and hardly ever caught.

Family MALAPTERURIDAE

The Electric Barbel (*Malapterurus electricus*) is only known in the Zambezi River below the Falls. It is a fascinating, but repulsive, bloated-looking catfish that delights the practical jokers among anglers. How many 'green' anglers have been asked to assist in landing an Electric Barbel and received an unpleasant and forceful shock for their pains? This species is one of half-a-dozen on the African continent which is capable of generating electrical pulses and can, I believe, discharge between 350 and 450 volts. This mechanism is used offensively to obtain food and in defence against would-be attackers. An underwater spear fisherman is credited with obtaining the largest specimen yet known – 6·4 kilograms. Details of the capture might make interesting reading!

Family MOCHOKIDAE

Disliked by the angler and commercial fisherman alike, the Squeakers nevertheless play an important role in the ecology of the river system. Although six species occur in the Zambezi, four above and two below the Falls, little is known of their biology. They are among the few fish species which successfully co-exist in the open river with the Tigerfish – possibly due to their bottom-frequenting habits and to their quite formidable dorsal and pelvic spine armament. The spines are serrated in different directions, fore and aft, one a cutting edge, the other a holding edge. To a greater degree even than the Catfish, the Squeakers are the true scavengers of the Zambezi. Though such an apparently uninviting meal, Squeakers form the main fish prey of the Whitebreasted and Reed Cormorants which take great trouble to swallow their prey head-first, the fish's spines folding back along the body.

Family POECILIIDAE

This group of very small top minnows is famed for their ability to control mosquito larvae populations and, of the five species involved, only two are found below the Falls. The most colourful species, *Nothobranchius taeniopygus*, is not a fish that favours large rivers but inhabits small temporary pools, to which its life cycle is adapted. Breeding occurs in these small pools and eggs are shed in late summer just before the pools dry up. The eggs desiccate and remain in the dried hard mud throughout the dry season to hatch when the pools refill the following rainy season. *N. taeniopygus* has not yet been located south of the Zambezi River but has been taken on the watershed between the Zambezi and Kafue Rivers near Monze and Mazabuka in Zambia. An undescribed species has been found in the Caprivi Strip near Katima Mulilo.

Family CICHLIDAE

Colloquially known as Bream throughout English-speaking Africa, this group is not related to the European Bream (*Abramis brama*), though it does bear a slight superficial resemblance. Some five genera totalling seventeen species are known from the Victoria Falls region and they can conveniently be divided into three groups:
a) Smallmouth Bream – *Tilapia* and *Oreochromis* spp. This is certainly the most important commercial fish group in the Zambezi and probably the whole of freshwater Africa, for that matter. Six species are recognised from the Falls vicinity and, due to stocking and recent natural invasions into Lake Kariba from the Upper Zambezi, five species are found below the Falls and five above. *T. ruweti* is confined above, and *O. mortimeri* below, the Falls. Our Zambezi species are typically riverine fishes and their early inability to adapt to the lacustrine environment on the formation of the new lake gave rise to concern. Latest indications are that recruit-ment is good – possibly due to recently established weedbeds which act as shelter for the fry and, since the introduction of the sardine (*Limnothrissa miodon*), predator pressure has lessened on the Smallmouths. The biology of this group is relatively well known as they have been extensively used in fish culture in central Africa during the last three decades.

A weight of 3·2 kilograms appears to be near to the maximum size attained by *Oreochromis*, and this weight has been recorded for two species. A Threespot Tilapia (*Oreochromis andersoni*) in the Upper Zambezi was caught on a spoon being trolled for Tigerfish. This was most unusual as this species is an algal feeder; the most probable explanation being that the spoon flashed past a male guarding its nest and was incidentally caught as it chased away the 'intruder'. The largest Kariba Tilapia (*O. mortimeri*), of 4·0 kilograms, was taken by gill net in Lake Kariba. The Redbreasted Tilapia is widely distributed throughout the Zambezi and central Africa and grows to only half the size of the two previous species. It is a herbivore and is widely used in tropical Africa to control the growth of aquatic plants in ponds and dams.

One of the more interesting attributes of Smallmouths is breeding behaviour. All species can be divided into either mouth-brooders or nest-guarders. *O. andersoni, O. mortimeri* and *O. macrochir* belong to the first group. The male of the species builds a saucer-shaped nest, then attracts the female. After she has laid her eggs and they are fertilised by the male, she takes them into her mouth where they remain until hatched. After hatching they stay in the vicinity of the mother for several weeks and, when danger threatens, pop back into her mouth for protection. *T. rendalli*, and presumably *T. ruweti*,

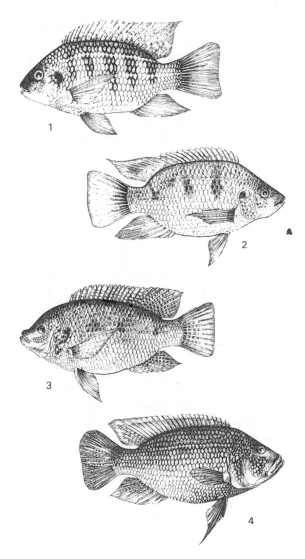

Fig. 4 1 Redbreasted Tilapia (*Tilapia rendalli*);
2 Mortimer's Tilapia (*Oreochromis mortimeri*);
3 Threespot Tilapia (*Oreochromis andersoni*);
4 Nembwe (*Serranochromis robustus jallae*).

scoop out a series of small holes – usually in a self-constructed basin – where the eggs are laid on the roof of one or more of the cavities. The parents remain over the basin and, by continuous fin movement, ensure a steady water circulation over the eggs. The newly hatched fry remain in the vicinity of the nest holes for a few weeks and utilise them as shelter when necessary.

b) Medium-mouth Bream – *Serranochromis (Sargochromis), Hemichromis, Pharygochromis* and *Pseudocrenilabrus*. The sub-genus (*Sargochromis*) comprises four species that feed predominantly on snails. The largest, the Pink Happy (*S. (S.) giardi*) can exceed 3·0 kilograms in weight and is rated highly by bait fishermen of the Upper Zambezi. It feeds primarily on bottom-living molluscs and, to the north in Barotse country, is named Seo and is recognised as the Paramount Chief's fish. Of potential importance as a biological control of the Bilharzia snail host are the Rainbow Happy (*S. (S.) carlottae*), and the Green Happy (*S. (S.) codringtoni*). Both species appear to prefer snails associated with vegetation rather than the bottom-frequenting species and preliminary research has indicated that, under certain conditions, either or both species can eliminate snails from small ponds or dams. Neither species attains the weight of the Pink Happy; 0·5 kilogram is near the maximum for the Rainbow Happy, whereas the Green Happy has been known to exceed 1·0 kilogram. The Zambezi Happy (*P. darlingi*) and the Southern Mouthbrooder (*P. philander*) seldom reach 10 centimetres in length and are widely distributed. They appear to favour shallow water where stones or vegetation afford some sort of protection from predation. Both are small species of no commercial importance but, as they are quite colourful, would make interesting aquarium subjects. As far as is known, all the above fish except *Hemichromis elongatus* are mouth-brooders and probably spawn at least twice during the summer months.

c) Largemouth Bream – No *Serranochromis (Serranochromis)* were recorded below the Falls prior to Lake Kariba and it is heartening to record, particularly for the angler, that at least three of the Upper Zambezi species have successfully invaded and appear to be colonising the lake. Largemouth Bream may be taken on fly or spinner, are excellent sporting species and will grace any table. Probably the most popular and most common in the Falls area is the Nembwe (*S. (S.) robustus jallae*). The unofficial angling record stands at 6·0 kilograms – a fish taken on a Bass plug in the Chobe River. Despite over two decades' experience of the Upper Zambezi, including a four-year fisheries survey of the whole system, I have never encountered a specimen in excess of 3·2 kilograms, the current Zimbabwe record from Lake Robertson, and would welcome further evidence of these large specimens. Deep, fairly quiet water next to a bank or rock fall appears to be the preferred habitat and the water must be fished deeply and slowly for best returns.

The Brownspot Largemouth (*S. (S.) thumbergi*) was confused with its larger relative, the Nembwe, for many years. It is superficially similar in colour and build, but differs in possessing three to four rows of teeth, as opposed to two rows in the Nembwe, and it has a sharper and slimmer profile. In the neighbouring Kafue River, where the Tigerfish is absent, the Brownspot Largemouth and African Pike dominate the open waters of the river. Because this role in the Upper Zambezi is filled by the Tigerfish, the Brownspot Largemouth and Pike are relegated to lagoons and backwaters and are consequently quite

uncommon. The one exception is a tributary of the Upper Zambezi where a barrier, some two miles from its confluence with the main river, appears to have inhibited the Tigerfish from populating the upstream section. Here *S. (S.) thumbergi* has reverted to its openwater predator role where it is numerous. It has not yet been recorded from below the Victoria Falls.

Some anglers claim that the Thinface Largemouth (*S. (S.) angusticeps*) is the best fighter of the family. Specimens of 2·5 kilograms indicate that it is second only to the Nembwe in size. Though recorded from Kariba it is not yet numerous there. Unlike the two previous species it prefers quieter water associated with aquatic vegetation.

The Purpleface Largemouth (*S. (S.) macrocephalus*) is, I think, the most attractively coloured of the group. In the breeding season the males exhibit a large maroon patch situated on, and just behind, the gill cover and this, combined with a bright yellow to orange anal and lower caudal fin, presents a pretty picture. In keeping with the other members of this group it has sterling sporting qualities but seldom exceeds 1·5 kilograms in weight. The last species, *S. (S.) longimanus*, is perhaps the most uncommon. Its resemblance to the Purpleface Largemouth probably has resulted in some confusion between the two. Its main diagnostic character is the pectoral fins which reach past the origin of the anal fin. Nothing is known of its breeding habits.

As far as we know all the *Serranochromis* build sandscrape nests in shallow water and are mouth-brooders and multi-spawners.

Family ANABANTIDAE

If for no other reason than their peculiar 'walking' habits, the two species of *Ctenopoma* that occur above the Falls are fascinat-

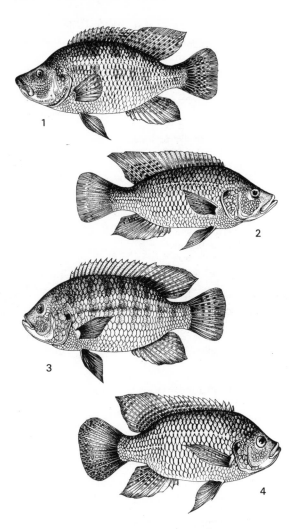

Fig. 5 1 Thinface Largemouth (*Serranochromis angusticeps*); 2 Purpleface Largemouth (*Serranochromis macrocephalus*); 3 Pink Happy (*Serranochromis giardi*); 4 Rainbow Happy (*Serranochromis carlottae*).

convenient grass stem or pebble, usually on damp vegetation, and propelling themselves along by vigorous tail action. *C. multispinis*, the larger of the two species, seldom exceeds 15 centimetres and is dull, mottled brown in colour. *C. intermedium* constructs a bubble nest at the water surface for eggs, like that of the African Pike. Both species prefer quiet water with good vegetation cover.

Family MASTACEMBELIDAE
The colloquial name of Shorttail Spiny Eel is a good description of *Afromastacembelus frenatus* though it is no relation to the true Eel (*Anguilla*). It frequents thick vegetation in quiet water, the roots of trees or virtually any nook and cranny. So far it has only been recorded above the Falls and a specimen of 38 centimetres would approximate its maximum size. A second species, *A. vanderwaali*, the Ocellated Spiny Eel, was discovered in 1977.

Acknowledgement
I wish to thank Dr and Mrs Rex Jubb for their kind permission to base the illustrations on their material and Mr M. Raath for reviewing the manuscript.

Select Bibliography

BELL-CROSS, G. 'The distribution of fishes in Central Africa', *Fish. Res. Bull, Zambia*, v, 1965, pp. 3–20.
BELL-CROSS, G. 'The fish fauna of the Zambezi River system', *Arnoldia (Rhod.)*, v, 29, 1972.
BELL-CROSS, G. and MINSHULL, J. L. *The Fishes of Zimbabwe*, Harare, 1988.
JACKSON, P. B. N. *The Fishes of Northern Rhodesia*, Lusaka, 1961.
JUBB, R. A. *Freshwater Fishes of Southern Africa*, Cape Town, 1967.
KENMUIR, D. *Fishes of Kariba*, Harare, 1983.

ing creatures. The possession of super-branchial organs enables the Climbing Perches to live in poorly oxygenated water and to make short excursions overland. This they do by engaging the gill cover hooks on a

FISH FAUNA OF THE ZAMBEZI RIVER SYSTEM — as at 1st July, 1988

U.Z. — Upper Zambezi system.   L.K. — Lake Kariba system

FAMILY	SCIENTIFIC NAME	COMMON NAME	U.Z.	L.K.
ANGUILLIDAE	*Anguilla bengalensis labiata*	African Mottled Eel	X	X
CLUPEIDAE	*Limnothrissa miodon*	Lake Tanganyika Sardine		X
MORMYRIDAE	*Mormyrops deliciosus*	Cornish Jack		X
	Petrocephalus catostoma	Churchill	X	X
	Hippopotamyrus ansorgii	Slender Stonebasher	X	
	H. discorhynchus	Zambezi Parrotfish	X	X
	Pollimyrus castelnaui	Dwarf Stonebasher	X	
	Marcusenius macrolepidotus	Bulldog	X	X
	Mormyrus lacerda	Western Bottlenose	X	
	M. longirostris	Eastern Bottlenose		X
KNERIIDAE	*Kneria auriculata*	Southern Kneria	X	X
	K. polli	Northern Kneria	X	
CHARACIDAE	*Hydrocynus forskahlii*	Tigerfish	X	X
	Brycinus lateralis	Striped Robber	X	X
	B. imberi	Imberi		X
	Micralestes acutidens	Silver Robber	X	X
	Rhabdalestes maunensis	Slender Robber	X	X
HEPSETIDAE	*Hepsetus odoe*	African Pike	X	
DISTICHODONTIDAE	*Distichodus mossambicus*	Nkupe		X
	D. schenga	Chessa		X
CITHARINIDAE	*Hemigrammocharax machadoi*	Dwarf Citharine	X	
	H. multifasciatus	Multibar Citharine	X	
	Nannocharax macropterus	Broadbar Citharine	X	
CYPRINIDAE	*Barbus afrohamiltoni*	Hamiltons Barb	X	
	B. afrovernayi	Spottail Barb	X	
	B. annectens	Broadstriped Barb	X	X
	B. barnardi	Blackback Barb	X	
	B. barotseensis	Barotse Barb	X	X
	B. bellcrossi	Gorgeous Barb	X	
	B. bifrenatus	Hyphen Barb	X	X
	B. codringtoni	Upper Zambezi Yellowfish	X	
	B. eutaenia	Orangefin Barb	X	X
	B. fasciolatus	Red Barb	X	X
	B. haasianus	Sicklefin Barb	X	X
	B. lineomaculatus	Line-spotted Barb	X	X
	B. marequensis	Largescale Yellowfish		X
	B. mattozi	Papermouth		X
	B. multilineatus	Copperstripe Barb	X	
	B. neefi	Sidespot Barb	X	
	B. paludinosus	Straightfin Barb	X	X
	B. poechii	Dashtail Barb	X	X
	B. puellus	Dwarf Barb	X	X
	B. radiatus	Beira Barb	X	X

FAMILY	SCIENTIFIC NAME	COMMON NAME	U.Z.	L.K.
	B. tangandensis	Redspot Barb	X	
	B. thamalakanensis	Thamalakane Barb	X	
	B. trimaculatus	Threespot Barb		X
	B. unitaeniatus	Longbeard Barb	X	X
	Varicorhinus nasutus	Shortsnout Chiselmouth		X
	Coptostomobarbus wittei	Upjaw Barb	X	
	Mesobolo brevianalis	River Sardine	X	
	Opsaridium zambezense	Barred Minnow	X	X
	Labeo altivelis	Manyame Labeo		X
	L. congoro	Purple Labeo		X
	L. cylindricus	Redeye Labeo	X	X
	L. lunatus	Upper Zambezi Labeo	X	
	L. molybdinus	Leaden Labeo		X
BAGRIDAE	*Auchenoglanis ngamensis*	Zambezi Grunter	X	
	Leptoglanis rotundiceps	Spotted Sand Catlet	X	X
	L. cf. dorae	Chobe Sand Catlet	X	
SCHILBEIDAE	*Schilbe mystus*	Silver or Butter Catfish	X	X
	S. yangambianus	Yangambi Catfish	X	
AMPHILIIDAE	*Amphilius uranoscopus*	Stargazer Mountain Catfish	X	X
CLARIIDAE	*Clarias gariepinus*	Sharptooth Catfish	X	X
	C. ngamensis	Blunttooth Catfish	X	X
	C. stappersii	Blotched Catfish	X	
	C. dumerilii	Okavango Catfish	X	
	C. theodorae	Snake Catfish	X	X
	Clariallabes platyprosopos	Broadhead Catfish	X	
	Heterobranchus longifilis	Vundu		X
MALAPTERURIDAE	*Malapterurus electricus*	Electric Catfish		X
MOCHOKIDAE	*Chiloglanis emarginatus*	Pongola Rock Catlet		X
	C. neumanni	Neumanns Rock Catlet	X	X
	C. pretoriae	Limpopo Rock Catlet		X
	Synodontis leopardinus	Leopard Squeaker	X	
	S. woosnami	Upper Zambezi Squeaker	X	
	S. macrostigma	Largespot Squeaker	X	
	S. nigromaculatus	Spotted Squeaker	X	
	S. zambezensis	Brown Squeaker		X
	S. nebulosus	Clouded Squeaker		X
POECILIIDAE	*Aplocheilichthys hutereaui*	Meshscale Topminnow	X	
	A. johnstonii	Johnstons Topminnow	X	X
	A. katangae	Striped Topminnow	X	X
	Hypsopanchax jubbi	Jubbs Topminnow	X	
APLOCHEILIDAE	*Nothobranchius taeniopygus*	Orangeband Killifish	X	
CICHLIDAE	*Hemichromis elongatus*	Banded Jewelfish	X	
	Pharyngochromis darlingi	Zambezi Happy	X	X
	Pseudocrenilabrus philander	Southern Mouthbrooder	X	X
	Serranochromis carlottae	Rainbow Happy	X	X
	S. codringtonii	Green Happy	X	X

201

FAMILY	SCIENTIFIC NAME	COMMON NAME	U.Z.	L.K.
	S. giardi	Pink Happy	X	X
	S. greenwoodi	Greenwoods Happy	X	
	S. robustus jallae	Nembwe	X	X
	S. angusticeps	Thinface Largemouth	X	X
	S. macrocephalus	Purpleface Largemouth	X	X
	S. thumbergi	Brownspot Largemouth	X	
	S. longimanus	Longfin Largemouth	X	
	Oreochromis andersonii	Threespot Tilapia	X	X
	O. macrochir	Greenhead Tilapia	X	X
	O. mortimeri	Kariba Tilapia		X
	T. rendalli	Redbreast Tilapia	X	X
	T. sparrmanii	Banded Tilapia	X	X
	T. ruweti	Okavango Tilapia	X	
ANABANTIDAE	Ctenopoma intermedium	Blackspot Climbing Perch	X	
	C. multispinis	Manyspined Climbing Perch	X	
MASTACEMBELIDAE	Afromastacembelus frenatus	Shorttail Spiny Eel	X	
	A. vanderwaali	Ocellated Spiny Eel	X	
(Totals)	106		86	64

CYPRINIDAE
(continued)

CICHLIDAE
(continued)

CHAPTER 14

The Insects

Elliot Pinhey

The species of insects to be found in any particular locality are dependent on the general form of vegetation and on the ecology of the area. Now, the Victoria Falls and the surrounding country are basically hot, dry savannah and Mopane (*Colophospermum mopane*) woodland. Entomologically, however, the fauna is greatly enriched by the presence of the Zambezi River with all its variations in current and the many quiet pools along its banks above the Falls where different species may breed. The river itself has created still other habitats at certain points: the so-called Rain Forest produced by the ample spray into a rich vegetation-insect community or microclimate; the deeply carved and luxuriant Palm Grove; and patches of thick forest along the river banks above the Falls as far as the rapids at Katombora Forest Reserve. Added to this there is the quieter Maramba River which joins the main river on the northern bank. During the rains there are generally swamps and pools or some slightly flooded margins which provide still other conditions for water-breeding insects.

It is not surprising that the richest insect fauna, comparatively speaking, is to be found in the aquatic groups, especially the Dragonflies, Caddis flies, Mayflies and water-breeding flies. Some of these groups are normally small in number of species but they make up for this in number of individuals, often vast. In the quieter waters there are also various aquatic beetles and bugs and some small delicate whitish pyralid moths, which breed in water, *Nymphula* and their more colourful relatives *Cataclysta* and *Aulacodes*.

The terrestrial species show, to some extent, a bias towards insects found on vegetation growing in the Kalahari Sand, which is the characteristic soil of this area.

There are, however, a great many wide-spread insect species. The most prominent and colourful are of course the Butterflies, particularly in the thicker bush or forest. It is obviously impossible to mention more than just a sprinkling of the more easily recognised species of insects since they are far too numerous and, moreover, several insect groups are still inadequately named and recorded from the area. For convenience the insects will be discussed under their respective groups.

One point that has to be emphasised, however, is that a certain area around the Falls has been declared as a biological sanctuary by the National Parks Departments of Zimbabwe and Zambia in order to preserve the fauna of all sizes and the flora. Although many of the insects are not significant rarities, yet visitors are not permitted to collect these, nor any other animal, nor plant life within the areas thus protected. Outside the National Parks, however, this ruling does not apply and one may capture insects at will.

Many visitors prefer to visit the Victoria Falls area during the dry season when it is cooler and there is less chance of a sudden downpour. The spray is then less dense and does not obscure the cascades. The richest insect fauna is seen during the hot rainy period, yet it is in the dry months from August to November, when many insects are in a dormant early stage of development, that a few of the more interesting butterflies are to be seen. These include a white butterfly, *Mylothris bernice attenuata* Talbot, and a beautiful Acraea, *Acraea anemosa alboradiata* Aurivillius (colour plate XVI). This Acraea is rarely seen elsewhere, but in September it is frequently abundant and has even been seen in the town of Livingstone, a few kilometres distant.

Now a few of the characteristic insects will be mentioned. One of the earliest general insect collections of the Falls area was made by Frank Oates, the species being recorded by Professor Westwood (1881). It is of interest to mention that four of the species of Acraea butterflies of the Falls were first recorded and described by Westwood in Oates' book. Other insects, especially dragonflies, were also first brought to light from specimens captured in the Falls vicinity.

Bristle-tails and Springtails (APTERYGOTA)
These are small or minute insects which never metamorphose and are usually only observed when logs and debris are turned over. There are numbers of Springtails (Collembola) and Bristle-tails (Thysanura) in the Rain Forest and in other moist areas. *Monachina zambesi* Wygodzinski of the latter order was first described from the Falls.

Dragonflies and Damselflies (ODONATA)
(Fig. 1, nos. 1–8)
About a hundred species of Odonata have been found in and around the Falls area. Damselflies, really only a subgroup of the Dragonflies, are usually smaller and slimmer than the average Dragonfly, but this is no criterion. The principal features of the Damselfly are the identical shape of all the four wings, narrowed at their bases, and the wide-apart eyes. In true Dragonflies the hindwing near the base is wider than the forewing; in fact the hindwing is more distinctly triangular. The eyes usually touch one another on the centre of the head, but this is not so in the family Gomphidae. This interesting family, with its eyes rather widely separated, is well represented on the Zambezi River.

Antlion adults (see Neuroptera) are often

mistaken for Dragonflies, but there are many differences. For instance, Dragonflies breed in water, their antennae are scarcely visible, the thorax is obliquely elongated and the wing-tips are rounded. Antlion adults breed in small sand-pits, under stones or on bark of trees. Their antennae are conspicuous, the thorax is not elongated and the wing-tips tend to be pointed. The flight of Antlions is floppy and they settle with wings down along the abdomen. Dragonfly flight is normally strong, even in most Damselflies, and they settle with wings either closed above the back, butterfly-like, or held out horizontally.

The largest of the Damselflies here, found in shady spots, is the long slender *Phaon iridipennis* (Burmeister). The thorax has metallic green bars; the wings, unusually broad for a Damselfly, are yellowish but reflecting iridescent blue and pinkish hues. Another common forest species is the splendrous *Platycypha caligata* (Selys), narrow-winged, with a short stumpy body and an upturned snout. The colourful male has a bright blue abdomen and the tibiae or middle portions of the legs are flattened into scarlet and white expansions. These decorations are often used for display during court-ship in this species. The many other Falls Damselflies are all small and slender-bodied.

Among the true Dragonflies the Gomphidae, with green or yellow body marked with black, and with separated eyes, are of

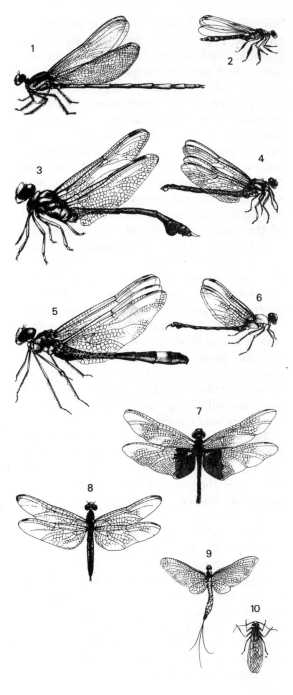

Fig. 1 Aquatic insects. Dragonflies: 1 *Phaon iridipennis* (Burm.) *m*; 2 *Platycypha caligata* (Selys) *m*; 3 *Crenigomphus cornutus* Pinhey *m*; 4 *Ictinogomphus ferox* (Ramb.) *m*; 5 *Paragomphus cataractae* Pinhey *m*; 6 *Macromia nyanzana* (Grünb.) *f*; 7 *Rhyothemis semihyalina* (Desj.) *f*; 8 *Eleuthemis buettikoferi* Ris *m*; Mayfly: 9 *Eatonica schoutedeni* (Navás); Stonefly: 10 *Neoperla spio* (Newman).

scientific significance. The most prominent are the large robust *Ictinogomphus ferox* (Rambur) and *Gomphidia quarrei* (Schouteden), which settle on twigs or reeds over the water; and the equally large but scarce *Phyllogomphus schoutedeni* Fraser which is occasionally seen flying across the tree-tops. The smaller, yellowish *Crenigomphus cornutus* Pinhey and the green *Paragomphus cataractae* Pinhey were described from the Falls region. The rare *Neurogomphus* may sometimes be not uncommon settling on vegetation further up the river. Smallest of the family is the slender *Lestinogomphus* which prefers the shelter of clumps of trees.

The large, long-bodied Emperor Dragonflies, which may hawk up and down, are widespread species. *Hemianax ephippiger* (Burmeister) and *Anax imperator* Leach have characteristic blue markings; *Anax speratus* Hagen is nearly all dull red; and, largest of all, the great black *Anax tristis* Hagen, marked with green and yellow. The strong-flying, metallic-bodied *Macromia*, which also hawk up and down, but a little way from the water, are well represented.

There are many species of the large family Libellulidae, more recognisable in the colourful males than in the more drab females. There are the powder-blue *Orthetrum,* the stout red-bodied *Crocothemis,* the more slender red or blue *Trithemis* and other genera. In *Trithemis annulata* (Beauvois) the male has a violet-red body; in *T. kirbyi ardens* Gerstaecker the body is scarlet, the wing-bases broadly orange. This last species is extremely similar to the gregarious *Brachythemis lacustris* (Kirby) which clusters on grasses over the river. Its closest relative, the common black-bodied *Brachythemis leucosticta* (Burmeister), has its clear wings crossed by a black band, and again this is

extraordinarily like the much scarcer black-banded *Parazyxomma flavicans* (Martin) which seeks the shelter of trees and shrubs.

Another black-bodied species, *Rhyothemis semihyalina* (Desjardins), has broad wings, the hindwing decorated with a large black basal area shimmering with metallic violet and green hues. It flutters like a butterfly over quiet pools. One of the rarer African Dragonflies, the blue-bodied *Eleuthemis buettikoferi* Ris, its forewing apex covered by a brown patch, is often common at quiet pools along the river. It is possible to confuse it with one of the female forms of the common *Hemistigma albipuncta* (Rambur) which, however, has brown apices to all the wings. Strongly flying *Zygonyx* often hover over the cascades and rapids in which they breed.

Stoneflies (PLECOPTERA) (Fig. 1, no. 10)
In tropical and subtropical Africa only a single species of Stonefly is known, *Neoperla spio* (Newman). It is brownish yellow, flattened, with the wings covering one another. The adults and the cast skins of their larvae may often be seen adhering to rocks and stones in the faster waters.

Mayflies (EPHEMEROPTERA) (Fig 1, no. 9)
Examples of seven different genera are at present known from the area, but the number of species cannot yet be stated. One of the larger ones which is fairly common is *Eatonica schoutedeni* Navás.

Grasshoppers and Crickets (ORTHOPTERA) (Fig. 2, nos. 1–7; Fig. 3, nos. 1–6)
Probably well over fifty species of these may be seen in the area, the majority being the Short-horn Grasshoppers, having short antennae. Crickets and Long-horn Grasshoppers have antennae longer than the body.

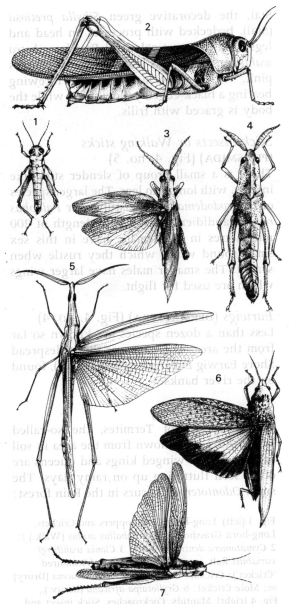

The largest Short-horn Grasshopper is *Ornithacris magnifica* (I. Bol.), a reddish brown species with yellow stripes, the hindwings maroon red in the basal area. It has the appearance of an enlarged Red Locust, but with an arched crest on the thoracic pronotum. Another large but more slender species, with the head narrowed and extended forwards, is *Truxaloides braziliensis* (Drury), with flat antennae. The male is small, pale brownish or greenish, with pale yellowish hindwings; the female larger, green or straw-coloured, with rosy red hindwings. This and some other species make a clacketty, rattling sound in flight. *Kraussaria prasina* (Walker) is pale green with brown markings.

The most abundant grasshopper is the much smaller *Morphacris fasciata* (Thunberg), which has red hindwings and a shiny black stripe along the side of the head and thorax. *Dictyophorus* are large and plump, with short red hindwings broadly margined with black. They belong to the colourful pyrgomorphid family, many of which exude a frothy liquid with a noxious odour. In the large grasshoppers of family Pamphagidae, *Lobosceliana* and *Lamarkiana*, both sexes have high sharp thoracic crests, the male has long brown wings but the female has no wings at all.

A scarcer wingless Lentulid Grasshopper, *Mecostibus mafukae* Uvarov, is only found after diligent search on branches of trees. The head is broad and shelved, the body tapering, flat below. When approached it sidles round the branch out of danger.

The Long-horned Grasshoppers are mostly arboreal, slender green species with long slender legs, for instance the green *Phaneroptera* and *Conocephalus*. *Cymatomera* are very broad, flattened and extraordinarily like the

Fig. 2 Short-horn Grasshoppers. 1 *Mecostibus mafukae* Uvarov *m*; 2 *Ornithacris magnifica* (Bol.) *f*; 3, 4 *Lamarckiana punctosa* (Walk.) *m*, *f*; 5 *Truxaloides brasiliensis* (Drury) *f*; 6 *Dictyophorus griseus* (Reiche & Fairmaire) *f*; 7 *Krausaria prasina* (Walk.) *m*.

bark on which they frequently rest. *Zabalius aridus* (Walker) is a large broad-winged green species, very leaf-like. Larger still, but more trim and slender, is the great green and brown *Clonia wahlbergi* (Stål), with brown spotted hindwings. It is a fearsome species to handle, armed with heavy spines on its long legs and with formidable jaws. On the ground or low vegetation bloated, almost wingless grasshoppers, such as *Enyaliopsis*, are often seen. They are called Armoured Crickets, because of the noise they make and the series of stout spines on the thorax. They can eject a noxious fluid.

There are several species of true brown or black Crickets in the area, some minute, others large; the huge Sand Cricket *Brachytrypes membranaceus* (Dr.), for instance, is a real monster. There are some delicate arboreal species of *Oecanthus*. The brown Mole Cricket *Gryllotalpa africana* (Beauvois), with powerful forelegs for digging, is a frequent visitor to light.

Cockroaches and Praying Mantids (DICTYOPTERA) (Fig. 4, nos. 1–3, 6, 7)

Apart from the cosmopolitan household Cockroaches known by such vernacular names as the German Cockroach and the American Cockroach there are here, as in other countries, many wild species. Some of these may be attracted to lights but they are not yet domesticated. *Pseudoderopeltis diluta* (Stål) is slender, pale orange brown, but it has many brown or black relatives of similar build. *Gyna maculipennis* (Schaum) is broad, mottled brown and yellow. The small black *Eustegaster poecila* (Schaum) is elegantly decorated with orange in the male.

Mantids are poorly known from the Falls at present. There are flattened grey bark species, *Tarachodes*, the browner *Popa spurca*

Stål, the decorative green *Sibylla pretiosa* (Stål), bedecked with processes on head and legs; and the most colourful *Pseudocreobotra wahlbergi* (Stål). This last is green, sometimes pink, with yellow markings, the forewing bearing a black-edged yellow spiral while the body is graced with frills.

Stick insects or Walking sticks (PHASMIDA) (Fig. 4, no. 5)

There is a small group of slender stick-like insects, with long thin legs. The larger species of *Bactrododema* and the still larger *Palophus reyi* (Grandidier), with a body-length of 200 millimetres in the female, have in this sex small round wings which they rustle when scared. The smaller males have larger wings which are used for flight.

Earwigs (DERMAPTERA) (Fig. 4, no. 4)

Less than a dozen species are known so far from the area. The largest is the widespread Shore Earwig *Labidura riparia* (Pallas), found on the river banks.

Termites (ISOPTERA)

A few species of Termites, the so-called White Ants, are known from the area in soil or timber. The winged kings and queens are often seen fluttering up on rainy days. The small *Odontotermes* occurs in the Rain forest;

Fig. 3 (left) Long-horn Grasshoppers and Crickets. Long-horn Grasshoppers: 1 *Zabalius aridus* (Walk.) *f*; 2 *Cymatomera denticollis* Sc. *f*; 3 *Clonia wahlbergi variabilis* Kalt. *m*; 4 *Enyaliopsis* spec. (Armoured 'Cricket'); Cricket: *Brachytrypes membranaceus* (Drury) *m*; Mole Cricket: 6 *Gryllotalpa africana* (Beauv.). Fig. 4 (right) Mantids, Cockroaches, Stick insect and Earwig. Cockroaches: 1 *Pseudoderopeltis dilutus* (Stål) *m*; 2 *Gyna maculipennis* (Schaum); 3 *Eustegaster poecila* (Schaum); Earwig: 4 *Labidura riparia* (Beauv.); Stick insect: 5 *Bactrododema* spec. *m*; Praying Mantids: 6 *Sibylla pretiosa* (Stål); 7 *Pseudocreobotra wahlbergi* (Stal).

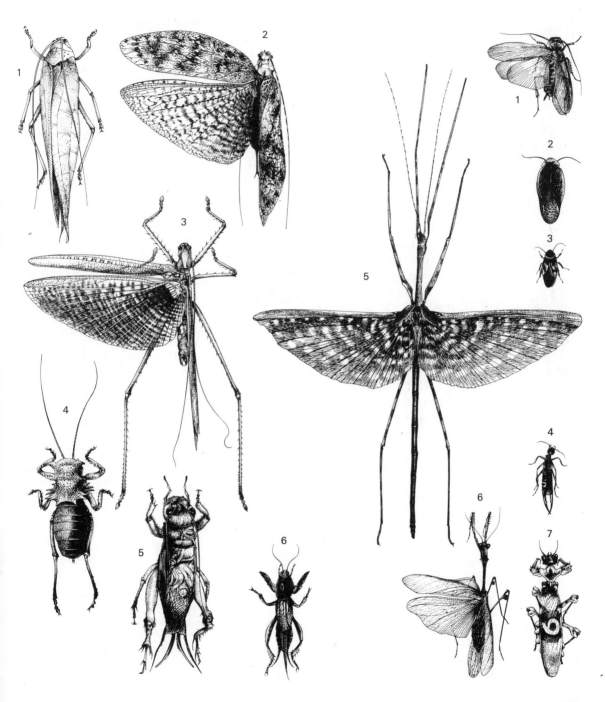

the Harvesters, *Hodotermes mosambicus* (Hagen), forage openly in grassland. Termites are the oldest known social insects and are, of course, quite unrelated to the more highly developed true Ants (see Hymenoptera).

Bugs (HEMIPTERA) (Fig. 5, nos. 6–12; Pl. XVI, no. 14)

The true Bugs, in the scientific sense, have sharp beaks or stylets for sucking juices. They do not bite their food in the way beetles or grasshoppers do. The Bedbug, a true Bug, is popularly said to 'bite' its victims, although more correctly it stabs with a beak. The Falls area has not really been searched properly yet for all the many Plant Bugs, Froghoppers, Leafhoppers and other numerous kinds, but there are surely a few hundred species when Aphids, Scale insects and other small Plant lice are taken into account.

The first group, *Heteroptera*, are flattened above, the forewing divided into a hardened basal half and clear outer half. These include numerous Shield and Stink Bugs, one of the most remarkable being *Pephricus livingstoni* (Westwood), resembling a broken dead leaf. The brown and red *Dysdercus* or Cotton Stainer Bugs and their spotted relatives, *Probergrothius sexpunctatus* (Cast.), are sometimes seen on or below the bulky Baobab trees. Assassin Bugs, which prey on other insects and on millipedes and have really vicious beaks, include the black-spotted brown *Petalochirus umbrosus* H. Sch., with flattened forelegs. Aquatic bugs are found in the quieter pools but may fly out and become attracted to light. There are the giant *Lethocerus*, up to 60 or 70 millimetres long; the Water Boatmen; Water Skaters of the genus *Limnogonus* and others.

The second group, *Homoptera*, have plain wings roofed along the body when at rest. Largest of these are the arboreal Cicadas or 'Christmas Beetles'. The males chant with a monotonous cacophony in the later months of the year. Genera here are *Ioba* and *Platypleura*. The Lantern Fly bugs include the long-snouted grey *Zanna punctatus* (Ol.) and the colourful *Druentia variegata* (Spin.) with a short upturned snout. The numerous Froghoppers on grass are represented by the red *Locris arithmetica* (Walker), the black and yellow *L. maculata* (Fabr.) and many others.

Lacewings, Antlions etc. (NEUROPTERA) (Fig. 5, nos. 1–5)

There is only a small number of species known from the area. The winged adults are frequently mistaken for dragonflies but their larvae are better known to the public since they often make small pits in sandy soil.

Largest of the Antlions commonly found

Fig. 5 (left) Antlions and Bugs. Antlions: 1 *Nemeura glauningi* Kolbe (Streamer-tailed Antlion); 2 *Cueta punctatissima* (Gerst.) (Speckled Cueta); 3 *Palpares cataractae* Peringuey *f* (Waterfall Lion); 4 *Tmesebasis lacerata* (Hagen) (Mottled Long-horned Antlion); Lacewing: 5 *Silveira marshalli* McL. (Marshall's Dusky Lacewing); Bugs: 6 *Ioba leopardina* (Dist.) (Leopard Cicada); 7 *Probergrothius sexpunctatus* Cast. (a Stainer bug); 8 *Pephricus livingstoni* (Westw.) (Livingstone's Leaf Coreid); 9 *Petalochirus umbrosus* H. Sch. (an Assassin bug); 10 *Zanna punctatus* (Ol.) (Dotted Lantern fly); 11 *Limnogonus* spec. (a Skater); 12 *Locris maculata* (Fabr.) (Maculate Locris).

Fig. 6 (right) Butterflies. 1 *Charaxes fulgurata* Aur. *m* (Fulgurate Charaxes); 2 *Salamis anacardii nebulosa* Trimen *m* (Clouded Mother O'Pearl); 3 *Acraea atolmis* Westw. *m* (Scarlet Acraea); 4 *Acraea aglaonice* Westw. *m* (Clear Spotted Acraea); 5 *Acraea atergatis* Westw. *m* (Streaky Tipped Acraea); 6 *Ypthima cataractae* van Son (Waterfall Ringlet); 7, 8 *Pentila pauli obsoleta* H. Sm. and melanic form (Paul's Buff); 9 *Teniorhinus harona* (Westw.) (Arrowhead Skipper); 10 *Nepheronia thalassina* (Boisd.) *m* (Cambridge Vagrant); 11 *Eronia leda* (Boisd.) *m* (Orange and Lemon).

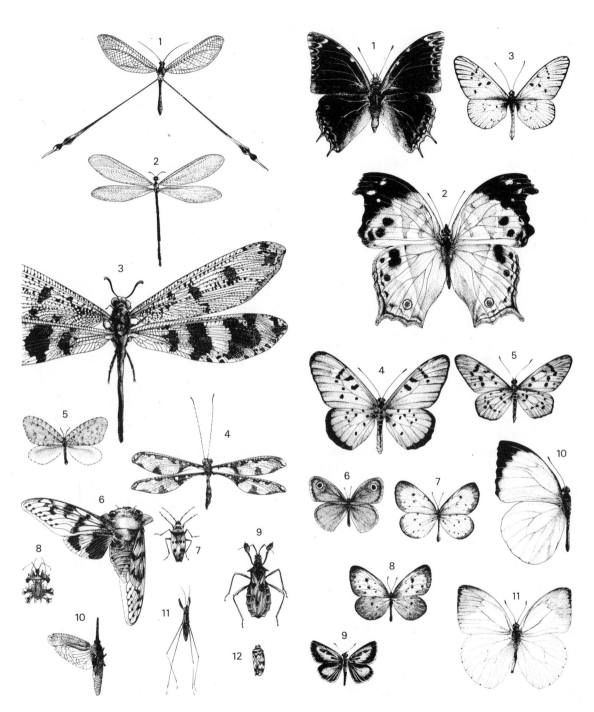

211

near the Falls and described from there is the great narrow-winged *Palpares cataractae* Peringuey, its wings covered with black patches. Like most Antlions its flight is slow and floppy. Smaller Antlions include the smoky brown speckled *Cueta punctatissima* (Gerst.) and *Banyutus lethalis* (Walker) with transparent wings.

Sometimes Long-horned Antlions, such as *Tmesebasis lacerata* (Hagen) with long slender antennae, may be observed flying from plant to plant or they may be seen at light. At night Streamer-tailed Antlions of the genus *Nemeura* occur in September or October. Their hindwings are drawn out into long slender tails broadened into straps at the tips.

Small Brown Lacewings and Green Lacewings may be disturbed from bushes. The larger and broader-winged Psychopsidae such as *Silveira marshalli* McLachlan may be attracted to lights.

Caddis flies (TRICHOPTERA) (Pl. XVI, no. 9)
For the small size of this order the Zambezi River in this area is distinctly rich. Approximately forty species are known so far, most of them brown in colour, like small brown moths with long antennae. There are, however, a few green species. One of them is the blue-green *Polymorphanisus elizabethae* (Navás). Much larger is the very pale green *P. bipunctatus* (Brancs.).

Butterflies and Moths (LEPIDOPTERA)
(Figs. 6, 7 and 8; Pl. XVI, nos. 1–8)
The total number of species of moths known in the area runs into several hundreds and there are seventy or eighty species of butterflies. The most noticeable butterflies are the large or largish Swallowtail Butterflies, some with, others without, tails on the hindwings; and the White family or Pieridae.

The most handsome of the Swallowtails is the Green Banded Swallowtail, *Papilio nireus lyaeus* Doubleday, black with a green or blue-green band across the wings and a short tail on each hindwing. The common yellow-spotted Citrus Swallowtail *P. demodocus* Esper has no tails; but the yellow-banded *P. constantinus* Ward, which looks somewhat like it in flight, has tails. *P. leonidas* Fabricius and *P. pylades corrineus* Bertolini are tail-less, the former black with numerous blue spots, the latter black and white. Two others are called Swordtails because of their slender tails, the bright green spotted *P. antheus* Cramer and the duller green spotted *P. porthaon* Hewitson.

The Whites include the common migrants *Catopsilia florella* (Fabricius) and species of *Belenois* sometimes seen on migration. More colourful are the Purple Tips, Lilac Tip and Red Tips of the genus *Colotis*. The Zebra White *Pinacopteryx eriphia* (Godart) is banded with yellow and brown. Very common around the Falls is the Cambridge Vagrant, *Nepheronia thalassina* (Boisduval), the male a delicate pale blue. A rarer relative is the white *N. argia varia* Trimen, whose female is brightened with deep orange and vermilion on the underside. *Eronia leda* (Boisduval) is a striking species, bright yellow with a broad orange tip to the forewing. The most prized of the Whites is *Mylothris bernice attenuata* Talbot, a narrow-winged white species with black marginal dots and an orange stripe below the forward margin of the forewing. It flies over the area very slowly, usually in the month of September, sometimes in great numbers. Other Whites include *Dixeia pigea* (Boisduval), the females decorated with orange and red.

In the family Nymphalidae the fast-flying tailed *Charaxes* are represented by nine or

Fig. 7 Swallowtail Butterflies. 1 *Papilio constantinus* Ward *m* (Constantine's Swallowtail); 2 *P. nireus lyaeus* Dbl. *m* (Green Banded Swallowtail); 3 *P. leonidas* Fabr. *m* (Veined Swallowtail); 4 *P. porthaon* Hew. *m* (Pale Spotted Swordtail).

ten species. The most striking of these is the great blue and black *C. bohemani* Felder, pale blue, margined with black. Three uncommon species occur in the area at times, the white-banded blackish *C. penricei* Rothschild, *C. fulgurata* Aurivillius, with a small greenish black male, and, at least further westwards of the Falls, the small scarce dark *C. gallagheri* van Son. Several common Commodores (*Precis*), Jokers (*Byblia*), the Diadem (*Hypo-limnas misippus* (Linnaeus)), the Guineafowl (*Hamanumida daedalus* Hübner) and the Clouded Mother of Pearl (*Salamis anacardii nebulosa* Trimen) are found here. The Common Gaudy Commodore (*Precis octavia sesamus* Trimen), is blue with red dots in the dry season, its underside black; but it is mainly red in the wet season.

The narrow-winged, black-speckled, red or orange-brown *Acraea* butterflies are noteworthy because four out of the nine local species, *A. atergatis*, *A. atolmis*, *A. axina* and *A. aglaonice*, were all described from the Falls by Westwood in 1881. The most striking of these, particularly in the dry season, is *A. atolmis*, the male bright scarlet or vermilion; the female, as usual, is of a duller brown shade. By far the most beautiful *Acraea* is *A. anemosa alboradiata* Aurivillius. This is perhaps the most attractive of all the Falls butterflies and rather a speciality of the region, pink with white markings. It is only to be seen from August to September. Others in the region are *A. natalica* Boisduval, *A. eponina* Cramer, *A. caldarena* Hewitson and the bright orange *A. acrita* Hewitson which

213

is often clouded with blue-black in the Zambezi Valley.

The Browns (Satyridae) are only represented by five or six species, including the large Evening Brown, *Melanitis leda africana* Fruhstorfer. *Ypthimomorpha itonia* (Hewitson) is a common small Ringlet in swampy country; but a more important relative is *Ypthima cataractae* van Son, which was described from the Falls. The Monarchs, Danaidae, are merely represented by the one abundant species, *Danaus chrysippus* (Linnaeus).

The Lycaenidae, which include the Blues and their relatives, is a miscellaneous but not very numerous family in this region. There are several small Blues to be seen among grass or bushes, but the most beautiful are some of the tree-loving species with slender tails on the hindwing. Bowker's Tailed Blue (*Iolaus bowkeri* (Trimen)) is bright pale blue chequered with black and white. The Azure Hairstreak (*Iolaus caeculus* (Hoppfer)) is bright blue or violet blue above and crossed by red lines on the underside.

The Barred Blues, with stripes on the underside, are represented by the common blue *Spindasis natalensis* Doubleday and Hewitson, and by the far scarcer brown species *S. cynica* Riley, which was found by R. W. Barney in 1938 in the Palm Grove and has not been seen since then. Quite different are the black-dotted yellow *Pentila*, rather Acraea-like. *P. tropicalis* (Boisduval) is a common narrow bordered species. *P. pauli obsoleta* H. Smith is a larger, black-margined species of which black aberrations (*f. cataractae*) are commonly encountered in the Palm Grove. They flutter very slowly a couple of metres above the ground and are easily discerned.

Several Skipper butterflies (Hesperiidae) may be seen, none of them particularly striking except perhaps the common 'Policeman' *Coeliades*; the Clouded Flat, *Tagiades flesus* (Fabricius), which settles flat on a leaf and has the hindwing white on the underside; and the White Cloaked, *Leucochitonea levubu* (Wallengren). The Arrowhead Skipper (*Teniorhinus harona*) was described by Westwood (1881) from the Falls.

Moths are extremely numerous and only a few can be mentioned. The two most noticeable Emperor moths (Saturniidae) are the large, long-tailed, green Luna moth, *Argema mimosae* Boisduval, and *Gonimbrasia zambesina* (Walker), tailess and green but with purplish suffused eyespots on the hindwing. Several common and widespread Hawk Moths (Sphingidae) are found, such as the Convolvulus, Death's Head, Silver Striped and Oleander Hawks. The nature of the country, the Kalahari Sand, the Teak trees (*Baikiaea*), suggest that the local and peculiar *Xenosphingia jansei* Jordan, known further south and west, will be found there. It is unusual in having strongly feathered (bipectinate) antennae and both sexes can be uniformly dull olive green or completely red. A very beautiful Hawk is *Leucophlebia afra* Rothschild and Jordan, the forewing pink with yellow stripes, the hindwing all orange.

A few day-flying moths may be seen flying in sunshine. The most colourful are the Agaristidae, although some of these are nocturnal. *Rothia butleri adulatrix* (Westwood), described from the area, is a large day-flier, like a Tiger moth, black with yellow bars, the hindwing bright red with a black border. *Crameria amabilis* (Drury) is smaller, the forewing red-brown with large yellow spots ringed with black. *Schausia coryndoni* Rothschild has the forewing dark brown finely irrorated with green and with

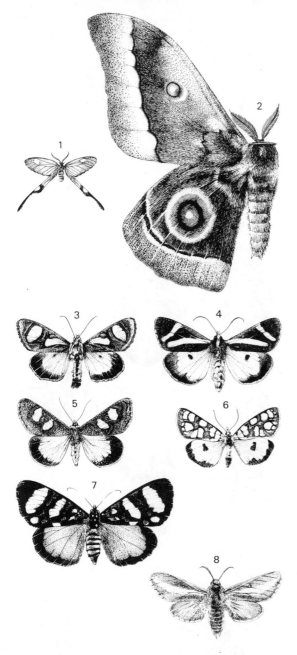

two prominent white spots; the hindwing is orange with a black border. *Aegocera trimeni* (Felder) also has a blackish green forewing, but it is decorated with a large yellow streak and a spot. *A. fervida* (Walker) has a red-brown forewing crossed by two oblique cream stripes. The orange hindwing has a red border in the male, black in the female.

The huge family Noctuidae is represented by many dingy brown or grey species, but one day-flier is the iridescent blue-black *Egybolis vaillantina* Stoll with orange spots across the forewings. One of several small semi-aquatic Pyraustidae is represented by *Aulacodes periopis* Hampson, banded with orange and decorated marginally on the hindwing with black dots. Only one more moth can be included here, one of the remarkable tailed relatives of the Burnet moths (Zygaenidae). This is the orange and black *Semioptila torta* Butler.

Beetles (COLEOPTERA) (Fig. 9; Pl. XVI, nos. 10–13)

Of these again there are hundreds of species, most of them black in colour and not of general interest to the public. There are, nevertheless, many which are large, colourful or otherwise noticeable. These include of course the famous Scarab or Dung Beetles (Scarabaeidae), always busily occupied, and their colourful Fruit chafer relatives; the numerous Ground Beetles, mostly Carabidae and Tenebrionidae; the Longhorn Borers and the Bullet-shaped Borers; various Leaf-eaters, Fireflies and aquatic beetles.

Largest of the Dung Beetles are the bulky *Heliocopris* which roll the manure into

Fig. 8 Moths. 1 *Semioptila torta* Butler (Twisted Tailed Burnet); 2 *Gonimbrasia zambesina* (Walk.) *m* (Zambesi Emperor); 3 *Aegocera trimeni* Felder (Trimen's False Tiger); 4 *A. fervida* (Walk.) (Fervid False Tiger); 5 *Schausia coryndoni* Roths. (Coryndon's False Tiger); 6 *Crameria amabilis* (Drury) (Amiable False Tiger); 7 *Rothia butleri adulatrix* (Westw.) (Butler's False Tiger); 8 *Leucophlebia afra* R. & J. (Rosy Banded Hawk moth).

spheres larger than tennis balls. A more flattened beetle is *Pachylomera femoralis* Kirby. In fact, if examined closely, it looks as if someone has dented it by treading on it. It is often seen flying and zooming through the bush. A common large Fruit chafer is the metallic green *Dicronorrhina derbyana* (Westwood), bedecked with white stripes. One of the fiercest-looking Ground Beetles is the great thick-bodied black Tiger Beetle *Mantichora*, which feeds on other beetles or on frogs. *Anthia burchelli* Hope is a large, striped runner capable of squirting an irritating fluid in defence. A small flattened relative is the brown and black *Graphopterus amabilis* Boheman. Various spheroidal, slow-moving ground beetles are the Tok-tokkies (Tenebrionidae), the males of which often tap out with their abdomens a nocturnal morse code of their own device to the females. A large species common at the Falls is *Tarsocnodes molossus* (Haag).

The numerous cylindrical Long-horn Beetles (Cerambycidae), include the beautiful *Prosopocera lactator* (Fabricius), pale blue with orange criss-cross markings, and the colourful *Purpuricenus laetus* Thomson, yellow and black with red and black head and thorax. These and the Bullet Beetles (Bupre-

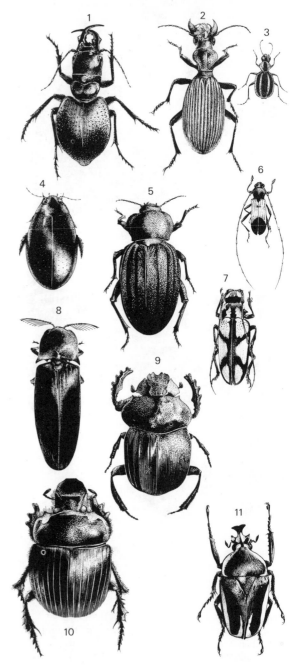

Fig. 9 Beetles. 1 *Mantichora* spec. (Giant Black Tiger); 2 *Anthia burchelli* Hope (Burchell's Anthia); 3 *Graphopterus amabilis* Boh. (a Ground beetle); 4 *Cybister immarginata* Aube (Immarginate Diver); 5 *Tarsocnodes molossus* (Haag) (Giant Tok-Tokkie); 6 *Purpuricenus laetus* Thoms. (Black Tipped Longhorn); 7 *Prosopocera lactator* (Fabr.) (Emerald Spotted Longhorn); 8 *Tetralobus rotundifrons* Guer. (Rotund Tetralobus); 9 *Pachylomera femoralis* Kirby (Common Dung Beetle); 10 *Heliocopris japetus* Klug (a Heliocopris); 11 *Dicronorrhina derbyana* (Westw.) (Derby Fruit Chafer).

XIV   Male (black) and female (brown)
Sable Antelope (*Hippotragus niger*).

XVb Tiger Snake (*Telescopus semiannulatus*).

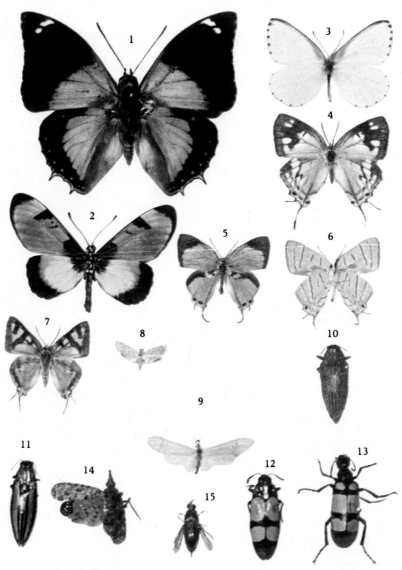

XVI   Insects of the Victoria Falls:

1 *Charaxes bohemani*
2 *Acreaa anemosa alboradiata*
3 *Myolthris bernice attenuata*
4 *Iolaus bowkeri*
5, 6 *Iolaus caeculus* (upper and underside)
7 *Spindasis natalensis*
8 *Aulacodes periopis*

9 *Polymorphanisus elizabethae*
10 *Evides pubiventris*
11 *Chrysechroa lepida*
12 *Agelia peteli*
13 *Mylabris oculata*
14 *Druentia variegata*
15 *Stilbum cyanurum*

stidae) are mostly borers in trees and shrubs, particularly *Terminalia*. Beautifully metallic green Bullet Beetles are *Evides pubiventris* Cast. and Gory, like exquisite iridescent green gems, and *Chrysochroa lepida* Gory, smoother green with orange stripes, but adorned on the head and thorax with glimmering traces of copper. *Agelia peteli* Gory is jet black with large yellow patches. It is one of the instances of mimicry, so common in African butterflies, whereby one species very closely resembles a totally unrelated species protected by being highly distasteful to its predators. The distasteful model in this case is one of several Blister Beetles (Meloidae), exuding the corrosive cantharadin, such as *Mylabris tricolor* Gerstaecker.

Lampyridae are the well-known Glow-worms and Fireflies. At dusk the Fireflies, *Luciola pumila* Boheman, fly erratically among trees, flashing their lights. When seen in close-up they are insignificant elongated beetles. Leaf-eaters (Chrysomelidae) are usually gregarious on foliage, often very colourful but small in size. Click-beetles (Elateridae), which can spring up when they fall inadvertently on their backs and right themselves, are represented by the large *Tetralobus* with fan-like antennae. The last beetles we can mention are the small Whirli-gigs (Gyrinidae) which gyrate on the surface of pools, and the submerged Water Tiger Beetles (Dytiscidae), for instance *Cybister immarginatus* Aube.

Flies (DIPTERA) (Fig. 10, nos. 2, 10–18)

Again there are hundreds of species yet, except for those which pester us in houses or the livestock in the lands, or those which 'bite' with their stylets, few are of interest to the average person. There are, however, some decorative and interesting species. To a specialist any insects can be of interest; the varied habits and customs of flies can be quite intriguing and many are surprisingly useful in this world. Like the parasitic Wasps (Hymenoptera) of the next and last group, many flies (Tachinidae), which somewhat resemble Houseflies but are more bristly, are parasitic on other insects, for instance on Army Worm caterpillars. Some again, also parasitic, are very like bees or wasps in appearance and frequently breed inside their unfortunate host's larvae.

Among 'biting flies' there are, of course, various species of Mosquitoes; and it is advisable, at least in the hotter months, to take suitable precautions against anophelines, using prophylactics and nets. Near the faster waters there may be tiny Gnats, Black Flies, *Simulium arnoldi* Gibb and *Culicoides* which may occasionally attack exposed legs. There are Horseflies (Tabanidae), such as the Clegs (*Haematopota*), with speckled brown wings, which settle quietly on an arm and suddenly stab; or the buzzing, disconcerting *Tabanus*. However, there are no Tsetse Flies (*Glossina*) within a great many kilometres of the Falls.

The Robber or Assassin Flies (Asilidae), which stab and prey on other insects but never attack man, include the large black, bristly *Hyperechia bifasciata* Grünberg, which is like a Bumble Bee and mimics the Carpenter Bee (*Xylocopa inconstans*) on which it preys. Bee Flies (Bombyliidae) are parasitic on other insects. Several species have decorative wing patterns. *Litorrhynchus basalis* (Ric.) is brown with brown wing markings resembling the wings of a common dragon-fly *Palpopleura lucia* form *portia* (Drury). *Ligyra mars* Bezzi is black with two gilt dots on the base of the abdomen. *Systropus snowi* Adams has a long slender waist, just like many wasps; while *Bombylius discoideus* (Fabricius) is much stouter, black with a white tail and more like a Bumble Bee.

There are some wasp-like Hover Flies (Syrphidae) which hover and buzz in the air and feed in their grub-state on plant-lice. Their Drone Fly relatives are often bee-like; *Senaspis haemorrhoa* (Gerstaecker) is a colourful example: black, with a red 'tail', a white waist and brown wings. Fruitflies (Trypetidae) occur in the area and a stouter-bodied family Otitidae is represented by the very noticeable but harmless blue-black *Bromophila caffra* Mcq., which has a gory red head and deep brown wings. Then there are the Stalk-eyed Flies, Diopsidae, for example, *Diasemopsis obstans* (Walker). This is a small black-bodied fly, with white bands on the abdomen, which swarms gregariously on swampy vegetation. The eyes and antennae are stretched apart on long slender stalks. Some delicate flies, Blepharoceridae, breed in the fastest currents, like the *Zygonyx* dragonflies.

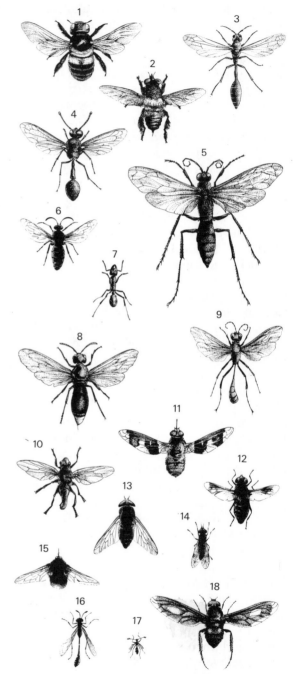

Fig. 10 Stingers and Flies. 1 *Xylocopa inconstans* Sm. (White Barred Carpenter Bee); 2 *Hyperechia bifasciata* Grünb. (Carpenter Robber fly); 3 *Belonogaster griseus* (Fabr.) (Grey Belonogaster); 4 *Eumenes maxillosus* de Geer (Eumenes wasp); 5 *Hemipepsis vindex* (Smith) (a Great Spider Wasp); 6 *Stizus dewitzii* Handl. (a Hunting wasp); 7 *Paltothyreus tarsatus* (Fabr.) (Stink ant); 8 *Synagris analis* Sauss. (Orange-tailed Synagris); 9 *Ammophila ludovicus* (Smith) a Hunting wasp); 10 *Bromophila caffra* Mcq. (Red-headed Stink fly); 11 *Litorrhynchus basalis* (Ric.) (a Mottled Bee fly); 12 *Senaspis haemorrhoa* (Gerst.) (Banded Syrphid); 13 *Tabanus taeniola* (Beauv.) (a Horse fly); 14 *Haematopota* vittata loew (a Clegg); 15 *Bombylius discoideus* (Fabr.) (a Bee fly); 16 *Systropus snowi* Adams (a Waisted fly); 17 *Diasemopsis obstans* (Walk.) (a Stalk-eyed fly); 18 *Ligyra mars* Bezzi (Martian Bee fly).

Stingers (HYMENOPTERA): *ants, bees and wasps* (Fig. 10, nos. 3–9; Pl. XVI, no. 15) This, the last insect order, includes the highly developed social ants and bees and, in other continents, the social wasps and hornets. The wasps here have only attained, in some species, a semi-social or colonial condition. Most of them are solitary in habits. A great many species of all these Stingers occur in the Falls area and probably hundreds of others, including some called Ichneumons, are parasitic, like Tachinidae and Bombyliidae of the Diptera (flies). These parasites are scarcely known at present. Wasps, which are predators or parasites, are among the most useful of all insects.

Ants (Formicidae), not to be confused with 'White Ants' (see Isoptera), are numerous near the Victoria Falls, as in most places, but several are very local species. One of the most notorious is the large Stink Ant, *Paltothyreus tarsatus* (Fabricius), since it advertises its presence with an offensive odour. It sometimes preys on termites.

The many groups of Wasps may be introduced by the large family Sphecidae, or Hunting Wasps, often erroneously called Hornets, a name vaguely attached to many other wasps. True Hornets do not occur in Africa except near the Mediterranean sea coasts. Several hunting wasps have very long slender waists, like the large *Ammophila ludovicus* (Smith) and the much smaller *Sceliphron,* with yellow-banded legs, which make mud nests in dwellings. *Stizus* have a more waspish body coloration, black and yellow. *Liris croesus* Smith is silky black with golden wings. These prey on insects and spiders, storing them in tunnels for their larvae. The family Pompilidae more normally prey on spiders. A few of them, *Hemipepsis vindex* (Smith) and *H. vespertilio* Gerstaecker

amongst others, are very large, blue-black, and are conspicuous in flight for the rattling noise they make, rather like some of the grasshoppers.

Vespidae are the wasps which make paper nests and include the semi-social species. *Eumenes maxillosus* de Geer is a large black species. Relatives make small clay-pot nests and are called Potter Wasps. *Synagris analis* de Saussure is velvety black with an orange 'tail'. *Belonogaster griseus* (Fabricius) is a long-waisted colonial species, belligerent in attitude as it rests on its paper nest.

The Honey Bee, *Apis mellifera* Linnaeus, need not be discussed but occasionally at the Falls and only too commonly in other dry savannah bush localities the tiresome little Stingless Bees (*Trigona*) are encountered. Known also as Sweat Bees, they walk all over exposed parts of the human anatomy, particularly the face, eyes and ears, and are most persistent on a hot sticky day.

Lastly, we will mention the Cuckoo Wasps (Chrysididae), such as *Stilbum cyanurum* (Forster), all metallic green in colour and parasitic on other insects. These are not related to the little known Ichneumons and other parasitic wasps, which may be referred to in this part of Africa as one of the 'great unknowns'. As any professional entomologist if Africa well knows, this continent is still wide open to the pioneering spirit. Much exploration has been done in opening up the hinterland of Africa and learning about its natural resources since Livingstone named the Victoria Falls. Yet, well over a century later, thousands of insects in the larger orders await discovery here or elsewhere on this continent.

Note: all illustrations in this chapter are reduced from life size.

Select Bibliography

ARNOLD, G. 'Some insects of the Falls area,' in J. D. Clark (ed.), *The Victoria Falls* (1st edn.). Livingstone, 1952, pp. 106–114.

DICKSON, C. G. C. *The Life Histories of the South African Lycaenid Butterflies,* Cape Town, 1971.

PINHEY, E. C. G. *Butterflies of Rhodesia,* Salisbury, (Look Around You series, no. 2), 1949.

PINHEY, E. C. G. 'Records of S. Rhodesian butterflies (up to March 1948)', *Occ. Pap. Nat. Mus. S. Rhod.* xv, 1949, pp. 276–341.

PINHEY, E. C. G. *The Dragonflies of Southern Africa,* Pretoria, (Transvaal Museum Memoirs, 5), 1951.

PINHEY, E. C. G. *Dragonflies (Odonata) of Central Africa.* Livingstone, (Occ. Pap. Rhodes-Livingstone Museum, 14), 1961.

PINHEY, E. C. G. 'Butterflies of the Federation' in A. J. Levin (ed.), *Guide to Rhodesia and Nyasaland.* Salisbury, 1961, pp. 90–106.

PINHEY E. C. G. *Hawk Moths of Central and Southern Africa,* Cape Town, 1962.

PINHEY, E. C. G. *Butterflies of Southern Africa,* Johannesburg, 1965.

PINHEY, E. C. G. *Introduction to Insect Study in Africa,* London, 1968.

PINHEY, E. C. G. and LOE, I. D. *A Guide to the Insects of Zambia,* Lusaka, 1973.

SWANEPOEL, D. A. *Butterflies of South Africa: Where, When and How they fly,* Cape Town, 1953.

VAN SON, G. *The Butterflies of Southern Africa, I. Papilionidae, Pieridae,* Pretoria, (Transvaal Museum Memoirs, 3), 1949.

VAN SON, G. *The Butterflies of Southern Africa, II. Danainae, Satyrinae,* Pretoria, (Transvaal Museum Memoirs, 8), 1955.

VAN SON, G. *The Butterflies of Southern Africa, III. Acraeinae,* Pretoria, (Transvaal Museum Memoirs, 14), 1963.

WESTWOOD, J. O. 'Appendix 4: Entomology' in F. Oates, *Matabele Land and the Victoria Falls,* London, 1881, pp. 331–365.

WHELLAN, J. A. 'Insects at the Victoria Falls,' in B. M. Fagan (ed.), *The Victoria Falls* (2nd edn.), Livingstone, 1964, pp. 109–128.

WILLIAMS, J. G. *A Field Guide to the Butterflies of Africa,* London, 1969.

There are many other papers of interest, for instance those by Dr V. G. L. van Someren on the *Charaxes* butterflies of Africa, published in recent years in the *Bulletin* of the British Museum (Natural History).

CHAPTER 15

Conservation of the Victoria Falls Environment

David W. Phillipson

From the foregoing chapters it will be apparent what a wealth of natural beauty and scientific interest there is in the Victoria Falls region. In an attempt to secure the preservation of this fascinating environment substantial areas of country surrounding the Falls in both Zambia and Zimbabwe have been declared National Parks. The extent of these is shown on the accompanying maps.

The Mosi-oa-Tunya National Park on the Zambian side covers approximately 6900 hectares; within this area is included the Mosi-oa-Tunya Zoological Park. The Mosi-oa-Tunya National Park differs from most other Zambian National Parks such as Kafue and Luangwa in having as its prime aim not the preservation of wildlife but that of the Victoria Falls themselves and their total physical environment. Because of the developments which have in the past been allowed within the present park area, such as the Customs and Immigration Post, hotel, Power Station and Boat Club, and also because the area is traversed by public rights of way in the form of main roads and the railway line, it is not possible to subject the main part of the Mosi-oa-Tunya National Park to such stringent conservation measures or control as prevail in other National Parks. Full National Park regulations do, however, apply in the Zoological Park. The Mosi-oa-Tunya Zoological Park has an area of approximately 1650 hectares and its single entrance is reached along Riverside Drive. The latter road is not included in the Zoological Park which, unlike its Zimbabwean counterpart, does not have a frontage on to the Zambezi. Certain areas of archaeological interest within the National Park are protected additionally by the Zambia National Monuments Commission.

In Zimbabwe similar situations prevail in

221

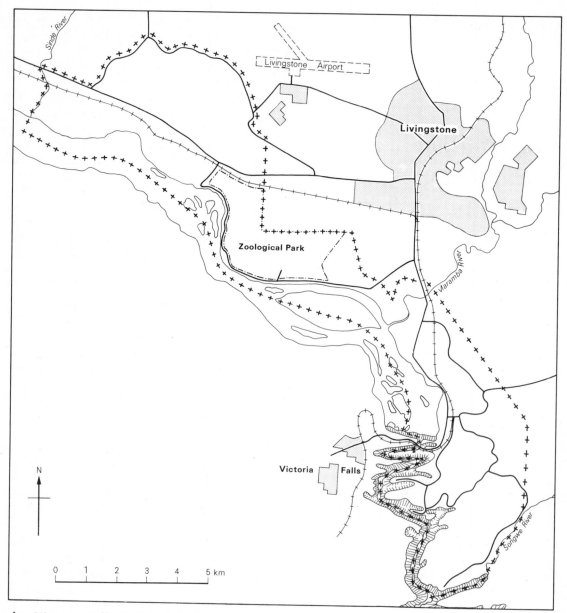

Labels on map: Sinde River, Livingstone Airport, Livingstone, Zoological Park, Maramba River, Victoria Falls, Songwe River

N

0   1   2   3   4   5 km

the Victoria Falls National Park which is, however, much larger than its Zambian counterpart, having a total area of almost 60 000 hectares. The Victoria Falls township

Fig. 1 (above) The Mosi-oa-Tunya National Park.
Fig. 2 (opposite) The Victoria Falls National Park.

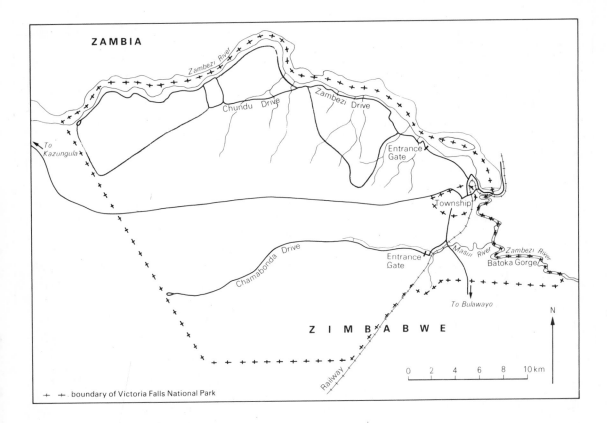

is an excluded enclave within the National Park and the area in the immediate vicinity of the Falls themselves is under the joint control of the Historical Monuments Commission and the National Parks Department. The greater part of the Victoria Falls National Park lying to the west of the main Bulawayo road is designated a Game Area and is subject to the general regulations prevailing in other National Parks except in so far as it is bisected by the main road from Victoria Falls to Kazungula.

There are two main drives in the Game Area. Zambezi Drive extends for 38 kilometres along the south bank of the Zambezi upstream of the Falls from the entrance gate situated immediately beyond Zambezi Camp six kilometres upstream of the Township. Chamabonda Drive leads in a generally westward direction for 24 kilometres from its separate entrance gate six kilometres south of the Township. For the first eight kilometres from the entrance Chamabonda Drive follows the valley of the Masui River. Ultimately it is planned to link the western ends of the Zambezi and Chamabonda Drives to produce a continuous loop-route with entrances at both the existing gates as well as where the new loop will cross the Kazungula road.

The regulations governing visitors to both National Parks, although differing in detail are very similar in all major respects.* Basically, within a National Park, no visitor should act in any way likely to cause damage or deterioration to any aspect of the natural environment. He should not camp or light a fire except in a place expressly authorised for that purpose; and he should carefully extinguish any fire before leaving it. No one should hunt, kill or disturb any form of wild-life (the sole exception to this regulation is fishing by rod and line only, which is permitted in some waters within the parks). Vegetation should not be damaged, nor should any plant or part thereof be removed from the park. Visitors should be particularly careful not to leave litter in any part of the park; not only is litter unsightly but it can also be dangerous to other visitors and to wildlife. Particularly in the vicinity of the Falls themselves visitors are earnestly requested to keep to the ample footpaths provided, as wandering away from these can easily cause irreparable damage to the unique vegetation of this area. Visitors to a National Park must at all times obey any lawful request or order of a National Parks official. Further legislation in both Zambia and Zimbabwe prohibits the collection or removal of archaeological specimens or other antiquities.

In the Mosi-oa-Tunya Zoological Park and in the Game Area of the Victoria Falls National Park more stringent regulations apply; these are posted at the respective entrance gates. In particular, visitors should note that entry into these areas must be by motor vehicle and at an authorised place and time; visitors are not allowed to leave their vehicles within the area except where this is specifically permitted; speed limits must be strictly observed; and no domestic animals or firearms may be taken into these areas.

As the number of visitors to the Victoria Falls steadily increases, the task of preserving the environment becomes progressively more critical and difficult. It must be realised that the requirements of human access, particularly by large numbers of tourists, and of strict conservation are to a certain extent incompatible. The responsible visitor should realise this and do everything in his power to minimise damage to the Falls environment, a considerable part of which has already been sacrificed for his supposed benefit.

The sensitive visitor will recognise that tourist, commercial and industrial development in the immediate vicinity of the Falls in both Zambia and Zimbabwe already far exceeds that which should ideally have been tolerated. Probably more irrevocable damage to the Falls environment has been done in the last decade than in the whole of the previous century; never again will man be able to see the wild beauty of the Victoria Falls unmarred by his own thoughtless activities. Let us hope that the visitor will ponder on this despoliation, and that the authorities will in future take a more responsible and long-term view of the need for constant surveillance if the beauty and scientific interest of the Victoria Falls are to survive for future generations.

* The detailed legislation is set out, for Zambia, in the National Parks and Wildlife Act, 1968, and the National Parks Regulations, 1972. For Zimbabwe, this information is contained in the National Parks Act, 1964, and the National Parks Regulations, 1968.